GRANTA

GRANTA 68, WINTER 1999

GRANTA PUBLICATIONS, 2-3 Hanover Yard, Noel Road, London N1 8BE
Tel 0171 704 9776 Fax 0171 704 0474
e-mail for editorial: editorial@grantamag.co.uk
Granta is published in the United Kingdom by Granta Publications and distributed in the United Kingdom by Bloomsbury, 38 Soho Square, London W1V 5DF.

GRANTA USA LLC, 1755 Broadway, 5th Floor, New York, NY 10019-3780
Tel (212) 246 1313 Fax (212) 586 8003
Website: www.granta.com
Granta is published in the United States by Granta USA LLC and distributed in the United States by Granta Direct Sales, 1755 Broadway, 5th Floor, New York, NY 10019-3780.

Granta, USPS 000-508, ISSN 0017-3231, is published quarterly in the US by Granta USA LLC, a Delaware limited liability company. Periodical Rate postage paid at New York, NY, and additional mailing offices. POSTMASTER: send address changes to Granta, 1755 Broadway, 5th Floor, New York, NY 10019-3780. US Canada Post Corp. Sales Agreement #1462326.

Printed in the United States of America on acid-free paper.

Design: The Senate
Cover photographs: Stephen Gill

ISBN 0-9645611-8-2

GRANTA 68

Love Stories

Introduction

The story by Raymond Carver that begins this issue of *Granta* was one of two discovered in the summer—July 1999—by Professor William Stull, of the University of Hartford, and his wife, Maureen Carroll. They found them in the William Charvat Collection of American Fiction at Ohio State University; via a dealer, Carver had sold a job lot of his papers to the university in 1984. Stull's was not the first Carver discovery in 1999. Earlier in the year Carver's widow, Tess Gallagher, unearthed another three unpublished stories in the writer's desk in his old home at Port Angeles in Washington state. She had put off the task of sifting through her husband's unpublished work for eleven years, fearing during that time, she later said, the distracting fuss among Carver enthusiasts and publishers that 'discoveries' would certainly prompt.

Raymond Carver was born in 1938 and died, aged fifty, in 1988. Literary celebrity came to him late, during the last decade of his life. Posthumously, he has become a legend and a sort of writer-saint. Pilgrims travel to his grave; there are picture books about his life and numerous studies of his work; he exists as a focus of worship and academic activity (Professor Stull is the leading Carver scholar). Perhaps no other modern American writer has had such a large influence in creative-writing schools and on how a younger generation think they should write. The way he lived has something to do with this: the writer as hero and martyr. Carver was born the son of poor parents, struggled with money, alcoholism and marital difficulty, suffered, found autumnal equilibrium with recognition and domestic happiness, died before he should have done. All true, and yet, compared to the work which grew from this experience, all beside the point. Carver wrote superb stories. Writing recently in the *New York Review of Books*, A. O. Scott called him 'the most beloved short-story writer of our time', his stories suffused with a personality that is 'affable, humble, battered, wise'.

Granta first published a Carver story—'Vitamins'—in 1981. Another six pieces followed in the years before his death. It would be fair to say if there is a '*Granta* school of writing', Carver's name would be closely identified with it, and that *Granta* played a large part in establishing his reputation on the eastern side of the Atlantic. The story overleaf, 'Call If You Need Me', does not let this reputation down. The terrain is familiar—you can glimpse it also in stories such as 'Blackbird Pie' and 'Chef's House'—but the writer's eye and sentences are as fresh as ever. I like to think this story would be there no matter who had written it, though only Carver could have.

IJ

GRANTA

CALL IF YOU NEED ME

Raymond Carver

DANNY LYON/MAGNUM PHOTOS

Call If You Need Me

We had both been involved with other people that spring, but when June came and school was out we decided to let our house for the summer and move from Palo Alto to the north coast country of California. Our son, Richard, went to Nancy's grandmother's place in Pasco, Washington, to live for the summer and work toward saving money for college in the fall. His grandmother knew the situation at home and had begun working on getting him up there and locating him a job long before his arrival. She'd talked to a farmer friend of hers and had secured a promise of work for Richard baling hay and building fences. Hard work, but Richard was looking forward to it. He left on the bus in the morning of the day after his high school graduation. I took him to the station and parked and went inside to sit with him until his bus was called. His mother had already held him and cried and kissed him goodbye and given him a long letter that he was to deliver to his grandmother upon his arrival. She was at home now finishing last-minute packing for our own move and waiting for the couple who were to take our house. I bought Richard's ticket, gave it to him, and we sat on one of the benches in the station and waited. We'd talked a little about things on the way to the station.

'Are you and mom going to get a divorce?' he'd asked. It was Saturday morning, and there weren't many cars.

'Not if we can help it,' I said. 'We don't want to. That's why we're going away from here and don't expect to see anyone all summer. That's why we've rented our house for the summer and rented the house up in Arcata. Why you're going away, too, I guess. One reason anyway. Not to mention the fact that you'll come home with your pockets filled with money. We don't want to get a divorce. We want to be alone for the summer and try to work things out.'

'You still love mom?' he said. 'She told me she loves you.'

'Of course I do,' I said. 'You ought to know that by now. We've just had our share of troubles and heavy responsibilities, like everyone else, and now we need time to be alone and work things out. But don't worry about us. You just go up there and have a good summer and work hard and save your money. Consider it a vacation, too. Get in all the fishing you can. There's good fishing around there.'

'Waterskiing, too,' he said. 'I want to learn to waterski.'

'I've never been waterskiing,' I said. 'Do some of that for me too, will you?'

We sat in the bus station. He looked through his yearbook while I held a newspaper in my lap. Then his bus was called and we stood up. I embraced him and said again, 'Don't worry, don't worry. Where's your ticket?'

He patted his coat pocket and then picked up his suitcase. I walked him over to where the line was forming in the terminal, then I embraced him again and kissed him on the cheek and said goodbye.

'Goodbye, Dad,' he said and turned from me so that I wouldn't see his tears.

I drove home to where our boxes and suitcases were waiting in the living room. Nancy was in the kitchen drinking coffee with the young couple she'd found to take our house for the summer. I'd met the couple, Jerry and Liz, graduate students in math, for the first time a few days before, but we shook hands again, and I drank a cup of coffee that Nancy poured. We sat around the table and drank coffee while Nancy finished her list of things they should look out for or do at certain times of the month, the first and last of each month, where they should send any mail, and the like. Nancy's face was tight. Sun fell through the curtain on to the table as it got later in the morning.

Finally, things seemed to be in order and I left the three of them in the kitchen and began loading the car. It was a furnished house we were going to, furnished right down to plates and cooking utensils, so we wouldn't need to take much with us from this house, only the essentials.

I'd driven up to Eureka, 350 miles north of Palo Alto, on the north coast of California, three weeks before and rented us the furnished house. I went with Susan, the woman I'd been seeing. We stayed in a motel at the edge of town for three nights while I looked in the newspaper and visited realtors. She watched me as I wrote out a cheque for the three months' rent. Later, back at the motel, in bed, she lay with her hand on her forehead and said, 'I envy your wife. I envy Nancy. You hear people talk about "the other woman" always and how the incumbent wife has the privileges and the real power, but I never really understood or cared about those things before.

Now I see. I envy her. I envy her the life she will have with you in that house this summer. I wish it were me. I wish it were us. Oh, how I wish it were us. I feel so crummy,' she said. I stroked her hair.

Nancy was a tall, long-legged woman with brown hair and eyes and a generous spirit. But lately we had been coming up short on generosity and spirit. The man she had been seeing was one of my colleagues, a divorced, dapper, three-piece-suit-and-tie fellow with greying hair who drank too much and whose hands, some of my students told me, sometimes shook in the classroom. He and Nancy had drifted into their affair at a party during the holidays not too long after Nancy had discovered my own affair. It all sounds boring and tacky now—it is boring and tacky—but during that spring it was what it was, and it consumed all of our energies and concentration to the exclusion of everything else. Sometime in late April we began to make plans to rent our house and go away for the summer, just the two of us, and try to put things back together, if they could be put back together. We each agreed we would not call or write or otherwise be in touch with the other parties. So we made arrangements for Richard, found the couple to look after our house, and I had looked at a map and driven north from San Francisco and found Eureka, and a realtor who was willing to rent a furnished house to a respectable middle-aged married couple for the summer. I think I even used the phrase second honeymoon to the realtor, God forgive me, while Susan smoked a cigarette and read tourist brochures out in the car.

I finished storing the suitcases, bags and cartons in the trunk and backseat and waited while Nancy said a final goodbye on the porch. She shook hands with each of them and turned and came toward the car. I waved to the couple, and they waved back. Nancy got in and shut the door. 'Let's go,' she said. I put the car in gear and we headed for the freeway. At the light just before the freeway we saw a car ahead of us come off the freeway trailing a broken muffler, the sparks flying. 'Look at that,' Nancy said. 'It might catch fire.' We waited and watched until the car managed to pull off the road on to the shoulder.

We stopped at a little café off the highway near Sebastopol. Eat and Gas, the sign read. We laughed at the sign. I pulled up in front of the café and we went inside and took a table near a window in the back of the café. After we had ordered coffee and sandwiches, Nancy touched her forefinger to the table and began tracing lines in the wood. I lit a cigarette and looked outside. I saw rapid movement, and then I realized I was looking at a hummingbird in the bush beside the window. Its wings moved in a blur of motion and it kept dipping its beak into a blossom on the bush.

'Nancy, look,' I said. 'There's a hummingbird.'

But the hummingbird flew at this moment and Nancy looked and said, 'Where? I don't see it.'

'It was just there a minute ago,' I said. 'Look, there it is. Another one, I think. It's another hummingbird.'

We watched the hummingbird until the waitress brought our order and the bird flew at the movement and disappeared around the building.

'Now that's a good sign, I think,' I said. 'Hummingbirds. Hummingbirds are supposed to bring luck.'

'I've heard that somewhere,' she said. 'I don't know where I heard that, but I've heard it. Well,' she said, 'luck is what we could use. Wouldn't you say?'

'They're a good sign,' I said. 'I'm glad we stopped here.'

She nodded. She waited a minute, then she took a bite of her sandwich.

We reached Eureka just before dark. We passed the motel on the highway where Susan and I had stayed and had spent the three nights some weeks before, then turned off the highway and took a road up over a hill overlooking the town. I had the house keys in my pocket. We drove over the hill and for a mile or so until we came to a little intersection with a service station and a grocery store. There were wooded mountains ahead of us in the valley, and pastureland all around. Some cattle were grazing in a field behind the service station. 'This is pretty country,' Nancy said. 'I'm anxious to see the house.'

'Almost there,' I said. 'It's just down this road,' I said, 'and over that rise.' 'Here,' I said in a minute and pulled into a long driveway with hedge on either side. 'Here it is. What do you think of this?'

I'd asked the same question of Susan when she and I had stopped in the driveway.

'It's nice,' Nancy said. 'It looks fine, it does. Let's get out.'

We stood in the front yard a minute and looked around. Then we went up the porch steps and I unlocked the front door and turned on the lights. We went through the house. There were two small bedrooms, a bath, a living room with old furniture and a fireplace, and a big kitchen with a view of the valley.

'Do you like it?' I said.

'I think it's just wonderful,' Nancy said. She grinned. 'I'm glad you found it. I'm glad we're here.' She opened the refrigerator and ran a finger over the counter. 'Thank God, it looks clean enough. I won't have to do any cleaning.'

'Right down to clean sheets on the beds,' I said. 'I checked. I made sure. That's the way they're renting it. Pillows even. And pillowcases, too.'

'We'll have to buy some firewood,' she said. We were standing in the living room. 'We'll want to have a fire on nights like this.'

'I'll look into firewood tomorrow,' I said. 'We can go shopping then too and see the town.'

She looked at me and said, 'I'm glad we're here.'

'So am I,' I said. I opened my arms and she moved to me. I held her. I could feel her trembling. I turned her face up and kissed her on either cheek. 'Nancy,' I said.

'I'm glad we're here,' she said.

We spent the next few days settling in, taking trips into Eureka to walk around and look in store windows, and hiking across the pastureland behind the house all the way to the woods. We bought groceries and I found an ad in the newspaper for firewood, called, and a day or so afterwards two young men with long hair delivered a pick-up truckload of alder and stacked it in the carport. That night we sat in front of the fireplace after dinner and drank coffee and talked about getting a dog.

'I don't want a pup,' Nancy said. 'Something we have to clean up after or that will chew things up. That we don't need. But I'd like to have a dog, yes. We haven't had a dog in a long time. I think we could handle a dog up here,' she said.

'And after we go back, after summer's over?' I said. I rephrased the question. 'What about keeping a dog in the city?'

'We'll see. Meanwhile, let's look for a dog. The right kind of dog. I don't know what I want until I see it. We'll read the classifieds and we'll go to the pound, if we have to.' But though we went on talking about dogs for several days, and pointed out dogs to each other in people's yards we'd drive past, dogs we said we'd like to have, nothing came of it, we didn't get a dog.

Nancy called her mother and gave her our address and telephone number. Richard was working and seemed happy, her mother said. She herself was fine. I heard Nancy say, 'We're fine. This is good medicine.'

One day in the middle of July we were driving the highway near the ocean and came over a rise to see some lagoons that were closed off from the ocean by sand spits. There were some people fishing from shore, and two boats out on the water.

I pulled the car off on to the shoulder and stopped. 'Let's see what they're fishing for,' I said. 'Maybe we could get some gear and go ourselves.'

'We haven't been fishing in years,' Nancy said. 'Not since that time Richard was little and we went camping near Mount Shasta. Do you remember that?'

'I remember,' I said. 'I just remembered too that I've missed fishing. Let's walk down and see what they're fishing for.'

'Trout,' the man said, when I asked. 'Cut-throats and rainbow trout. Even some steelhead and a few salmon. They come in here in the winter when the spit opens and then when it closes in the spring, they're trapped. This is a good time of the year for them. I haven't caught any today, but last Sunday I caught four, about fifteen inches long. Best eating fish in the world, and they put up a hell of a fight. Fellows out in the boats have caught some today, but so far I haven't done anything today.'

'What do you use for bait?' Nancy asked.

'Anything,' the man said. 'Worms, salmon eggs, whole kernel corn. Just get it out there and leave it lay on the bottom. Pull out a little slack and watch your line.'

We hung around a little longer and watched the man fish and watched the little boats chat-chat back and forth the length of the lagoon.

'Thanks,' I said to the man. 'Good luck to you.'

'Good luck to you,' he said. 'Good luck to the both of you.'

We stopped at a sporting goods store on the way back to town and bought licences, inexpensive rods and reels, nylon line, hooks, leaders, sinkers, and a creel. We made plans to go fishing the next morning.

But that night, after we'd eaten dinner and washed the dishes and I had laid a fire in the fireplace, Nancy shook her head and said it wasn't going to work.

'Why do you say that?' I asked. 'What is it you mean?'

'I mean it isn't going to work. Let's face it.' She shook her head again. 'I don't think I want to go fishing in the morning, either, and I don't want a dog. No, no dogs. I think I want to go up and see my mother and Richard. Alone. I want to be alone. I miss Richard,' she said and began to cry. 'Richard's my son, my baby,' she said, 'and he's nearly grown and gone. I miss him.'

'And Del, do you miss Del Shraeder, too?' I said. 'Your boyfriend. Do you miss him?'

'I miss everybody tonight,' she said. 'I miss you too. I've missed you for a long time now. I've missed you so much you've gotten lost somehow, I can't explain it. I've lost you. You're not mine any longer.'

'Nancy,' I said.

'No, no,' she said. She shook her head. She sat on the sofa in front of the fire and kept shaking her head. 'I want to fly up and see my mother and Richard tomorrow. After I'm gone you can call your girlfriend.'

'I won't do that,' I said. 'I have no intention of doing that.'

'You'll call her,' she said.

'You'll call Del,' I said. I felt rubbishy for saying it.

'You can do what you want,' she said, wiping her eyes on her sleeve. 'I mean that. I don't want to sound hysterical. But I'm going up to Washington tomorrow. Right now I'm going to go to bed. I'm exhausted. I'm sorry. I'm sorry for both of us, Dan. We're not going to make it. That fisherman today. He wished us good luck.' She shook her head. 'I wish us good luck too. We're going to need it.'

She went into the bathroom and I heard water running in the tub. I went out and sat on the porch steps and smoked a cigarette. It was dark and quiet outside. I looked toward town and could see a faint glow of lights in the sky and patches of ocean fog drifting in the valley. I began to think of Susan. A little later Nancy came out of the bathroom and I heard the bedroom door close. I went inside and put another block of wood on the grate and waited until the flames began to move up the bark. Then I went into the other bedroom and turned the covers back and stared at the floral design on the sheets. Then I showered, dressed in my pyjamas, and went to sit near the fireplace again. The fog was outside the window now. I sat in front of the fire and smoked. When I looked out the window again, something moved in the fog and I saw a horse grazing in the front yard.

I went to the window. The horse looked up at me for a minute, then went back to pulling up grass. Another horse walked past the car into the yard and began to graze. I turned on the porch light and stood at the window and watched them. They were big white horses with long manes. They'd gotten through a fence or an unlocked gate from one of the nearby farms. Somehow they'd wound up in our front yard. They were larking it, enjoying their breakaway immensely. But they were nervous too; I could see the whites of their eyes from where I stood behind the window. Their ears kept rising and falling as they tore out clumps of grass. A third horse wandered into the yard, and then a fourth. It was a herd of white horses, and they were grazing in our front yard.

I went into the bedroom and woke Nancy. Her eyes were red and the skin around the eyes was swollen. She had her hair up in curlers and a suitcase lay open on the floor near the foot of the bed.

'Nancy,' I said. 'Honey, come and see what's in the front yard. Come and see this. You must see this. You won't believe it. Hurry up.'

'What is it?' she said. 'Don't hurt me. What is it?'

'Honey, you must see this. I'm not going to hurt you. I'm sorry if I scared you. But you must come out here and see something.'

I went back into the other room and stood in front of the window and in a few minutes Nancy came in tying her robe. She looked out the window and said, 'My God, they're beautiful. Where'd they come from, Dan? They're just beautiful.'

'They must have gotten loose from around here somewhere,' I said. 'One of these farm places. I'll call the sheriff's department pretty soon and let them locate the owners. But I wanted you to see this first.'

'Will they bite?' she said. 'I'd like to pet that one there, that one that just looked at us. I'd like to pat that one's shoulder. But I don't want to get bitten. I'm going outside.'

'I don't think they'll bite,' I said. 'They don't look like the kind of horses that'll bite. But put a coat on if you're going out there; it's cold.'

I put my coat on over my pyjamas and waited for Nancy. Then I opened the front door and we went outside and walked into the yard with the horses. They all looked up at us. Two of them went back to pulling up grass. One of the other horses snorted and moved back a few steps, and then it too went back to pulling up grass and chewing, head down. I rubbed the forehead of one horse and patted its shoulder. It kept chewing. Nancy put out her hand and began stroking the mane of another horse. 'Horsey, where'd you come from?' she said. 'Where do you live and why are you out tonight, Horsey?' she said and kept stroking the horse's mane. The horse looked at her and blew through its lips and dropped its head again. She patted its shoulder.

'I guess I'd better call the sheriff,' I said.

'Not yet,' she said. 'Not for a while yet. We'll never see anything like this again. We'll never, never have horses in our front yard again. Wait a while yet, Dan.'

A little later, Nancy was still out there moving from one horse to another, patting their shoulders and stroking their manes, when one of the horses moved from the yard into the driveway and walked around the car and down the driveway toward the road, and I knew I had to call.

In a little while the two sheriff's cars showed up with their red lights flashing in the fog and a few minutes later a fellow with a sheepskin coat driving a pick-up with a horse trailer behind it. Now the horses shied and tried to get away and the man with the horse trailer swore and tried to get a rope around the neck of one horse.

'Don't hurt it!' Nancy said.

We went back in the house and stood behind the window and watched the deputies and the rancher work on getting the horses rounded up.

'I'm going to make some coffee,' I said. 'Would you like some coffee, Nancy?'

'I'll tell you what I'd like,' she said. 'I feel high Dan. I feel like I'm loaded. I feel like, I don't know, but I like the way I'm feeling. You put on some coffee and I'll find us some music to listen to on the radio and then you can build up the fire again. I'm too excited to sleep.'

So we sat in front of the fire and drank coffee and listened to an all-night radio station from Eureka and talked about the horses and then talked about Richard, and Nancy's mother. We danced. We didn't talk about the present situation at all. The fog hung outside the window and we talked and were kind with one another. Toward daylight I turned off the radio and we went to bed and made love.

The next afternoon, after her arrangements were made and her suitcases packed, I drove her to the little airport where she would catch a flight to Portland and then transfer to another airline that would put her in Pasco late that night.

'Tell your mother I said hello. Give Richard a hug for me and tell him I miss him,' I said. 'Tell him I send love.'

'He loves you too,' she said. 'You know that. In any case, you'll see him in the fall, I'm sure.'

I nodded.

'Goodbye,' she said and reached for me. We held each other. 'I'm glad for last night,' she said. 'Those horses. Our talk. Everything. It helps. We won't forget that,' she said. She began to cry.

'Write me, will you?' I said. 'I didn't think it would happen to us,' I said. 'All those years. I never thought so for a minute. Not us.'

'I'll write,' she said. 'Some big letters. The biggest you've ever seen since I used to send you letters in high school.'

'I'll be looking for them,' I said.

Then she looked at me again and touched my face. She turned

and moved across the tarmac toward the plane.

Go, dearest one, and God be with you.

She boarded the plane and I stayed around until its jet engines started and, in a minute, the plane began to taxi down the runway. It lifted off over Humboldt Bay and soon became a speck on the horizon.

I drove back to the house and parked in the driveway and looked at the hoofprints of the horses from last night. There were deep impressions in the grass, and gashes, and there were piles of dung. Then I went into the house and, without even taking off my coat, went to the telephone and dialled Susan's number. □

GRANTA

HABIBI

Ruth Gershon

Tel Aviv

ERICH HARTMANN/MAGNUM PHOTOS

1.

Can you still find this day, Habibi, among your possessions? Among the souvenirs of your trip to Sweden, the textbooks from the time you tried to teach yourself Russian, the chess set left behind in the youth hostel, the photographs of the girls whose names you can't remember? Or is it hidden in the darkness behind the shutters, put out of sight with the degree you dropped out of, the stories you didn't finish?

I can still find it here, in London, in the flat you never visited, in the kitchen, where I can't make an omelette without asking you, do you want cheese in it, shall I chop some parsley? It is here even when I'm not, for I go out now as you do, leaving the light on and the radio playing, so that I can come home to the illusion of company.

Of course I know that I'm better off as I am. Without a secret to keep from my mother. Without a lover to come between me and my children, me and my colleagues, me and my sensible, understandable, usable life. My life that I keep trying, keep failing, to bring into line with expectations that I keep trying, keep failing, to make my own.

The security officer looked about sixteen. I put the suitcase down in front of her and said, automatically, 'Shalom.' And then, embarrassed by the happy smile and the long stream of Hebrew, 'Please. My Ivrit is absolutely terrible, I can only say a few words. I'm sorry.'

'But that's absolutely amazing. I was so sure you were an Israeli. Well, have a nice flight.'

'And that was all?' said Jill, who arrived a few weeks afterwards. 'Do you know, I was interrogated for half an hour? and they asked me how many Muslim students I taught? and then turned over my suitcase, and went through everything, and left me to repack it?'

'Oh, how awful. I suppose I got through simply because I was Jewish-looking. That's awful. I'm so sorry.'

But it didn't feel all that awful. Actually, I rather liked it.

No one had seemed ready for me, although the arrangements had been made long before. The seminars would not now begin for over a month. I was welcome to use the University library and the canteen.

Here was a list of restaurants and cafés. Here were the keys to the flat. The landlord was away. They had phoned me in London, they thought it was only right to ask me if I minded: the landlord was an Arab; he was often away, he worked at night, I would hardly see him.

It was the coldest winter Tel Aviv had had for a hundred years. The plate-glass outer wall of my room did not catch even the midday sun. At night I wore pyjamas, bedsocks, shawls, and clenched myself around a hot-water bottle. By day I tried to keep a step ahead of the other readers in the library, moving from one desk to another to stay in the pools of sunlight that fell in favoured places. I swallowed endless cups of coffee, and in the evenings, huge bowls of cabbage soup.

I was not invisible. I was something better: literally, unremarkable. Tourists asked me for street directions, students asked me how to use the catalogues, bus drivers swore at me for not producing the correct pass; they looked startled only when I came out with my one grammatical Hebrew sentence apologizing for the fact that I could not speak the language.

My face fits, I told myself. No one finds my presence awkward, anomalous. No one expects anything in particular from me. It will be all right for me to be irreligious, and middle-aged, and alone, and without a wedding ring. I don't need a membership card. I don't need a letter of recommendation. I have it written all over my face.

Maybe that's why I'm a coward at home, maybe that's why I can't go to a pub or a café on my own, saying no, not that one, it's too posh, not that one, it's too sleazy, and here there are only men, and here only men with very young girls, and this place might be nice but it's a little bit weird, and the other is so near where I live that it looks as if I don't have anybody. Maybe I guessed right all along, and I really was out of place, had something to apologize for; skin more green than pink; features too large for a small thin head.

Still, you can have enough of blending into the background. Everywhere I went I carried a stack of stationery. If you write home, at least you are having half a conversation; if you write lots of postcards it shows that you've got friends somewhere in the world, doesn't it? And if you write in your notebooks, perhaps someone will notice you and think that you're an intellectual, that you've got your own agenda, even that you might be quite well known in your own country...somebody might just want to talk to you.

Two weeks went by without a meal shared, without more than a slight nod and a smile in another's direction. I was cold and I was losing weight.

And then you came.

I had left the library early, because I felt too weak and shivery to last the day out. You were in the street talking to one of the neighbours. The sun was shining brightly. You were not much taller than me, and your black hair framed your face, like mine. You guessed who I was and you gave me the sweetest smile. I had seen that smile of welcome and recognition in a dream once, and woken up wondering if I had to die and go to heaven to see it again.

We went upstairs and into that tiny white-tiled kitchen where I'd only stayed long enough to boil water for myself; and you told me that you'd been in the country near Nazareth, visiting your family, and you began unpacking food from your bags. You took out soft flat bread with herbs worked into it that you warmed in a little electric cooker, and a wide-mouthed jar of olive oil in which balls of soft cheese were floating, and you sliced up cucumbers and tomatoes and made us mugs of tea.

What did you tell me first? That your father was an imam, that you had had the strictest upbringing of any boy in your village, that you weren't allowed a visit from a Christian schoolfellow, not even if you needed his textbook for that night's homework. You had left home, and gone to a Jewish university. You taught Arabic now, and got translation work; sometimes it paid very well, sometimes not.

You wanted to write more. You had projects that you had started but not completed; you needed to be more disciplined, to set yourself deadlines.

'I'll help you to finish something,' I said. 'It's my speciality. I can cure writer's block and I can make my friends finish what they've started. They call me the great El Nago. You'll see!'

'I will let you cure me,' you said, and you looked as happy as a child.

The next day you asked if I was in a hurry to get to the library, and I said, not really. We went to your favourite café. You ordered mint tea, and it came in the glasses with metal holders that we'd used for lemon tea at home; but in place of the lemon there were sprigs of mint with tiny, soft leaves. I said it was the best I had ever tasted and you said you liked experimenting with these kinds of teas, you had pot plants, geranium, sage, that you used for infusions. We would have some in the evening.

It surprised you to learn that I was Jewish. I started to talk about being brought up Orthodox, not being able to shake it off entirely in spite of everything I'd done since then, always feeling rival claims upon me; and I hoped you'd pick it up, see how much we had in common; but you refused the invitation, changed the subject.

You hoped I wasn't too uncomfortable in the flat, you actually liked the weather to be extraordinary, found the winds and storms thrilling, and the snow! This year you had seen it for the first time in your life, and you had dashed back to your village to see how it would look, and it was amazing: exactly the same and yet completely different at the same time.

'I like it better today,' I said. 'I like bathing in sunshine.'

'Well, here you're paddling, at least.'

After that, the street where we lived was always warm to me, always baking in the sun. I was in love with the solid, stoical, shabby buildings rising above pock-holed pavements: a block housing a newspaper, a trade union headquarters, residential apartments on top of rows of shops and smaller offices; nothing there that you could photograph for a postcard, that shrieked happy holidays. I was in love with the succession of cafés and with the Levantine tattiness of the tiny grocery shops, all side by side and selling exactly the same lines; with the hardware stores, piling their tangled heaps of plastic, rope and metal goods on the floors and in the windows, as if there had just been a fire or flood on the premises.

Above all I was in love with the bookshops, their second-hand shelves stuffed with the remnants of collections brought from Berlin and Vienna, discarded by children and grandchildren. Were the owners all dead now, or stored in old people's homes? I visited the books daily, almost as a duty, as if we were somehow related. I bought political essays, and little books of poetry with handblocked covers; in a small skip I found disbound sections of a part work, issued 'to private subscribers only' in the 1920s by the Berlin Institut für Sexualwissenschaft.

'The illustrations are missing,' the proprietor apologized. 'They were sold separately. The customer was an artist.'

'That was an excuse,' I replied.

'I'm inclined to agree with you.'

I would purchase what was left. I would take them away, give them a good home, these aged great-aunts and uncles, confused in the sunlight, fitfully remembering their old romances and ardours, falling into tatters, dying in a strange land. I would take them back from one exile to another.

Sitting now in a parallel universe, in a sturdy Thirties block overlooking a row of shops, I could almost lean out and touch the bookstores and the cafés. I could stop writing and walk up the hill, where I would see, in ones and twos, clothes carefully arranged, heads under wigs for reasons of pride and not religion, the last frail relics of that wretched exodus, drinking their coffee and chocolate.

I could stop writing and go out, leaving the radio on; give myself an errand, see other people, maybe even bump into someone I know.

2.

It was wonderful not to be teaching for a term, not to hear myself repeating the same old words until they tasted like ashes in my mouth; not to have to read, appalled, those very words in my students' essays, to see what I had once thought well-judged conclusions exposed as the crudest of aphorisms; not to have to mark those essays, when all I really knew was that some of my students longed to use their minds and others didn't. Every once in a while, not often enough, I would have a group to teach who followed their thoughts wherever they led, who argued about history as if their lives depended on it, who could sharpen their wits on their own ignorance. They were the ones who could transform my seminars into the dinner-table disputations I sat through every evening as a little girl, not forcing me into a show of professionalism, of authority, of adulthood, of anything except my own curiosity and pleasure. In such hours of freedom I could almost accept the rest of it.

But now what pleasure, what freedom, to be under your roof, taking my time, laying out the files of notes that I'd begun to accumulate more than fifteen years before, and finding exactly what I was looking for: the threads that bound disparate facts together, that showed how they belonged to each other; the repeated details of women's domestic lives, the ordering, caring relationships, all transformed by private conscience into public agency; the working out of nineteenth-century religion in nineteenth-century politics. Wasn't this all the happiness I needed, this landscape yielding to my exploration, revealing its structures and its beauties endlessly, for as long as I had the will and the patience to look for them?

And there was another happiness, unacknowledged, that crept into bed with me every night; for the first time since the children had left home I was not alone under my roof; as I put out my light, yours burned in your room and the radio kept up its accompaniment to your own reading and writing.

I came back one evening from the library and found an Arabic class about to start in your living room; you called out from the kitchen that you were making lentil soup to have with your students afterwards, and would I join you?

We squashed somehow around the tiny table. 'Visiting Fellow, very posh,' you said to introduce me, but they already knew who I was. Nechama had read my work, she would be coming to hear my seminar presentation, would be speaking next month, as I would, in the international conference at the University. She told me of her own research on the first women kibbutzniks, and of her job in adult education. Ari was her partner, but it seemed they had little time to spend together: he reported for B'Tselem, monitoring civil rights in the occupied territories. They both looked as if they were thinner and poorer than they might have chosen to be. They both turned towards me with recognition, spoke to me as family, as one of their own.

I wanted to say: but I'm a fraud; or at least, not that good. I can claim only the barest degree of kinship on account of the demonstrations I turn out for in a resigned, embarrassed way, the evenings I spend at meetings in drab halls, the hours of my life given up to taking minutes, raising funds, catering socials, impaling my conscience on the contradictions in the system; while they, they were continually risking the anger and rejection of parents, brothers, sisters, not just their own flesh and blood, but that flesh and blood clothed in state uniforms, translated into laws, buried in the land beneath their feet. I knew I would have flinched from that, drawn back in silence, slid into an easier life.

Unless it had just happened, one thing after another, almost without conscious choice, obvious things like joining CND at school and the Labour Party afterwards and the International Socialists after that; like demonstrating against the Vietnam War; like marrying out and leaving the community and breaking everyone's heart; like getting divorced; another life not having happened.

The next morning you travelled in to the University with me. We caught the bus near the beginning of its journey, and found seats at the back. The bus filled up rapidly. Near the University, an elderly woman got on. Grey hair, thick pebble glasses, no stick; from Germany or Austria was my guess. None of the passengers sitting near her offered her their place. Her angry eyes swept the length of the bus. As no one else stirred, you got up and signalled to her. Making her way to the back she shouted loudly, in Hebrew that even I could understand:

'This is the only Jew on the bus! The rest of you are all Arabs!'

She sat down beside me and patted my knee as I smiled weakly and avoided your gaze.

I was ravished by your directness.

There were almost no preliminaries. When you saw me in the morning you would ask me if I slept well, if the neighbour's car had disturbed me, but as soon as I had answered you were ready with whatever had preoccupied you in the night: the uses of the subjunctive and the conditional modes in English; the difference in meaning between 'barbaric' and 'barbarous'; the development of the calendar and the sense of time in antiquity; did I still believe in God.

'I still can't not believe.'

'And you pray? How can you? It is self-abasement, it is organized humiliation. My father will not accept me as his son until

I make my prayers behind him in the mosque.'

Did you want an answer? I couldn't give one.

'I'm sorry. You didn't come here to have your landlord arguing with you. I did believe in Him until 1967. Then I stopped. You must get on with your work.'

You were always calmer when I got back in the evening. If you had no students we would sit in the kitchen while you told stories, stories of your travels, every night a different place: Stockholm, where you had been able to find an exiled relative without even knowing his new address, much less his new name; Geneva, where you had met Arafat, who came from a village near yours; every evening, you cast your spell, like Scheherazade.

Did you know your own strength or could you, like her, never trust it, always waiting for the axe to fall?

One evening you asked me:

'Have you ever been to Spain?'

'Only to the seaside, really.'

'I went to southern Spain ten years ago. I went into a mosque in Cordova and there was a young man playing a kind of pottery flute. I took a hotel near the mosque, I got up early every morning to go and hear him; for hours I stood so still a bird could have perched on my head. I'd like to live there, to write there. I don't think I'll ever produce anything if I stay in Tel Aviv.'

'Couldn't you write down your stories here?'

'Not here, no. To write them down…it would be like pretending I was in some other place. And I'm here, that's just the truth, it is what it is.'

It was very late when I came in the next evening, but the door of your room was open. You were in your bed, smoking in the yellow light, reading newspapers; not naked. You called me in, motioned me to sit down on the bed; there seemed to be no reason not to. Had I been to Jerusalem, you asked.

'Not since 1963, in the days when it was divided.'

'It is still divided.'

'Yes, I know, but you know what I mean.'

'Do you dream about Jerusalem?'

'When I was younger and very religious, yes, I did. We're commanded to, almost.'

'Let me tell you a story. I have a friend who is an Oriental Jew. One of his relatives lived in a village in the north; he had never been as far south as Jerusalem. Some cousins who lived there arranged for him to visit them. They took him to all the sights: the Tower of David, the Dome of the Rock, the Wall, everything. Then they all returned to their flat to rest and eat. And he was found sitting in a corner, crying. He said: "I am still missing Jerusalem." All his life he had yearned for something he still had not seen.'

I could not move. A bird could have perched on my head. I forced myself to speak.

'I'm tired, I have to sleep now.'

'Sweet dreams.'

A time came when I was spending more time working in my room, preparing my lectures. You would go out on your morning errands and then, finding me at home, would resume your interrogations.

Had I read *Tin Soldiers on Jerusalem Beach*? What did I think of a psychotherapist who analyses the dreams of Palestinians and of Jews as if they come from the same place, the same experience? who listens with equal empathy to the victim of the holocaust and its perpetrator?

And I, feebly: the discipline cannot be wholly value-free; it must surely rest on an assumption that the desire to hurt others is a sign of disturbance and ill health; but can a doctor refuse anyone treatment? I don't know.

And you, changing tack: how about you, Hannah? Do you feel that things are right with you?

My children are grown-up and well. I can manage my job. I have good friends, I don't get ill. Yes, I am quite happy.

And then, one midday, you came in at my door, your small body propelled by its own tension, needing to be caught before it crashed into something, and asked:

'Do you ever think about committing suicide?'

'Why? Does someone else want my room?'

You took the shock full on the face, and gasped with laughter, and said:

'Oh Hannah, I like you very much.'

I had stayed away for thirty years. There had been only the one visit, in the early Sixties, backpacking, still Orthodox, hardly questioning the deal. Oh, I knew that it was mostly taken by force, that we had been the bully boys, that we had thrown you out. I had a kind of look-at-me-not-feeling-guilty bravado about it. We got what we wanted the same way everyone else does. We had done it, and I wasn't going to care.

But it wasn't an empty space for all that. It wasn't the numbness that I found whenever anyone appealed to me to deplore the division of Germany; that didn't even let me wince at the thought of the fire-bombing of Dresden. Happy shall he be, that taketh and dasheth thy little ones against the stones. No, it wasn't that. I just didn't want to think about it, I wanted the refugee camps to dissolve, for your fellow-Arabs to take care of you all, the way that we Jews looked after each other.

I suppose I began to think about it just about the time that you were losing your belief in God. Being by 1967 against all imperialism, having friends who were Muslims or Arabists, seeing my people as others saw us. And then I turned my face away completely: it was too much to contemplate, too much to be responsible for. I would never go back.

Yet when this invitation came, I said to a friend: I don't know why, but I want to accept. Do you disapprove?

And he answered: Now that the Wall is down, everything has the power to change. We are free to try different things.

Do you think so, Habibi? Will there be change, will your faith be restored? Will things be right with you?

You were careful of your home, you would not let the dust settle over your rooms, shaking the mats out daily over the balcony, sweeping the floors, clearing out rubbish, tending your plants, and always with that bright baroque music in the background.

Your mother had always kept a little garden. Was she still alive?

No, she died a few years back. She reached a certain age, her husband took a second wife, the kitchen had to be divided; she was never well after that.

You loved to cook. You would show me the things she showed you, the best way to cut an onion, how to tell if an egg is fresh.

You made me an omelette at the weekend, and divided it between us.

'No,' I protested, 'you're giving me too much.'

'I want you to have it,' you said. 'Come on. It's not the partition of Palestine.'

Oh Yussuf. If I were living here permanently (and that's a subjunctive, the expression of a wish, a doubt, a possibility), I would not be able to give up this conversation (and that's a conditional). I would not be able to separate myself from you, to leave this table which is becoming ours.

'Oh Yussuf,' I said, 'I like you very much.'

And you said, 'Let's go for a walk on the beach.'

3.

We waited until long after dark, until the roads were empty of young men's cars and stereos, and the streets had lost their sociability, their crowds of gossiping Russians, their soldiers on leave.

'Why do you walk so fast?'

'In England everyone says I walk slowly.'

In England I married someone who was impatient of me, found me too slow for him. If we went for a walk together, he had to stride ahead. We never held hands.

You were holding my hand. I didn't walk so fast. We got closer to the beach, and the wind was blowing, and I didn't feel cold.

We reached the sand and decided to go north.

The cafés overlooking the sea had shown out their last customers, but the lights were still on. You knew the Arabs putting away the dishes, piling chairs on tables, sweeping the floors; you yourself used to work in one of the cafés a few years back. You let go my hand, and went to speak to a youth locking up, whose eyes darted continually between your face and mine, seeing that my face was

Jewish, checking that I didn't understand Arabic. Eventually I turned and looked the other way.

You parted from him and we went on. The big hotels began to loom up on our right.

'All these horrible hotels,' you said, 'it's not so long since there were sheep and goats grazing here. Not so long since Tel Aviv was just a little outgrowth of Yafo.'

'And if the Arabs had won? You think there would never have been any hotels? You think that no one's little house would have been bulldozed to make way for them?'

'It wouldn't have been the same.'

'You might still have hated it.'

'Yes, I might. I would.'

'What were you talking to your friend about?'

'About another friend. He lives in Gaza and can't get a permit to come in to work since this last business.'

This last business; a man with a knife who cut down a Jewish girl and the Arab who ran in vain to save her. Two or three days ago, four or five miles away.

Walking on in silence, thinking about it, trying not to think about it.

The beach wasn't empty, there was another couple, a long way off, coming towards us. Are they a couple? There is something strange about them. What are they wearing? Are they in Purim party clothes? Is that a wig?

They were both men. One of them carrying a rifle.

They passed us by without a glance.

Soldiers on leave; going home from a party. Of course.

I said, 'What did you think?' and you said, 'I thought they might not be Jews.'

'If they hadn't been Jews, would you have put in a good word for me?'

'They wouldn't have heard a word, would they? The guy who tried to rescue that Jewish girl; don't you think he was shouting in Arabic? But when you've made up your mind to do something, every second counts, you see nothing, you hear nothing. I've thought about it, what it must be like.'

Yes, you have thought about it. Among your subjunctives and your conditionals, how could that thought not have found a place in your mind?

'I'm cold now,' I said. 'I want to go home.'

The wind was blowing. We had our hands in our pockets and we walked quickly.

At lunchtime the next day you brought in a newspaper.

'Look!' you said excitedly.

'I can't see anything, Yussuf: I can't read it.'

'You can read that much at least,' showing me a bordered advertisement, and above your index finger, in printed Hebrew characters, my own name.

'Oh, it's me.'

'See, you're famous.'

'Only as one of the speakers at the conference.'

'Do you want to cut it out?'

Of course I did. I cut it out and xeroxed it and arrowed it in red and sent it home to my mother, to my brother, to say, look, this is me, transformed, translated, white as snow. Won't you be pleased with me now?

Ah, my brother. Two years ago, just after my divorce, I went to his house and one of his oldest friends said: 'I didn't know Simon had a sister.' My brother, prince among men, who admits me with difficulty to his court; what would make me stop, give up pleading my cause, give up hoping to please him?

After the advertisement appeared, I had my first dinner invitation.

'I told you, you're famous.'

'I'm not. They're just graduate students who've read my book.'

They had too, every word of it. They were young and lively and enjoyed my company and each other's without fencing for position. Their conversation was like their food, produced in huge quantities and devoured with the eagerness of four-year-olds. What was the situation with Thatcherism, what were the prospects for change? Had I read Hobsbawm's new book? Did my journal still keep 'socialist' on the masthead? Would I be interested in reading some of their chapters? They were working on militarism, on imperialism, on collusion, collaboration, popular consent to war; on social control, and passive and active resistance. Would I? Yes, charmed and flattered to be needed, I would.

They wanted to know where I was staying, what I thought of Tel Aviv. I began to talk about the street where we lived, about the one café with Arab as well as Jewish customers, about Yussuf. How I had not thought before about the situation of non-Jewish citizens, the gap between legal rights and social acceptance; how it made me wonder again about the first 'emancipated' Jews of Europe, why they persisted in the face of the snubs, the coldness, the slights, the insults they must have had to endure from neighbours, from professional colleagues…

I tailed off. Leah broke the silence.

'So why does he live in Tel Aviv?'

'I suppose because he went to university here, and this is where his contacts are.'

'Well, it's not very usual for an Arab to live in Tel Aviv.' She was sitting bolt upright, and her voice was metallic.

So here we are again. I didn't ask for this, I didn't go looking for this, did I? I didn't ever say I wanted this to happen. But here we are, dear God, with an iron blind coming down, with these people thinking that they see me and hear me, but they don't, because I'm not here any more, because I've been removed to another place.

For a moment I think of letting my protest ascend to you, God, that you let this happen. You bring me to some haven and you say, be happy here. And then you send me down roads that end in brick walls, on paths that lead to precipices. Just once, just once you could have let my affections lead me into safety. But I won't even bother to cry out, to plead with you, to beg you, not again, please, not again.

And I drew back in silence, not asking, what are you talking about, are you proposing that he live on a reservation, do you want apartheid even between citizens, you, who claim so much kinship with a Western intelligentsia? Impossible to confront them, to be one against so many, to spoil a nice evening.

I stayed silent, pinioned by a truth so unimaginable that it hardly needed concealing, a profanity that would have defiled me in their eyes had they been open; the truth that it had happened, Yussuf, my brother, my love; that my heart had begun to make its home with you; and that, being in that place, I must accept again, again, a decree of exile.

4.

I do remember, I don't remember. I came in one night and you were sitting on your bed, crushed, defeated. A class had been cancelled and a commission had gone somewhere else. You had advertised two weeks running for someone to rent my room when the summer began and I went home. None of your Arab friends needed a place and none of the Jewish callers had been willing to rent from an Arab.

'I wish you could stay here all the time, Hannah.'

'I wouldn't have a job, so I couldn't help you with the rent.'

'Stay here anyway. Look for a job. It would be nice.'

I sat down next to you.

When we were ready to undress, you said, 'You're tired. Lie on your front. I'm going to give you a massage.' And you rubbed me with thumbs and palms and fingers until every edge and corner and boundary dissolved. And I rolled over and found you ready.

'Oh! I had no difficulty with you, no difficulty at all. Did I last an hour, half an hour?'

'I wasn't looking at my watch. Does it matter?'

'No. Are you happy, Beautiful?'

'Yes, you can look at me and know that I'm happy.'

'I like your skin.'

'It's like yours. I like yours.'

'Don't go to work tomorrow.'

You turned away suddenly, shrouded yourself in your sheet and fell asleep.

'Did I tell you,' you said, in the morning, 'that my mother's name was Hanan?'

'And my father's name was Yosef.'

'People often mistake me for an Oriental Jew. But no one would ever take you for an Arab. If you marry me, you'll have to Islamize.'

'I'll see you pray behind your father first.'

'Well, perhaps we won't marry.'

Touching each other lightly, outlining each other with our fingertips.

'I sometimes wonder,' I said, 'whether all this would have happened if the Jews had been more respectful of Mohammed in the first place. When he told them he was being visited by the Angel Gabriel.'

'What do you mean?'

'Well, if they hadn't said, go away, you crazy Arab, which is probably what they did say, he might just have stayed around and become a convert.'

'I suppose so.'

'So after all this time, we would both have been Jews.'

'You do talk a lot, Hannah.'

'I talk a lot?'

'Hold me tight now. Make me big. I want to fuck you again.'

All that day we kept the shutters closed.

I became limp, while you drank in more and more energy.

'Listen,' you said, jumping up, 'I'm going to play a tape. Guess what it is.'

Women's voices, lute strings, a small drum.

'Is it Arabic?'

'No.'

'Spanish?'

'Yes, Andalus, thirteenth century.'

We lay back and clapped our hands together as the music rippled over us.

'Listen to the next track. They use a fountain of water in the accompaniment.'

Rippling and washing and soaking and drowning as the sun fought to get in between the cracks at us.

'Yussuf,' I said, 'why don't you ever play Arabic music?'

'I do sometimes. Mostly not. I don't like to think about what is missing. Can you understand that? In classical music there's nothing of me, nothing that's mine. It's neutral, it's painless.'

You sat up and began to dress. 'Let me tell you a story. A friend of mine was a baby in 1948. His family lived in a small town, but it was prosperous. His father used to talk about the house they had lived in, how fine it was, how beautiful its situation. But in 1948 they had been driven out. When he grew up, his father often asked him to visit the town with him, and for a long time he refused. When he finally agreed, and they made the journey, the street was unrecognizable, the house a ruin. My friend said to his father: "You should never have brought me here. Now I have lost forever all my most precious memories."'

'I've been thinking,' you said in the kitchen, as we ate at last, 'that it wouldn't be so bad to become a Jew.'

'What? Isn't it bad enough to be a Muslim?'

'I didn't mean in the religious sense, I meant culturally, to be part of a diaspora. It's got to the point with me where I write in Hebrew as my first language; but I conceive and write it in an Arabic way. That's like Yiddish, isn't it? German written in a Hebrew way? For the Palestinians to create such a literature, such a culture, as the Jews did, that would be worth a few hundred years of exile.'

'I'm not sure it's worth a holocaust.'

'Well, no, I wouldn't want to go that far. But to have no country, except one you dream about and pray for, that must be a good thing. Not to hope for a revolution that will make everything right, not to take up an armed struggle that you are never going to win; just to believe in a Messiah and for him, even, to wait patiently; what an achievement, Hannah; one of the pinnacles of human civilization. Maybe we could repeat it. Maybe the further you go from your starting point, the less you think about your losses. You're happy in London, aren't you?'

'Yes.'

'Maybe if I was living and writing somewhere else, I would be happy too; in Spain; in America; anywhere, so long as I wasn't here.'

'London, even?'

'Yes, London, even.'

5.

Despite all our exhaustion, the miracle was visible on our faces: that astonished shedding of the despairs and disappointments of an adult life, that dissolution of grudges and resentments in the warmth of happiness, the right to happiness even, suddenly restored.

You began to write, rising early and going off to the beach with your notebook. You would come back exultant, full of a fantasy of a future world with only one man left alive in it, or thinking himself so. Every day the story grew in dreamlike detail. Every day you translated the latest passage and read it aloud to me.

Shoshana and Daniel, your old university friends, invited us round to watch a video: a French costume drama, highly rated. We sat close together, one cigarette passing between us without a word or glance exchanged, as if it were the habit of decades; and the drama's solemn silences and profound sentiments reduced the two of us to childish hysterics until at last we all became infected, and the film became the funniest ever made.

'We must see Hannah again while she's here,' Shoshana said. 'Give us a few days to find a babysitter, and we'll come round for the evening.'

An Arab friend came by, Daoud, a Christian from Nazareth who knew London well. 'Yussuf has talked to me such a lot about you,' he said, and his eyes did not dart anxiously between our faces as we talked. He drove us down to Yafo to visit the relatives with whom he was staying. You wouldn't let anyone else sit beside me on the crochet-covered sofa, and you laughed as you asserted proprietorship. They served us coffee on tables inlaid with mother of pearl and everyone chatted with us in English. The television came on, a repeat episode of a serial not to be missed, and you explained the story to me: it was an Egyptian thriller set in the time of Nasser, based on the true exploits of a man who spied against Israel.

'You see,' you whispered, 'you are in the same country, but you are on another planet now.'

As we drove back, Daoud asked me, 'Where have you been in Israel, Hannah? Have you been to Nazareth? No? Yussuf, you must bring her next weekend. It's easy, we have three bedrooms, so you can sleep with my son, and Hannah with my daughter.'

'We'll talk about it, Daoud,' you said. 'We'll ring you back.'

'No,' I said, 'we can decide now. I'd love to go.'

'What about your conference?'

'It will be over by then.'

'Won't people want you to stick around afterwards, have dinner, that sort of thing?'

'No; the people here will only bother with the visitors from Harvard and Yale, the ones with the patronage. Small fish they throw back.'

'Good,' said Daoud, 'that's settled, then. Come up on the Friday bus.'

Another exile, another patriotism. Must it be?

One man in the world, and in his features, in his speech, in his way of wearing clothes even, I am connected to, tied to, possessed by a people. Every voice in your accent seems to speak to me; every face belongs to me, makes me smile with recognition as if we are related, as if I expect to be recognized.

I already know that every news item will be headlined in bold, will compel my attention if I think it concerns you. I will have a right to it, I will claim it. It will include me, embrace me. Even a list of names, a page of figures, will be enough; when I type them out, the keys will send sparks through my fingers.

Taking more minutes, editing more bulletins. Going to more meetings, showing up at yet more demonstrations.

Nothing is for nothing; no one is welcomed for the sake of their brown eyes. You would have told them I was educated, that I edited a journal, that I wrote for the literary reviews. You would have presented me as a friend for Palestine. To be invited to another planet in order to speak for it back on earth.

Do I want it, do I want another patriotism, another confinement within the stockade of injured innocence, another life dictated to by the tears of others? Do I want to become their good Indian, to be excused for being Jewish, to be praised for being remade?

Oh, there are membership tests wherever you go. We can't have an exile that's just for the two of us.

A few days later I remembered Shoshana and Daniel. 'We'd better phone them, hadn't we, in case they booked a babysitter for Friday?'

'Don't bother,' you said.

'Why not?'

'Listen, Hannah. I want to explain. Shoshana and Daniel have lived round the corner from me for years, and they ask me round, but they never, never, come round to my flat. It's always too much trouble to get babysitters. And I've asked Shoshana to drop in sometimes with the baby, in the afternoon, but she never does. And now, because of you, because I am in a couple, I am all of a sudden legitimate, you understand? I wasn't good enough, I wasn't kosher, before. I can't stand that, that's not friendship at all.'

If it was true, it was true. If you felt it, it was enough.

I knew the rest, but I asked anyway.

'And Nazareth?'

'No. I can't bear to do it. I don't want you to look at my people as a tourist spectacle. I'm not going to make a holiday out of what has been done to my people. If you want to take a trip we can go to the Negev: I don't mind that, because it's empty.'

'I didn't come here to be a tourist. You know that perfectly well.'

'And another thing, I don't want people in Nazareth to stare at me as I go round with you.'

'What is all this? You've been round with film crews, haven't you, and with that Swedish woman who was making a television documentary?'

'That's different and you know it's different. You and I look like a couple, it's obvious. We can't go.'

Well, I suppose I wouldn't take you for a walk down Golders Green Road on a Saturday afternoon, if it comes to that. So reasonable, all your refusals. But oh, Habibi, it's part of love, this sharing of space, this joint occupation, this facing of others together, side by side; must we refuse it so soon?

'Are you angry with me?' you asked. 'Do you hate me?'

'No. I understand,' I said, and didn't cry until you went out again.

6.

The sun blackened the room with shadows. I was packing, taking myself off the shelves, folding my months away tidily, removing all tracks and traces, returning the room to its former state.

Except, of course, that I was too vain to vanish. I planted hints and mementoes in your bedroom: a pile of fresh aerograms so that you would have no excuse for not writing; a photograph of my session at the conference; a postcard reproduction of a Matisse that we looked at together in a gallery.

And the room that was so cold when I first came to it was not its former self; it was almost choking in its own warmth. I opened the glass door on to the balcony, reminding myself that the dust would blow in and I would need to sweep the floor again before the morning.

The sun baked the street hard, muffled sound, stifled movement, stilled even birds and insects. Nothing stirred the branches. Only one creature, a skinny little cat with large ears set wide apart, seemed alive, threading her way in slow motion between parked cars.

An image fired in a kiln, which my life did not change, which would not be changed by my leaving.

Why, leaning over the balcony, did I believe I belonged here? Did the cells of my body, the ones that made my hair and skin and eyes dark, recognize this dust, this heat, the smell of that cypress, the shape of that cat, the colours of the lemon tree? Had our cries, year upon year, that our hearts yearned for Zion sprung from an actual physical anguish, did they declare a biological truth? I remember, as if it were my own memory, that Zeida, my mother's father, wanted to spend his last years studying the Law in Jerusalem. What did he remember, as if it were his own memory? You told me, Yussuf, that memories can be destroyed as well as given life, but I wasn't convinced; we are as much composed of the memories of others as of their eggs, their sperm, their genes.

This is, this ought to be our home. We should not, either of us, have to leave.

You put your head in at the door.

'Do you need any extra bags?'

'No.'

'But you bought presents, didn't you?'

'They're all little things except for the books, and I've got a bag for those.'

'This bag's stronger. I'll pack the books for you.'

'Stop winding me up, Yussuf. You know they'll ask me if I packed my own bags.'

'Well, I just want to put in one bomb, just one little bomb, to blow just one little hole in the fuselage. You'll carry that for me, won't you?'

'Stop it.'

'Oh, you lovely English socialists, always playing by the rules, always so law-abiding. Would you keep the lousy laws if you lived here?'

'I don't know. I don't live here.'

You looked around the room. 'I wish you did.'

You took the phone off the hook and we went back to your bed.

'When are you coming back?'

'Do you want me to come back?'

'Don't be stupid. You know I do. And I can't afford to come to England this year.'

'At the end of the summer, then. Before the start of term, if you ask me.'

'I'm no good at writing.'

'You're very good at writing.'

'Not like that. I told you; I don't like to think about what is missing, about what I've lost.'

'I won't be lost, if you write to me!'

'I'll phone. Oh, the phone; I'd better put it back on. No I won't. Let's have a shower first.'

Dipping and spluttering and hugging and stroking. One more luxury, one more forgetting of the world and time.

'Oh, this is nice. But when you come back we'll go swimming. We'll go down to the beach when everyone else is leaving and we'll see if we can be in the water when the sun sets into it. Shall we?'

'Yes. And stay in as long as we like without thinking that we're wasting water.'

'You're right.' You switched the shower off. 'Is that the doorbell?'

It must have been ringing for a long time, because whoever it was now began banging frantically.

Struggling to put clothes on over damp, resistant skin, to brush and dry our sopping hair; you finished first. You opened the door. It was Daniella Blum, the faculty secretary, out of breath, annoyed.

'I've been trying to get through to you all afternoon.'

Looking from one wet head to the other, disconcerted.

'You are going home tomorrow, aren't you, Hannah? It's just that Brigitte went home yesterday, and they called us from the airport; they were giving her a terrible grilling because she had papers from some student organization in Berlin they didn't like the sound of. And they gave us a bad time too. And we think you shouldn't say that you've been staying at Yussuf's. You can give them my address when they ask you where you lived for the past three months.'

She handed me a slip of paper. 'Here you are. Perhaps it would be a good idea to learn it by heart?'

'Where is it? I don't know any of these names. Show me on the map.'

I fetched the street plan from my holdall and unfolded it on the desk.

'There it is; and my flat's on the third floor. I don't see that it matters. Just remember the address and the phone number and give them my name.'

I looked at the map again and folded it up. 'This will sound silly, Daniella, but I actually don't like telling lies. At least, not other people's. I'm not very good at it.'

'Lies, truth,' you shouted. 'They've got nothing to do with it. Hannah has been renting a room from an Israeli citizen. Even under the lousy legal system of this country that is not a crime. The University placed her here. Is the University telling me I'm not a citizen? That my residence here is criminal? Should I maybe wear some kind of yellow badge in future, so that you don't make the mistake of treating me as an equal?'

'Yussuf, I'm just trying to make life easier for Hannah.'

'You're just trying to make life easier for yourselves.'

'Daniella, Yussuf, listen.'

Daniella was white as a sheet. She really was frightened: of the police; of Yussuf; perhaps even of me.

'I meant what I said about being a bad liar. If I give Daniella's address I shall look and sound guilty. And they probably know I've been staying here anyway. Better to go into the airport having nothing to hide, nothing to feel guilty about. What have I been doing but renting a room?'

Daniella looked again from my wet head to yours.

'Well. Everyone thought I ought to warn you.'

'Thank you. I appreciate that.'

She left. You were still angry. 'Why did you have to be so nice to her?'

'Why not? She was frightened. Yes, she was, Yussuf. Not everyone is brave, not everyone is like Nechama and Ari.'

'Oh, you need to be brave to mix with dirty Arabs, is that it?'

I didn't say anything. I wasn't brave enough to say, only as brave as you needed to be to take me to Nazareth.

The security officer looked about sixteen.

'Are these your bags?' Yes.

'Did you pack them yourself?' Yes.

'Have they been under your supervision since you packed them?' Yes.

'Are you taking anything home for anybody else?' No.

'Where have you been staying?' Here is the address.

'With whom have you been staying?'

I gave her the surname. Her brow furrowed slightly.

'What is the first name?'

I told her. She looked at me with disbelief.

'I have to go and fetch a senior officer.'

Her senior officer looked about twenty-one. He went through the first litany of questions, and then began his own.

'How did you meet this man?'

'I didn't. I came as a visiting fellow of the University, and they arranged my accommodation.'

'How did you know him?'

'I didn't. I didn't meet him until I went to stay there.'

'Who is he, what does he do?'

'He is a former student of the University. He teaches and translates. Why don't you ask him? I can give you the phone number.'

'Where does he come from?'

'I don't know the name of the village. He is a citizen. Why don't you ask him?'

'Why did you stay there?'

'I've told you. I was placed there.'

'What did you do while you were there?'

'Wrote lectures and papers.'

'Who did you meet?'

'How long have you got? I have been here three months. I don't even know the name of everyone I met.'

'Well, we will have to fetch a more senior officer. We can't let you get on the plane yet.'

Frozen with hostility and distaste, the pair of them.

And suddenly it welled up in me, an ecstasy of anger, against these children with their powers to call me an enemy of the people, these children whose parents weren't even born when I was being called names in the playground.

'What are you saying, and who are you saying it to? *Ani Yehudit.* I am Jewish. I do not endanger the state. I am also old enough to take security precautions seriously. I have told you everything and I have broken no laws or regulations. Now, what do you intend to do?'

The girl mumbled: 'But we have to do this. You understand.'

'Yes, of course you have to do this, and of course I understand. There are people who want to destroy us. I am not one of them.'

They looked at each other. The boy shrugged, and said: 'Well, have a nice flight.'

Oh, Yussuf, do you hate me?

7.

The first few weeks were going to be easy. You phoned the night I got home, so tenderly, so sweetly: 'Would you like a hug, Hannah?

and a kiss?' and I slept like a baby, and went back to the world, running, not walking, glowing with the knowledge that I was no longer alone. I poured monologues of joy into the ears of intimates, bombarded Tel Aviv with bulletins and streams of consciousness. I danced on air, I was carried through the days by the current that we had created. And, of course, I was beautiful: men wanted me; yes, this is normal, I thought, this is only to be expected; I am always someone who is loved, who is in love.

I wrote and told you that I was living in the words of a prayer, the one I learned before I was old enough to read, when my brother Simon stood in his stripy pyjamas, satin *coppel* on shining black hair, reciting one word at a time for me to repeat after him: loving with all my heart and with all my soul and with all my might, sitting in my house and walking by the way, and lying down and rising up. That must have been the one time that most of the letter was in Hebrew.

And I didn't expect you to answer one letter in five, in ten, even. I vowed not to fret, not to fidget, not to nag for a response, to keep myself busy, not to worry for at least a month. I could do that, surely, couldn't I, with my full life, with my full heart?

I cracked after a fortnight.

Late at night, I phoned. I took you completely by surprise. It was as if a ghost had laid hands on you. And then we managed to babble; you said that people had been teasing you about me, people like Daniel and the woman who ran the café; I said I was due for promotion, I would come in September if you could remember my name, ha-ha; you asked if there was anything you could send me and I said, send me yourself in a letter. I love you very much, I said. You said it too: I love you, *modik*, sweetheart. Goodbye, we said.

It wasn't you, it wasn't us. I felt sad, stupid, ridiculous. I had been banished from your mind, while you still occupied all my senses, my ear listening for your step, my hand longing for your grasp. I cried myself to sleep and dreamed that a letter from you arrived at last, stapled together; as I unpicked the staples, snow began falling from the envelope.

I told myself I would not think about you.

It should have been easy. I accepted an invitation to speak at a

German university halfway through the term. A large audience applauded my lectures on women and the political process over the last century, and crowded round me afterwards to ask questions, to get my address. I was taken to lunch, taken to dinner, shown round the city. At the end of each day, you were not there. At the end of each day was nothing.

I came home. I would not think about you.

I went out more, bought myself new clothes. As I tried them on I imagined how your eyes would widen at that first sight of me in them, at the airport. Every evening I came home alone from the cinema, the theatre, the restaurant, and as I opened my front door I pretended that I was not looking for a letter from you. Every night I went to bed early, willing myself to fall asleep before the hour when people in Israel might think of making cheap long-distance calls.

I would not crack, I would not write to you.

Except on your birthday.

I would not crack again, it was for you to break the silence.

I let the cat follow me everywhere, walk all over the desk while I was working, sit on my lap whenever she wanted to. When I got up I would give her a pat and put her down gently. Oh, that moment when lovers go to sleep; they have finished their lovemaking, they have finished their talking, they want to slip away, and they give each other a little kiss or a pat as they turn aside.

Sadness grew inside me like a baby. It was omnivorous. It fed on good food and drink, the smell of herbs in the garden, outings in the sunlight, walks in the warm evenings. Every pleasure recalled you, told me that my sadness was greater than I had imagined only the day before, that it would grow every day, no matter what I did; as I sat in my house, as I walked by the way, as I lay down, as I rose up.

I lived through another month.

I watched films of the occupied territories on television. I saw ululating women, in their headscarves, mourning their sons, screaming for more of them to become martyrs. Illiterate, maybe, like your mother, your sisters, my own grandmother? Were they my family, as well as yours? I saw men and boys, wounded or imprisoned for gestures of defiance, futile demonstrations of all the manhood that was left to them. I saw a celebration of betrothal, the dignity of bride and groom retrieved in ancient ceremonies and costumes, the pride of making new generations asserted in the teeth of humiliation. Where would you find your manhood, where would your pride be, if you were to take a foreign wife, in exile, bereft of all those customary honours?

I would not, must not write again.

But I opened the paper one morning and read that a Jew had stabbed an Arab in the street in Tel Aviv, quite suddenly, with no time for a warning voice in any language. I had to know that you were all right. You had to know that I had to know.

You have other things to do, I wrote, you do not like to think about that which is missing. But the news is frightening and your silence makes me miserable. Tell me you are all right, tell me we shall not meet again; that will be sufficient; I will say goodbye as a sister to a brother.

I lived for another six weeks.

I struggled to be unpossessed. I set traps for my unconscious. I was not allowed to think of the future. I was permitted only to remember the past. This thing that was growing inside me would shrink, would shrivel. I myself would be both its murderess and its corpse.

Slowly, I began to live like other people. Enjoying the gossip. Liking my students again. Calming their examination nerves, rereading their dissertations, gratefully accepting the piles of marking, the hours of invigilation, all the duties which I could perform interchangeably with my colleagues, and which relieved me of the burden of a particular existence.

I began to plan a restful, reasonable summer, visiting old friends in Scotland. We would talk about children growing up and leaving home, about the financial crisis in higher education, about teaching loads and declining doctoral standards. It would be really nice.

I had almost won my victory when the phone rang.

You were ashamed, you said. You had been inhuman. You could not write because you were at a crossroads, in a crisis, you did not know what to do. The election had brought you no work. I said, I could come if you really wanted me to. You said, I am not creative; I am not anything; I would not please you so much as before. I said,

I was unhappy in Tel Aviv before I met you; perhaps it is my turn to cheer you now. Should I come in October? All right, September. Goodnight, we said.

Surely I would not do it? I was within weeks of making myself whole. Would I willingly, knowingly, risk it all, choose that seething sickness in preference to a normal, healthy life? Surely not. But then again, gambling has always been a Jewish vice.

The combined forces of the Women's Studies Department of a London polytechnic could not arrive at a consensus.

'I don't think you should go,' Vi said, 'if he's made so little effort to keep in touch.'

Jill agreed: 'You can't build a bridge from just one side of the river.'

'That's right,' Vi said. 'You're making all the running.'

Both of them talking like the problem page of *Jackie*. How to make sure of that second date. The importance of playing hard to get. Both of them happily married to the men they first thought of. But they would never have thought of Yussuf. What does *Jackie* have to say about a second date with a guy whose birthplace was razed to the ground by your folks, in the month that he was born?

'Anyway,' said Sarah, 'How can you possibly be in love with someone in another country, with someone who isn't there. It's not a relationship. It's insane, really. A fixation, anyway.'

'And what will you do,' asked Carol, 'if it actually does work out? If you settle in Israel, or if he comes to London? You won't be able to tell your mother, or the rest of your family, will you?'

'No, I won't,' I admitted, 'but that's the easy part.'

And it would be. They wouldn't know, they wouldn't want to know. I would go on visiting my mother on Saturdays, telling her those little bits and pieces of myself that she might find interesting and acceptable. I would go on thanking Simon every birthday for the cheque in the card, wishing him long life on the anniversary of Daddy's death. Not much danger that a phone call, a visit from any of them, might catch me unawares.

'I would go if I were you,' said Kate, who had just ended her second marriage, and was still as beautiful as on the day we met at the Freshers' Fair. 'What does it matter if you never marry again, if you see each other only once or twice a year? What matters is that you have a relationship that means something to you.'

'You should go,' said Juliet, whose husband had committed suicide. 'If something is real, you must stay with it to the end.'

I didn't know if it was real to you, Yussuf. I only knew that it was real to me.

And so I came out of the airport in my new pearl earrings, and my new pearl-grey suit, and your eyes widened and shone, and you looked so happy that I could have sworn you loved me too. We went back to the flat and the wind blew the perfume of the cypress in over the bed, and we made love with great haste, and you kept hold of my hand in your sleep, all night long.

8.

You had shaved your head completely.

'What did you do that for? It doesn't suit you. Grow it again, you'll look much nicer.'

'You mean, not so ugly.'

'I mean, much nicer. And much younger.'

You gave me a sideways glance. 'You are mocking me.'

'Only a little bit.'

It was nearly midday and we had finally got up and into the kitchen. You were boiling water.

'After I had it shaved I met a girl I know, and she had just done the same. She did it after she was raped. She asked me if I had been raped.'

You made the tea.

'Had you been raped?'

'Don't be stupid.'

I looked in the fridge; there was some yogurt, some cheese, a little bread.

'You haven't been back to your family lately, have you?'

'Not home, not for food. I've been to hospital, I mean, to visit my father in hospital. He's been very ill, he's still there. I wanted to do something for him, to please him, and I said that I'd cut my hair, and I'd return to the mosque when Allah wills. That was for him, just for him, but he had to make a triumph, a party of it, to boast about it when the others came... Well, now he's lost the power of speech, and I'm not sorry, Hannah; I'm glad. I hate the old man; and the rest of them. They hate me, or they ignore me, except when they need someone to speak to an official, to sort out a licence, then they get on the phone...'

Suddenly you stood up, pulled your Filofax from your jacket and began ripping out pages and throwing them on the floor.

'I'm finishing with them, finished! They don't exist for me!'

'Stop, Yussuf, stop,' I said.

'Why should I?'

'Because that page has my address on it. Don't you want that any more, either?'

You sat down. 'Oh, Hannah, I'm sorry. I told you I wasn't as good as the last time you were here.'

I went into my room and came back with a packet of gummed rings. I picked up the pages and smoothed them and began mending the tears and putting them back in the file.

'Hannah, do you carry those things around with you everywhere?'

'Yes.'

'You British are wonderful.'

I put the contents of the fridge on the table, and when we had got through them, you said, 'I'm going out. I'm going to collect some work, some translation. What will you do?'

'I have some books to review. If I get tired of them, I'll go out and see if Nechama is around. And I'll pick up some groceries.'

'OK.' You hesitated on the threshold. 'Are you angry with me for going?'

'Should I be?'

'No.' You kissed me and left.

I went to the market, as much to be wrapped round in colours and smells and noises as to stock up with fruit and vegetables. Jostled and deafened and comforted and reassured, I picked up bread and butter and a chicken from the supermarket, got home and started cooking.

We finished the chicken in one sitting.

'Oh, Hannah, this is wonderful. However did you manage to fit it all inside the cooker?'

'You haven't been eating, have you?'

'No. It's been very hot, remember.'

'You need to eat, remember.'

'What does the word "nag" mean?'

'You know what it means.'

'No, I don't. Is it something to do with "hug"?'

'You know perfectly well that "nag" is me telling you to eat properly, and to answer my letters. This is a hug.'

Afterwards, we settled down to look at the work you had brought back with you. It was a set of scripts, in English, for a television series in natural history. You were to translate it into Arabic for use in schools. You were full of questions, wanting to be sure that you understood the technical terms, that you had selected the correct definition where the dictionary offered alternatives.

'I think I'd like to see the films themselves before I'm quite certain of some of this,' I said.

'A friend down the road has a video player. I'll arrange it. I think we'd enjoy watching the series anyway, don't you? Oh, Hannah, this is good. You're better than the best dictionary, you know. Really you are. The way you talk about things: you're so educated. I wish I was. I wish I were.'

'Yussuf, *modik*, why shouldn't you be? Why don't you finish your degree? Would it take you so long? If you did, I'm sure you could put together a research proposal that would get some funding. And then you wouldn't have to worry quite so much about the rent. For a couple of years at least. And while you were doing the research you could find some time for your own writing.'

'Oh, Hannah, always so full of ideas. I'm too tired to talk. I'm going to bed.'

You shrouded yourself, and we slept.

As soon as you woke up, you wanted to make love.

'Lie on your front, lie flat. No, don't look like that; I don't want to bugger you. I just want to take you from behind, I like it better that way.'

It doesn't do much for me, I felt like saying. It's fairly uncomfortable, and you keep falling out. But I got on with it; tolerant, obliging, resigned.

'We should find lots more ways of fucking, do it in different places. Always the same is boring.'

'I'm not bored.'

'We should do it on a table.'

'Well, that's all right for whoever's on top.'

'We could pretend things, act things. Oooh! Surgical operation!'

What is this, Yussuf? Some shopping list you wrote out before I arrived? Some practice schedule for your next three affairs? You've hardly let me touch you yet, we've hardly started this conversation, this singing without words, this being us. I could gaze, and stroke, and fondle you forever without being bored. I don't want you to be something else, I don't want to pretend to be something else. Don't we already have enough parts to play?

I rolled out of bed and started getting dressed as if I hadn't been paying attention.

'You are so dull, so boring, Hannah. Just like your clothes.'

'What on earth is wrong with my clothes?'

'All those long skirts. You look like one of the religious.'

'Maybe it looks like that in Tel Aviv. But in London skirts this length are actually fashionable.'

'Oh! I know nothing. Dirty Arab.'

'This isn't much of a conversation. I'm going to have some breakfast.'

You came up behind me in the kitchen and put your arms around me. 'I love it when you come, Hannah. I love the music of your voice. I love it when you cry like a child.'

We stood and rocked from side to side. We went back to work. You switched on the radio, the classical band as always, and we sat at our desks without speaking for most of the day.

It took us a week to work through all the scripts. Then Natan, one of your journalist friends, gave us the use of his flat and his video player, and we watched and worked for four hours after supper. In the last hour Natan came back and watched with us; we replayed the final section which we liked the best, on animals which had successfully colonized urban habitats.

'Have you seen the colony of bats near the park on King George Street?' Natan asked. 'Late at night, after most of the traffic has died down, you can see hundreds of them in the open.'

'What's the time now?'

'Two o'clock. Let's have a drink and then wander down there.'

We had gone about half a mile when Natan stopped. He was looking at a building plated with new metal shutters. The sign on the door was a garish yellow decorated with heart shapes, and bearing a non-committal legend: Tel Aviv Institute.

'Wasn't that a grocery store last week?' you asked.

'Well, it's not now,' said Natan. 'It has to be a new bordello.'

'Surely not,' you said. 'Not this close to the centre.'

'Well, what else can it be?'

'Well, OK,' you said, 'it's hard to imagine what else it can be.'

And then you said, 'How much does it cost, Natan, do you think?'

'Why do you want to know?' I demanded.

'Just out of academic interest. I hear about these things from friends.'

'And why should Natan know?'

'Natan's a journalist.'

'Well,' Natan said, 'I wouldn't really know about it either. But whatever it used to cost, it's gone down since the Russians arrived.'

We walked on, and I thought of other shops in other streets, full of lacquered spoons and Babushka dolls and gleaming new Russian china, chess sets, rugs; but behind the shop windows old irons, toasters, lamps, hairdryers, and racks of second-hand shoes; the desperate jettisoning of small comforts for uncertain reward.

We finally reached an island in the road, and a clump of gnarled trees. They had been growing there for five or six hundred years, Natan said. They had a fruit, a kind of wild fig, and for this the bats came. There was no problem about sighting them. They were huge, maybe half a metre from wing tip to tip, and livid in the orange street-lights. They swooped incessantly through the trees, over to the park and back again, snapping and grabbing, so fast that I could hardly see their heads. They flew low as well as high, and I prayed they wouldn't come near me.

We began at last to walk slowly back down King George, on the park side, in sight of the picnic areas, with their wooden tables and benches. A blanketed figure was stretched out on one of the tables.

'Homo Sovieticus,' said Natan, and laughed.

When we got back we did not wait to take our clothes off but made love frantically, noisily, clumsily, like animals, on the kitchen floor.

9.

In the morning, you said:

'This is ridiculous, pathological.'

'What is?'

'Us. Lying here, making love, when next week you're going home and we don't even know when you're coming back. When can we be together again? What will you be doing in the Christmas vacation?'

'I haven't thought about it, darling. I was just hoping that you would be able to find the air fare to London soon.'

'We could meet in Cyprus at the end of term. We could have a little holiday.'

'But I really don't think I can afford another air fare. And I certainly can't afford a hotel room.'

You were silent.

'Sweetheart, if you come to London, you can stay with me and it won't cost you anything. I could even find out if you're allowed to work, and what sort of visa or permit you need. Then you can be earning as well.'

'I don't want to do any more restaurant work, Hannah.'

'Of course you don't. I'll ask my friends about translation and teaching.'

'I could come for a month or two, maybe. Will it be cold?'

'Probably. And wet. You'll want that tweed jacket of yours.'

'Which?'

I got up and pulled it out of the wardrobe.

'This one. It's really good; Harris tweed. Where did you get it?'

'An American friend of mine left it here, he didn't want it any more.'

'Try it on. There, look at yourself. It's good, it suits you.'

We put it away and went back to bed.

'Have you got a car, Hannah?'

'No. You don't need one in London. I don't, anyway. And I can't really afford to run one.'

'Well, how will we get out of town?'

'There's always the train if we want it.'

'We will want it, we don't want to be stuck in one place like we are here, in Tel Aviv. It's so boring.'

I sat up in bed. 'I haven't been bored.'

'You must borrow a car from your friends.'

'That might not be possible.'

'Why not?'

'I don't know, it just might not. I can't promise anything.' I got out of bed. 'London is one of the biggest cities in the world, you know. Most people don't find it boring.' I put my clothes on. 'We finished the bread and milk yesterday. I'm going out to get some.'

You had the tea waiting when I got back. 'I'm sorry, Hannah. Of course we can have a lovely time in London without a car.'

'We can have a lovely time anywhere, *modik*.'

'It's true. If we wrote down all we did, it wouldn't seem like very much to anyone else. But it always seems as if we have a full agenda.'

'What are we doing today?'

'I have to go out, Hannah. I've got to find out about next term's teaching. I'm going to the adult education institute to see Nechama, she thinks she has some students for me. She thinks more and more people are wanting to learn Arabic. Who knows, maybe times really are changing. What will you do?'

'This review. I've finished making my notes on the books.'

'I'll see you later, then.'

I wrote for three or four hours, and then ran dry. I knew I wouldn't get anything else done that day, wouldn't be able to revise or add anything until the next morning. I stared out over the balcony, not seeing anything, not thinking anything, all senses suspended, at a halt. Perhaps it was time to eat and sleep, but it was too hot to eat, too hot to rest properly. Fruit would be nice, but we didn't have any. Shopping had more or less been left to me until the money came through for the scripts. Maybe going to the market would be pleasanter than sweating indoors, maybe there would be a current of air out in the streets, nearer the beach.

By the time I got to the market a river of sweat was streaming down my back and between my buttocks and all my clothes were plastered to me. I could no longer remember my Ivrit numbers. The Arab stallholders, ululating their wares and prices, carolling to each other across the aisles, became brusque and impatient as I stumbled over my words. They refused to sell me anything below a weight which suited them, and I bought too many grapefruit—I was the only one who liked them—and grapes which had passed their best. I knew that you would be scornful, and that I would bite my tongue not to remind you that I had paid for it all.

My load was too heavy. I kept putting the bags down, flexing my numbed fingers, wriggling my shoulder blades back into a better position. The last time I stopped I was opposite the café, our café. You were sitting outside, chatting animatedly with a group of women. Sharp faces, smart clothing. Journalists, perhaps? The sort of women you would have taken to Nazareth? The sort you would sleep with when I wasn't there? You had already told me, quite casually. I was different; we were a romance; but if I wasn't there you would still have physical needs. You had no sooner said it than I had blotted it from my mind. But I was looking at it now.

You didn't see me. I went on walking, heaved the stuff up the three flights to our door, unpacked it, ate one of the grapefruit, went to my room, and fell asleep.

It was dark when you got back.

'You haven't cooked supper,' was all you said, when you found me in my room.

'Nor have you.'

'Will you cook for me in London?'

'I'm going to cook you all sorts of things in London. English things, Jewish things. But we can take turns, like we do here.'

'I cook more than you do.'

'No you don't, Yussuf.'

'Yes, I do. And I do all the cleaning.'

'That's true. But I do all the shopping.'

'I'm thinking, Hannah, your flat in London must be very dirty, if you're so lazy.'

'What is this?'

'I think you must be a very lazy person.'

'Yussuf, I go into work practically every day of the year. I don't sit around half the day talking in cafés. I earn the money for air fares, I earn the money for groceries, I earn the money to pay the mortgage on my flat, and when I have the time and energy I clean it. When you work as hard as me you can start to call me lazy!'

I was screaming at the top of my voice. You ran out, slamming the door.

We slept in our own rooms. I got up early and phoned Jerusalem. Jill had given me the number of a friend at the Hebrew University. It was short notice; but, yes, she would love to see me, and perhaps I could have dinner and stay overnight?

You passed me in the hall.

'I'm going to Jerusalem, I'll be back some time tomorrow.'

'Oh, very fine! Stare at my people under occupation. Buy some bargains while you're about it.'

'I'm going to visit someone. I'm not going shopping, and I'm not going into the East. If I do any sightseeing, it'll be in Mea She'arim. Since I wear such horrible clothes, nobody there will want to throw stones at me.'

'I'm not interested, Hannah. I don't want to hear what you're doing, I don't want you to tell me about it when you come back. I'm tired of you telling me things, telling me things, always talking. You talk too much. Like a teacher.'

'That's not what you said a week ago.'

'A week ago, that's a whole week more I've had of you being here, all the time. When I go out, you come with me; when I come in, you are already there; when I stand up, you stand up; when I sit down, you sit down. When I go to bed, you come with me. I'm sick of it, it's crazy.'

'Well, you don't have to wait for me to catch my plane, Yussuf. Just go back to the cafés, go back to your hard-working life and your smart girlfriends, and get them to buy your groceries for you!'

I went out, without crying.

10.

I got back the next afternoon. The flat was dark, no music playing. I went to my room, and it was some time before I realized you were in yours. The phone rang, a voice asked for you, I knocked on your door to check.

You were sitting on the bed in the darkness and silence, curled up like an embryo, shrivelled, withered. I made an excuse to the caller and sat beside you.

'I didn't like it when you screamed at me, Hannah. I don't like you to be angry with me. My mother never screamed. Only my father did. Why did you?'

'Because you said horrible things about me. Because I believed them. Because I'm no good really, is the truth. I think I'm just shit. That's it, that's how it is.'

'You think you are shit? You with the job and the children and the conferences and the invitations?'

'You don't know me, you don't know all my mistakes. I'm no good at all.'

'That's not sensible, Hannah.'

We lay down, arms and legs entwined, clutching each other's bodies like spars. After a time your clasp loosened, and I began to hold you and rock you, and we were making little noises, like sucklings in a litter, when you said:

'Oh *modik*, I don't know anything, I don't know who I am, I don't know what I am any more. Arab, Jew, man, woman, I don't know.'

I rocked you again, and then I said, 'I want to give you a massage.'

We both took our clothes off and you lay on your front. I worked the way you had taught me, starting with your feet, stroking, rubbing upwards, pushing my palms into and over the soft places of your flesh, pressing and kneading around your spine, up to your beautiful shoulders, your dear neck, my fingers brushing every crease and bump and hair and freckle, until the whole of my own body was on fire and you rolled over and said:

'I'm ready now: now I want to hear you scream.'

We were very lazy the next day. We ate toast and jam in bed, and I did some sewing, and you told me stories of your childhood; of going in a cart to buy enormous quantities of plums very cheaply, and sitting in the cart with your brother, gobbling up the plums, continuously, like animals, while your mother turned them into jam. I told you about me and Simon, city children, looking for adventures in bomb sites and air-raid shelters; always knowing, despite the brass bands and the victory parades, that we had been slaughtered; never knowing what had happened to you. How I had gone away from home and walked on the other side, as you had; loved still, perhaps, but never forgiven.

We lay and looked at pictures in books: prints and photographs, and wonderful pages of Arabic calligraphy. We found an atlas with Hebrew lettering, and pored over the pages for England and France. I started to tell you about the French region I knew best, how we would go there and stay with friends, how it had once been conquered by the Moors; and you showed me how much further north they had conquered, and where the great battles had taken place.

Later on, you said: 'I don't feel like swimming. But let's watch the sun set into the sea.'

We walked down to the beach and sat on a blanket, not talking, just looking, as the sky turned pale and pink. The sun came towards the sea, spilling blood into the water, leaking it over the shining sand. You had brought your binoculars so we could look at the stars; we waited until we saw Venus rising. Darkness gathered round us and we started for home, walking slowly, buying ice creams, sweets, nuts and cakes for each other as we went.

Before we fell asleep, I said: 'If your people had reached further north, perhaps we would all have been Arabs by now.'

'Oh Hannah, you silly. Last time it was, maybe we both could have been Jews. We are what we are, sweetheart. Things are what they are. You mustn't try to pretend that they're something else.'

'We have reason to try.'

'Reasons aren't enough. If reasons were enough—well, we'd have something perfect, like communism should have been. No more talking, darling. Go to sleep.'

Can you still find this day, Habibi, among your possessions? Or can you no more fish it out than that same sun out of the sea?

The phone rang an hour after I got back from the airport. There was a time lag: you would begin, I would start answering, you would be beginning again and not hear me, we fought against air, and at last found the rhythm of it.

'Would you like a hug, Hannah? and a kiss?'

'Yes. And will you hold my hand in the night?'

'Yes.'

We said other things: I that I would start making enquiries with the Home Office and among my friends; you that Ari had business in London and would call on me in about a month.

I didn't tell you that I had done my *Ani Yehudit* routine again at the airport, that I had browbeaten the fresh-faced security officers until they said, oh all right then, do us a favour, open the bags and just go through them yourself while we watch you. They ended up shamefacedly wishing me a happy new year (which I had told them I was spending with my family in Golders Green, a detail they liked).

What didn't you tell me, my love?

I did make the enquiries, I read the job adverts and sent off for particulars, feeling slightly embarrassed, feeling that, even over the phone, it was obvious that I was asking For My Arab Lover. If anything, I felt even more awkward with my friends; as if I were coming across as the heroine, daring all, making any sacrifice for her beloved; as the kind of girl for whom, in more heroic times, love, passion and the struggle were fused in a single flame. But I just wanted you, Yussuf. I wanted an end to the absurdity of cooking without you, sleeping without you, not knowing your news.

Of course you didn't write, or call. I waited patiently: Ari was coming. I prepared a little package for him to take back to you; a long letter, herbs from my own balcony. I waited patiently for Ari, and the package he would bring for me.

Ari came, and I made him a meal. We talked as we hadn't found time to before, about the prospects for the peace process, about the situation in Yugoslavia, about his own life, the time he had spent in prison for his political activities, how he had wondered if he would ever give up and emigrate.

I waited patiently, but finally, I said: 'So; how is our friend Yussuf?'

And he went and stood by the fridge, supporting his back on a piece of the wall that juts out there. And he said that there were two ways of answering the question. You could say that Yussuf was fine, he was functioning OK, or you could say, no, Yussuf was not OK.

He told me that someone was starting a new journal and wanted you to write an article for it, but you wouldn't, because you couldn't get an exact guarantee of the political position of the editor. Someone else had wanted to interview you for a special feature on people who had walked away from a religious upbringing, but you had placed impossible conditions on them, and they had given up.

'I don't think he will ever consent to publish anything, Hannah; he will always find a way to refuse.'

I gave Ari the package, in exchange for nothing. You had sent nothing for me. Not a letter, not a tape, not a leaf, nothing.

I counted the days, I knew when you would have received my package. I counted the days, and then stopped counting.

I still had the presents you gave me when I left; the blue and white mug that was my favourite, the bar of soap that your sister made from olive oil. I didn't use the soap often, I wanted it to last. Some nights I would drink from the cup and wash with the soap before I went to bed. Yes, I was trying to conjure you.

I wrote you letters, but I didn't post them. Actually, it was the same letter, cut and polished and refined over and over again. A letter of protest; a letter of dismissal. A death warrant; and I wouldn't send it until I was convinced that it was time to get it over with. There are only so many practice runs, rehearsals, imitations of the real thing that a person can take. I made an end of it, as the year came to an end, and sent the letter.

Your silence is unforgivable, I said, because you know how much it hurts me. If you want to come to London, you will have to find another Englishwoman to help you.

I've gone back to real life, Yussuf. I'm very busy. The place where I teach became a university, and it's got big financial problems now. We're working flat out to get more students; if the new Women's Studies MA isn't a success, we're looking at departmental mergers and early retirements. At the weekends, if there's any time to spare, I collapse with the same group of friends; it's comfortable, it doesn't tire me, I always know what to expect.

Kein eyin ha'ra, my mother's health is good, no emergencies there for the moment, though I know a more demanding time lies ahead. The children are abroad, but there's the telephone and now e-mail too, so most weeks we're in touch.

I don't torment myself with thoughts of you. There is nothing so special about this story, there are many such, of men who say, 'I'll call you,' and then fall silent. No need to bring politics, religion, history, into it. Holiday romance, I can say; I'm old enough to know better.

I don't expect you to think of me. If you hate your own memories already, you're not going to create any more; you won't clutch another vacancy to your heart. You won't accept the love of a wife when you have walked away from the mosque, from the Party, from the armed struggle, from all the props that were offered you. Why strive to keep anything, when so much has been lost, and what is left is mutilated? Why finish anything, if you are the last man on earth, and no one but you will ever know about it?

I always knew that you would refuse me. You would never allow the power of casting spells to triumph over the thrill of resisting them. You would never keep a day of harmonies and pleasures while you had the strength to hurl it into the fathomless sea of your discontent.

But I still keep my wishes for you, Habibi; that, despite everything, you will make something, complete something, keep something of your own: a story; a child.

No, I don't torment myself. I think of you only when I see an Arab, when I see a Jew, when I read a newspaper, when I watch the television, when I go to a café, when I cook a meal, when I clean the flat; when I lie down and when I rise up; when the sun shines and when it doesn't.

I will go back some day, but as a tourist, or at least as a holidaymaker. My niece has married and settled in Eilat. Time will pass, and we will sigh over the peace process and take her children to the beach.

And if, against the odds, it were to happen: a new state, a new parity, a new possibility of citizenship; what would become of you? No longer an exotic, a curiosity in the land where you were born; no longer bound to fascinate a certain sort of woman, or man. There will be no tragedy left, no oppression visible, to dignify your discontent. Your story will dwindle into the commonplace. Even the bitter fruits of exile will be taken from you. Your sufferings will become so much unwanted baggage, like the past dissidence of Eastern Europeans, irrelevant now. What will you do, how will you grow old?

These are my last questions, this is my last letter. I no longer want an answer. I live normally now. I find it's possible, after all, to live without you; to live without a dream of belonging. I keep my memories of a homeland; but I live at last, almost, without looking for it. □

GRANTA

FAMOUS PEOPLE

Orhan Pamuk

TRANSLATION BY ERDAG M. GÖKNAR

GALATA BONMARSESI

Life is dull if there's no story to listen to or nothing to watch. When I was a child, if we weren't staring out of the window at the street and the passers-by, or into the apartments of the building opposite, we were listening to the radio, on top of which a small porcelain dog perpetually slept. Back then, in 1958, there was no television in Turkey. But we'd never admit to not having it. We'd optimistically say, just like we said about one of the legendary Hollywood movies which took some years to reach Istanbul: 'It hasn't come yet.'

Staring out of the window was such an essential habit that when television finally did arrive, people started watching it as if they were still looking outside. My father, my uncle and my grandmother talked and argued in front of the television without looking at one another, and described what they saw, as they used to do when gazing out of the window.

'At this rate, the snow will be really thick,' my aunt would say, for example, watching the snow that had been falling since morning.

'That halva-seller's come to Nishantashi again!' I'd say, peering through the other window at the tramlines.

On Sundays, we would go upstairs to my grandmother's apartment for lunch along with my aunts and uncles who, like us, lived on the building's lower floors. I'd wait for the food to be brought in, staring out of the window. I'd be so excited to be among this noisy gathering of relatives that the living room—dimly lit by the crystal chandelier hanging over the dining table—would brighten before my eyes.

My grandmother's living room was always in semi-darkness, like those on the other floors, but to me it seemed even gloomier. Maybe this was because of the net curtains and heavy drapes that hung in terrifying shadows at the edges of the balcony doors that were always kept closed. Or maybe it seemed that way to me because of the stuffy, cluttered rooms that smelled of dust and were filled with old worn wooden chests, screens inlaid with mother-of-pearl, colossal oak tables with elegant claw feet and a baby grand piano whose lid was covered with framed photographs.

After lunch one Sunday, my uncle, who was smoking a cigarette in one of the dark rooms that opened off the dining room, announced: 'I have two tickets for the football match, but I'm not

ROBERT CAPA/TOPHAM PICTUREPOINT

going. Why doesn't your father take both of you.'

'Yes! Take us to the game, Dad!' said my older brother from the other room.

'It will give the boys some fresh air,' my mother said.

'Why don't *you* take them out,' said my father.

'I'm going to visit my mother,' my mother said.

'We don't *want* to go to Grandma's,' said my brother.

'You can take the car,' said my uncle.

'Come on, Dad, please,' said my brother.

There was a long, awkward silence, as if my father could sense what everyone in the room was thinking about him.

'Give me the keys, then,' my father said to my uncle.

Later, downstairs on our floor, my father smoked and paced the long hallway while my mother dressed us in thick patterned wool socks and made us put on two sweaters each. My uncle's elegant cream-coloured 1952 Dodge was parked in front of the Teshvikiye Mosque. My father agreed to let us both sit in the front seat. The engine started at the first turn of the key.

There wasn't a queue at the stadium entrance. 'This ticket is for both of them,' my father said to the man at the turnstile. 'One is eight, the other is ten.' Afraid to catch the ticket-man's eyes, we walked inside. There were plenty of empty seats in the stands. We sat down.

The teams were already on the muddy field and I liked seeing the players running back and forth in their white shorts warming up. 'Look, that's Little Mehmet,' my brother pointed out. 'He was called up from the junior team.'

'I know that, thanks.'

Sometime after the game began, when the entire stadium had grown mysteriously quiet, I stopped concentrating on the players and my mind began to wander: Why do footballers all wear the same strip but keep their own names? I watched the names as they ran around. Their shorts were gradually getting muddier. Later, I saw the slow-moving funnel of a ship passing behind the bleachers as it made its way through the Bosporus. There was no score at half-time, and my father bought us a paper cone of roasted chickpeas and a pitta bread with melted cheese.

'Dad, I can't finish all of my pitta,' I said, showing him what was left in my hand.

'Just put it down,' he said. 'No one will notice.'

At half-time we stood up and moved around, trying to keep warm along with everybody else. Just like my father, my brother and I put our hands in our trouser pockets and turned our backs to the field. We were watching the other spectators when a man in the crowd called out to my father. My father cupped his hand to his ear, gesturing that he couldn't hear over the din.

'I can't come now,' he said, pointing to us. 'I'm with the kids.'

The man in the crowd wore a purple scarf. He came down the rows, stepping over the backs of seats, pushing and prodding people out of his way, to sit beside us.

'Are they yours?' he asked after they had embraced and he had kissed my father on both cheeks. 'They're so grown-up. It's unbelievable.'

My father didn't reply.

'How did you manage it?' the man said, looking at us in disbelief. 'Did you get married straight after school?'

'Yes,' said my father without looking at him. They talked some more. The man with the purple scarf placed a single unshelled peanut in each of our palms. After he left, my father sat in silence.

The teams were back on the field wearing clean shorts when my father said, 'Come on, let's get back home. You two are cold.'

'I'm not cold,' my brother said.

'No, you boys are cold,' my father insisted. 'Ali's cold. Come on, let's see you get up.'

As we left, bumping knees and treading on toes, we trod on the cheese pitta I'd dropped on the ground. Walking down the stairs, we heard the referee's whistle signalling the start of the second half. 'Are you cold?' my brother asked me. 'Why didn't you say you weren't cold?'

I didn't answer.

'You idiot,' my brother said.

'You can listen to the second half on the radio at home,' said my father.

'It isn't on the radio,' my brother said.

'Hush,' my father said. 'On the way back I'll take you through Taksim Square.'

We were silent. After passing the square, our father parked the car by the off-track betting window, as we'd guessed he would. 'Don't open the doors for anyone,' he said. 'I'll be right back.'

He got out. Before he could lock the doors from the outside, we pushed down the locks from the inside, but my father didn't go to the betting window. He ran down the cobbled street and crossed to the other side where he went into a shop with posters of ships, large plastic model planes, and pictures of beaches in the window.

'Where's Dad going?' I said.

'When we get home, do you want to play Tops or Bottoms?' my brother asked.

When my father came back, my brother was playing with the gear lever. We quickly drove to Nishantashi. He parked the car in front of the mosque again. As we passed Aladdin's, the cut-price shop, my father said, 'Why don't I buy you two something? But not that Famous People series again.'

'Oh, please, Dad, please!' we said jumping up and down.

My father bought us ten pieces each of the gum that came with pictures of famous people folded up with it. Back home in the lift I thought I'd pee out of excitement. It was warm in the apartment and our mother hadn't come back yet. We unwrapped the gum quickly and dropped the wrappers on the floor. I ended up with two Marshal Fevzi Çakmaks, one Chaplin, one of the wrestler Hamit Kaplan, a Gandhi, a Mozart, a De Gaulle, two Atatürks, and a number 21, Greta Garbo, which my brother didn't have. My total was 173 famous people, but I was still twenty-seven short of a complete set. My brother ended up with four Marshal Fevzi Çakmaks, five Atatürks, and an Edison. We each tossed a piece of gum into our mouths and began reading the captions on the back of the pictures:

Marshal Fevzi Çakmak
Commanding Officer, Turkish War of Independence
(1876–1950)
Mambo Candy & Gum Co.
A leather football will be awarded to the lucky person
who collects all 100 Famous People

My brother held the 165 pictures he'd collected in a stack in his hand. 'Let's play Tops or Bottoms,' he said.

'No.'

'I'll give you twelve of my Marshal Çakmaks for one Greta Garbo,' he said. 'Then you'll have a total of 184.'

'Nope.'

'But you have two Greta Garbos.'

I didn't say anything.

'When they give us our inoculations tomorrow at school, you'll be in a lot of pain,' he said. 'So don't come crying to me, all right?'

'I won't.'

After we'd had dinner in silence, we listened to the Sports World programme and found out that the game had ended in a two-all draw. When my mother came into our room to put us to bed and my brother was sorting out his school bag, I ran into the living room. My father was gazing out into the street.

'I don't want to go to school tomorrow, Dad,' I said.

'How come?'

'We're going to have our jabs,' I said. 'They make my temperature go up, and then I have a hard time breathing. Mum knows about it.'

He didn't answer, but just looked at me. I ran and got him a pen and paper from the drawer.

'Are you sure your mother knows?' he asked as he placed the paper on top of the Kierkegaard he was always reading but never finished. 'You'll go to school, but you won't get the jabs,' he said. 'That's what I'm writing.'

He signed the note. I blew on the ink, folded it up and put it into my pocket. I rushed back into our bedroom, put the note into my bag, then climbed on to my bed and started jumping up and down.

'Behave yourself,' my mother said. 'Go to sleep, now.'

At school, right after lunch, the whole class assembled in two columns and we headed back down to the foul-smelling cafeteria to be inoculated. Some of us were crying, others were in a state of frightened anticipation. When I caught a whiff of the iodine coming up from below, my heart quickened. I left the line and went to the teacher at the top of the stairs. The class clattered past us making a tremendous commotion.

'Yes,' said the teacher. 'What is it?'

I took the note my father had written from my pocket and handed it to the teacher. She read it with a frown. 'But your father isn't a doctor,' she said. She thought for a moment. 'Go upstairs. Wait in 2A,' she said.

Upstairs in 2A there were six or seven other excused children like myself. One was staring in terror out of the window. From the corridor came an endless din of crying and turmoil. A fat kid with glasses was eating sunflower seeds and reading a Kinova cartoon book. The door opened and Seyfi Bey, the skeletal assistant principal, entered.

'No offence to you students who are perhaps genuinely sick,' he said. 'This is for those of you who are faking. One day you'll all be called on to serve your country, maybe even die for it. If those of you who have avoided your shots today don't have a proper excuse then, you'll have committed an act of treason. Shame on you!'

We were silent. Glancing at Atatürk's picture, my eyes began to water.

Later we went back quietly to our classrooms. The ones who had been inoculated were long-faced. Some had their sleeves rolled up, others had tears in their eyes, and they were pushing and bumping into each other.

'Those of you who live nearby can go home,' said the teacher. 'Those of you who need someone to accompany you will wait here until the last bell. Don't hit each other in the arm like that! School is cancelled tomorrow.'

We cheered. Downstairs at the main gate some of the students who were leaving rolled up their sleeves and showed off their iodine stains to the doorman, Hilmi Effendi.

As soon as I was outside on the street with my bag in my hand I began to run. A horse-drawn cart was blocking the pavement in front of Karabet's butcher's shop. Running between the cars, I crossed to our side of the street. I ran past Hayri's fabric shop and Salih's flower shop. Our doorman, Hazim Effendi, let me in.

'What are you doing home at this hour?' he said.

'They gave us our jabs,' I said. 'Then they let us out of school.'

'Where's your brother? Did you walk back alone?'

'I crossed the tramlines by myself. There's no school tomorrow.'

'Your mother isn't home,' he said. 'Why don't you go up to your grandmother's.'

'I'm sick,' I said. 'I want to go to our floor. Let me in.'

He took the key from the hook on the wall and we went into the lift. In the time it took to go upstairs, the lift was filled with his cigarette smoke, which burned my eyes. He let me into the apartment. 'Don't fiddle with the lights,' he said, closing the door behind him as he left.

Though there was nobody there, I shouted, 'Is anybody home? I'm home, I'm home!' I dropped my bag, pulled open my brother's desk drawer and began to examine the film-ticket collection he'd never show me. After that I became so engrossed in the scrapbook where he pasted newspaper clippings of football games that I panicked when I heard the front door being unlocked. I knew it wasn't my mother by the sound of the steps. It was my father. I carefully replaced my brother's tickets and scrapbook so he couldn't tell I'd disturbed them.

My father walked into his bedroom, opened his wardrobe, and looked inside.

'Oh, you're at home?'

'No, I'm in Paris,' I said, the way they did at school.

'Didn't you go to school today?'

'Today was inoculation day.'

'Where's your brother? All right then, let's see you go and sit quietly in your room.'

I did as he said. Resting my forehead on the windowpane, I looked outside. From the sounds he made, I realized that he was taking down one of the suitcases from the hall cupboard. He went back into his room. He took his sports jackets and trousers out of the wardrobe; I recognized the hangers by their tinny sound. He opened and closed the drawers where he kept his shirts and socks. I heard him put them all into his suitcase. He went in and out of the bathroom. He shut the suitcase and locked the metallic clasps with a perfect click. He came to find me in my room.

'What are you doing in here?'

'Staring out of the window.'

'Come over here,' he said.

He pulled me on to his lap and together we looked outside. The tips of the tall cypress trees between us and the opposite apartment building began to sway slowly in a gentle breeze. I liked the way my dad smelled.

'I'm going far away,' he said. He kissed me. 'Don't tell your mother anything. I'll tell her later.'

'By plane?'

'Yes,' he said, 'to Paris. Don't say anything to anyone.' He took out a large two-and-a-half lira note and gave it to me. 'Don't mention this to anyone, either,' he added, and kissed me again. 'Or that you saw me here...'

I immediately pocketed the money. When he lowered me from his lap and picked up his suitcase, I said, 'Don't go, Dad.'

He kissed me again and left.

I watched him from the window. He walked towards Aladdin's store, then hailed a passing taxi. Before he bent down to get into the car, he glanced back at the apartment building and waved to me. I waved back and he disappeared.

I stared at the empty street. A tram went by and then the water-seller's cart pulled by its plodding horse. I rang the bell, calling for Hazim Effendi.

'Did you ring the bell?' he asked when he arrived. 'Don't play with the bell.'

'Take this two-and-a-half lira!' I said. 'Go to Aladdin's and buy me ten pieces of the Famous People gum. And don't forget to bring back the fifty kurus change.'

'Did your father give you the money?' he asked. 'Your mother won't be angry, will she?'

I didn't answer. From the window, I watched him go into the store. A few minutes later he came out and on his way back he ran into the doorman of the Marmara apartments on the opposite side of the street. They chatted.

When he came back he gave me the change. I unwrapped the gum straight away: three more Marshal Fevzi Çakmaks, one Atatürk, one each of Lindbergh, Leonardo da Vinci, Sultan Süleyman the Magnificent, Churchill and General Franco, and another number 21, Greta Garbo, which my brother didn't have. My total now was 183. But I was still missing twenty-six cards for a complete set.

While I was admiring the number 91 Lindbergh photo for the first time, taken in front of the plane he'd flown across the Atlantic, I heard someone unlocking the door. My mother! I quickly threw away the gum wrappers that had dropped on the floor.

'We had our jabs. I came back early,' I said, 'You know, typhoid, typhus, tetanus.'

'Where's your brother?'

'His class hasn't been inoculated yet,' I said. 'They sent us home. I crossed the street by myself.'

'Does it hurt?'

I didn't say anything.

Before long, my brother came home. He was in pain, and he lay on the bed on his right side frowning as he fell asleep. By the time he woke up it was almost dark outside. 'Mum, it really hurts,' he said.

'You'll have a fever by evening,' said my mother from the living room as she ironed. 'Ali, does yours hurt as well? Lie down and be still.'

We lay motionless, resting. After a nap, my brother sat up and read the sports section of the paper and told me that we'd missed seeing four goals yesterday because of me.

'If we hadn't left, they might not have scored *any* goals,' I said.

'What?'

After another nap my brother offered to trade me six Marshal Çakmaks, four Atatürks, and three other pictures I already had for one Greta Garbo.

I refused.

'Do you want to play Tops or Bottoms?' he asked then.

'OK, let's play.'

The game went like this: you sandwiched a stack of Famous People pictures between your palms and asked 'tops or bottoms?' If the other person said 'bottoms' you took out the picture at the bottom of the stack, let's say it was a number 78, Rita Hayworth, for example. Say number 18, the poet Dante, was on top. Then bottoms would win the round because it had the higher number and you'd have to give up one of your least favourite pictures. We traded pictures of Marshal Fevzi Çakmak until evening. At dinner time my mother said, 'One of you go up and take a look, maybe your father's come home.'

We both went upstairs. My father wasn't there. My uncle and my grandmother were smoking. We listened to the news on the radio and read the sports section. When my grandmother and uncle sat down to dinner, we went back downstairs.

'Where have you been?' my mother said. 'You didn't eat anything upstairs, did you? I'd better give you your lentil soup now. You can eat it slowly until your father arrives.'

'Isn't there any toast?' my brother said.

My mother watched us as we silently ate our soup. I could tell she was listening for the lift by the way she cocked her head and avoided our eyes. When we'd finished, she looked into the pot and said, 'Do you want any more? I should probably have mine before it gets cold.' But instead, she walked to the window that overlooked Nishantashi Square and gazed down in silence. She came back to the table and started eating her soup. My brother and I were talking about yesterday's game when suddenly she said, 'Shush! Isn't that the lift?'

We listened carefully. It wasn't the lift. A tram went by, faintly jiggling the table and the water in the glasses and the jug. As we were eating our oranges, we actually did hear the lift. It came nearer and nearer, but passed us on the way to my grandmother's on the top floor. 'It went upstairs,' my mother said.

When dinner was over, she said, 'Take your plates into the kitchen, but leave your father's place.' We cleared the table. Our father's empty dinner plate remained on the table.

My mother walked to the window facing the police station and gazed outside. As if she had suddenly come to a decision, she cleared away my father's plate, his knife, fork and spoon, and took them into the kitchen. She didn't wash the dishes. 'I'm going up to your grandmother's,' she said. 'Don't fight.'

My brother and I began a round of Tops or Bottoms.

'Tops,' I said, starting off.

He showed me the picture at the top of his stack first: 'The world-renowned wrestler Yusuf the Giant, number 34,' he said. Then he looked at the bottom of the stack, 'Atatürk, number 50,' he said. 'You lose. Hand one over.'

The more we played, the more he won. He quickly took nineteen number 21 Marshal Fevzi Çakmaks and two Atatürks from me.

'I quit,' I said angrily. 'I'm going upstairs with Mum.'

'She'll be mad.'

'You're just afraid of staying here by yourself, chicken!'

The door to my grandmother's apartment was open as usual. They'd finished dinner. The cook, Bekir, was washing the dishes and my uncle and grandmother sat facing each other. My mother was standing at the window overlooking Nishantashi Square.

'Come here,' she said, without moving her gaze from the window. I quickly squeezed into the space between my mother's body and the window, the space that seemed to be reserved just for me. I leaned my body against hers and, like her, began to stare out at Nishantashi Square. My mother put her hand on my forehead and stroked my hair.

'I know your father came home, and you saw him around noon,' she whispered.

'Yes.'

'Did he tell you where he was going, my love?'

'No,' I said, 'he gave me a two-and-a-half lira bill.'

The darkened shopfronts on the street below us, the car headlights, the absence of the traffic policeman from his usual spot, the wet cobblestones, the letters that made up the advertisements hanging from the trees, they were all so very lonely and sad. When it started to rain, my mother was still slowly stroking my hair.

I realized that the radio which always sat between my uncle and grandmother, the radio that was always on, was silent, and this frightened me.

'Don't just stand there, my dear girl,' said my grandmother after a while. 'Come here, please, and sit down.'

Meanwhile, my brother had also come upstairs.

'Go into the kitchen, you two,' my uncle said. 'Bekir,' he called. 'Make a ball for them, so they can play football in the hall.'

In the kitchen, Bekir had finished the dishes: 'Have a seat,' he said. He began to crumple and shape a ball from the newspapers he had fetched from the small glassed-in balcony off my grandmother's room. 'How's this?' he asked, when the ball was about the size of his fist.

'A bit bigger,' said my brother.

Bekir wrapped a few more sheets of newspaper round the growing wad. Through the half-open door, I noticed that my mother had sat down across from my grandmother and uncle. Bekir wound the string he had taken from the drawer tighter and tighter round the newspaper ball, making it perfectly round, and then tied a knot. To smooth out the remaining jutting corners of newspaper, he dampened the ball with a wet rag. Unable to contain himself, my brother grabbed it.

'Oh, man, it's hard as a rock.'

'Put your finger there,' said Bekir.

My brother carefully put his finger on the place where the string had been knotted and Bekir finished the ball off by tying one final knot. He tossed it into the air and we began kicking it.

'Out in the hallway,' said Bekir. 'You'll break everything here.'

We played furiously for a long time. I imagined I was Lefter of Fenerbahçe and could dodge my opponents like he could. Making wall passes, I ran into my brother's sore arm. He hit me, too, but I felt nothing. We were covered in sweat and the ball was coming apart. I was beating him five–three when I really laid into his arm. He fell to the ground and began crying. 'When this stops hurting, I'll kill you,' he said from where he lay.

I ducked into the living room. My grandmother, my mother and uncle had moved into the den. My grandmother was on the phone, dialling.

'Hello, dear,' she said in the same distant tone she adopted when she said 'my dear girl' to my mother. 'Is this the Yeshilkoy airport terminal? Yes, dear, we want to ask after a passenger on one of today's flights to Europe.' She gave my father's name and waited, winding the telephone cord around her finger. 'Go and get me my cigarettes,' she said to my uncle. When he left the room, my grandmother lifted the receiver away from her ear slightly.

'My dear girl, please,' she said to my mother, 'you would know, is there another woman involved?'

I couldn't hear my mother's reply. My grandmother regarded her as if she hadn't said anything at all. The person on the other end spoke and my grandmother said angrily to my uncle, who had returned with cigarettes and an ashtray in his hand, 'They're not giving me an answer.'

My mother must have been alerted to my presence by the expression on my uncle's face. She grabbed me by the arm and dragged me out into the hall. Sliding her hand from the nape of my neck down my back, she could feel how much I was sweating, but she didn't seem to care that I might catch a chill.

'Mum, my arm hurts,' said my brother.

'We'll go downstairs now, and I'll put you to bed.'

Downstairs, on our floor, the three of us moved silently. Before going to bed, I went into the kitchen in my pyjamas for a drink of water then walked into the living room. My mother was in front of the window, smoking.

'You'll catch a cold walking about in your bare feet,' she said when she heard me. 'Has your brother gone to sleep?'

'He's asleep. Mum, I want to tell you something.' I waited to position my body between my mother and the window. When my mother moved, creating that perfect space, I squeezed in. 'Dad's gone to Paris,' I said, 'and do you know which suitcase he took?'

She didn't say a thing. In the stillness of the night we watched the rainy street.

My maternal grandmother's house stood directly across from the Shishli Mosque, on the last tram stop before the station yard. Today, Shishli Square is filled with bus and minibus stands, multi-storey department stores covered in an orgy of signs, tall ugly buildings riddled with offices and armies of sandwich-carrying employees who flood the pavements like ants during the lunch hour. Back then, it was a large, peaceful cobbled square, a fifteen-minute walk from our home. Walking under mulberry and linden trees, holding my mother's hands, it seemed as if we had reached the very edges of the city.

One side of my grandmother's four-storey stone house, which was shaped like a matchbox standing on end, faced west, towards old Istanbul; the other side faced east, towards the mulberry orchards and the first hills of Asia across the Bosporus. After her husband died and after she had married off her three daughters, my grandmother took to living in just one room of this house, which was packed from top to bottom with tables, armoires, pianos and piles of worn-out furniture. One of my aunts, my mother's oldest sister, would have meals prepared for my grandmother and bring them to the house herself or send them in containers with a driver. My grandmother wouldn't even venture into the other rooms, which were covered in a thick layer of dust and silky spider's webs, to tidy up, let alone go downstairs two flights to make herself something to eat. Just like her own mother, who had spent the last years of her life alone in a large wooden mansion, my grandmother wouldn't allow a caretaker, a housekeeper, or a maid to enter the house after she'd been stricken by this mysterious plague of loneliness.

Whenever we came to visit, my mother would ring the bell for a long time and bang on the heavy door, until finally my grandmother opened the rusty shutters of the second-storey window facing the mosque and peered down at us. Because she couldn't rely on her failing eyesight, she had us call to her and wave.

'Move away from the door, boys, so your grandmother can see you,' my mother would say. She'd walk to the middle of the pavement with us, waving and shouting, 'Mother, it's me and the boys, it's us, can you hear us?'

We'd know that our grandmother had seen and recognized us from the sweet smile that would light up her face. She'd turn quickly back inside, walk into her room, remove the large key she kept under her pillow and, after wrapping it in newspaper, toss it out of the window to us. My brother and I would jostle each other to be the one to catch it.

This time, since my brother's arm was still hurting him, he didn't try for the key and I ran and grabbed it off the pavement and handed it to my mother. She turned it inside the lock with difficulty. The large iron door opened slowly as we applied our combined weight to it, and from the darkness within came the stagnant smell of mould, age, and stuffiness—a smell I have never encountered anywhere else. On a coat stand next to the door hung my grandfather's fur-collared coat and felt hat that my grandmother had put there to scare away thieves, and off to one side rested his boots, which always frightened me.

We saw our grandmother in the distance, standing at the top of the dark wooden staircase that went straight up two flights. In the whitish light filtering through the frosted art-deco glass, she stood, cane in hand, not moving, a ghost in the shadows.

As she climbed the creaking stairs, my mother didn't say a word to her mother. ('How are you, Mother darling?' she'd say on other visits. 'I've missed you, Mother darling.' 'The weather's so very cold, Mother darling!') At the top of the stairs, I kissed my grandmother's hand and brought it to my forehead, as we used to do then, trying not to look at her, or at the large protruding mole on her wrist. Once again we were frightened by the sight of her single remaining tooth, her long chin and the hairs on her face, and as we entered her room, we stuck close to my mother and sat on either side of her. My grandmother climbed back into the large bed where she spent the majority of her day, wearing her long nightgown and thick woollen vest, and smiled at us with an expectant look that said, 'Go on, then, entertain me!'

'Your stove isn't working so well, Mother,' said my mother. She picked up the tongs and stoked the wood in the stove.

My grandmother waited a moment. 'Leave it right now,' she said. 'Tell me some news. What's going on in the world?'

'Nothing at all!' my mother said.

'Don't you have anything to tell me?'

After we were silent for a time, my grandmother asked, 'Haven't you seen anyone?'

'Not really, Mother,' said my mother.

'For the sake of Allah, isn't there any news?'

There was a pause.

'Grandma,' I said, 'we had our jabs.'

'*Did* you?' said my grandmother, opening her blue eyes wide. 'And did it hurt?'

'My arm's sore,' said my brother.

'Oh my goodness!' said my grandmother, smiling.

Another long silence. My brother and I stood and looked out of the window at the distant hill-tops, the mulberry trees and the old empty chicken coop in the backyard.

'Don't you have a story for me?' my grandmother asked my mother, imploringly. 'You must go up to your mother-in-law's floor. Doesn't anyone drop in there?'

'Lady Dilruba came to visit yesterday afternoon,' my mother said. 'She played bezique with the children's grandmother.'

Delighted by this, my grandmother said what we knew she would say: '*She* was raised in the palace!'

Of course, by 'palace' we understood her to mean Dolmabahçe Palace, not the colourful Western palaces that I'd read about for years in storybooks and newspapers. It was much later that I realized my grandmother's belittling implication that Lady Dilruba had been a *cariye*, a lady slave in the sultan's harem, not only demeaned Lady Dilruba, who had spent her youth in the harem and was later made to marry a businessman, but also my father's mother, who was her friend. Next they moved on to the subject that was guaranteed for discussion on each visit: once a week my grandmother lunched alone at Aptullah Effendi's famous and expensive restaurant in the Beyoglu district, after which she'd complain at length about everything she'd eaten. The third regular topic of conversation was introduced by my grandmother's sudden question: 'Boys, does your grandmother give you parsley to eat?'

As our mother had prompted us beforehand, we said in unison: 'No, Grandma, she doesn't.'

As usual, my grandmother explained how she had seen a cat urinating on parsley in a garden, adding that in all probability that very parsley, without being properly washed, had been served in who knows what idiot's meal, and she further explained how she squabbled with the greengrocers of Nishantashi and Shishli who still sold parsley, trying to convince them they should stop.

'Mother,' said my mother, 'the children are restless, they want to explore. Why don't I unlock the room across the hall?'

To prevent a thief getting into the house, my grandmother kept every door locked. My mother opened up the large, cold room which looked out over the tramlines and for a moment we all stood surveying the armchairs and divans covered in white sheets, the rusting dusty lamps, the chests, the yellowed stacks of newspaper, and the drooping handlebars and worn-out seat of a girl's bicycle which leaned forlornly in a corner. But this time she didn't happily pull something out of the chests to show us, as she would do when she was in better spirits. ('Your mother used to wear these sandals when she was little, my darlings.' 'Look, here's your aunt's school frock!' 'Do you want to see the piggy bank your mother had when she was small, my darlings?')

'If it gets too cold, come back into the other room,' she said as she left.

My brother and I ran to the window and looked out at the mosque across the road and at the deserted tram stop in the square. Then we read about old football matches in the papers. 'I'm bored,' I said a bit later. 'Do you want to play Tops or Bottoms?'

'Do you want to lose again?' my brother said without lifting his head from the paper. 'I'm reading now.'

After last night's game, we'd played again in the morning and my brother had continued to beat me.

'Please.'

'On one condition. If I win you give me two pictures, if you win, you get one.'

'No.'

'Then I'm not playing,' said my brother. 'As you can see, I'm reading the paper.'

He ostentatiously held his newspaper the same way the English detective had in the black and white film we'd seen recently at the Angel Theatre. After gazing out of the window for some time, I decided to accept my brother's rules. We took our Famous People stacks out of our pockets and began the game. I was winning at first, then I lost seventeen more pictures.

'I always lose this way,' I said. 'If we don't play like we used to, I'm giving up.'

'OK,' said my brother, imitating the detective. 'I was going to read the papers anyway.'

I went to the window and carefully counted my pictures: I had 121 left. Yesterday, after my dad had gone, there were 183! Why should I go on feeling so fed up? I accepted his terms.

At the beginning, I won some, then he began to beat me. As he added the pictures he'd taken from me to his pile, he tried to stop himself from smiling so I wouldn't get angry.

'If you want we can play by different rules,' he said a bit later. 'Whoever wins takes one picture. If I win I get to choose the picture, because I don't have some of the ones you do and you never give those up.'

I accepted, thinking I'd start to win. I don't know how it happened: I lost three times in a row and before I knew it, I'd given up two of my number 21 Greta Garbos and a number 78 King Farouk, which my brother already had. I wanted to win them all back at once so I upped the stakes. That's how I rapidly lost, in two rounds, my number 63 Einstein—which he didn't have—number 3 Rumi, number 100 Sarkis Nazaryan—the founder of the Mambo Gum and Candy Company—and number 51 Cleopatra.

I couldn't even swallow. Afraid I was going to cry, I ran to the window and looked outside. Five minutes ago, everything was so beautiful: the tram approaching its stop, the distant apartment buildings between the autumn chestnut trees with their falling leaves, the dog lying on the cobblestones lazily scratching itself. If only time would stop. If only I could go back five squares like in the horse-racing game we played with dice, I'd never play Tops or Bottoms with my brother again.

'Let's play once more,' I said without taking my forehead off the windowpane.

'I'm not playing,' he said. 'You'll cry.'

'I *swear* I won't cry, Jevat,' I said earnestly, walking up to him. 'Only, let's play fair, like we did at first.'

'I'm reading the paper.'

'All right,' I said. I shuffled my dwindling stack of pictures. 'With the rules we last played by,' I said, 'tops or bottoms?'

'No crying allowed,' he said. 'All right then, tops.'

I won and he handed me a Marshal Fevzi Çakmak. I refused it. 'Please give me number 78 King Farouk.'

'No,' he said. 'That's not what we said.'

We played two more rounds and I lost. I shouldn't have played a third round: I surrendered my number 49, Napoleon, my hand trembling.

'I quit,' he said.

I begged him. We played twice more. When I lost, instead of giving him the pictures he wanted, I tossed the rest of my pile over his head. All of those number 28 Mae Wests and number 82 Jules Vernes, number 7 Sultan Mehmed the Conquerors and number 70 Queen Elizabeths, number 41 the journalist Celal Saliks and number 42 Voltaires that I had thought about one by one, painstakingly hidden and carefully collected every day for two-and-a-half months, flew into the air like butterflies and fell hopelessly to the ground.

If only I had a completely different life somewhere else. I headed towards my grandmother's room, then turned and quietly went down the creaky stairs thinking about our distant relative, an insurance salesman, who had killed himself. My father's mother had explained to me that people who commit suicide were condemned to a dark place underground and couldn't go to heaven. When I was almost at the bottom of the stairs, I stopped and stood in the darkness. Then I turned round again and went back upstairs and sat on the top step by my grandmother's room.

'I'm not well off like your mother-in-law,' I heard my grandmother say. 'You'll just have to take care of your children and wait.'

'But I'm asking you again, Mother, I want to move back in here with the children,' my mother said.

'You can't stay here in this dusty, haunted, thief-ridden house with two boys,' said my grandmother.

'But don't you remember, Mother, in the last years of Father's life, after my sisters married and left, how happy the three of us were living here together!'

'Mebrure, my dear, you'd only flip through your father's old magazines all day,' my grandmother said.

'I'd get the large stove downstairs lit and the whole house would warm up in two days.'

'I warned you about him before you got married,' said my grandmother.

'It would only take a couple of days to get rid of all the dust and dirt in the house, with the help of a maid.'

'I won't allow any pilfering maids to enter this house,' said my grandmother. 'Besides, it would take you six months to clean this place and get rid of all the spiders. In the meantime your wayward husband will have returned.'

'Is that your last word?' said my mother.

'Mebrure, my love, if you and the children move in here, how would we get by, the two of us?'

'But Mother, how many times have I asked you, begged you, to sell the property in Bebek before the government expropriates it?'

'I can't bring myself to go to the Land Registrar's office, sign my name, and give my photograph to those disgusting men.'

'But Mother, we sent you a lawyer, just so you wouldn't have to deal with that,' my mother said, her voice rising.

'I didn't trust that lawyer at all, not at all,' said my grandmother. 'You could tell from his face he was a swindler, I'm not even sure he was a real lawyer. And don't raise your voice at me.'

'Fine. I won't say anything else,' said my mother. She called to us, 'Children! Get ready, hurry, we're leaving.'

'Wait, where are you going?' said my grandmother. 'We haven't talked about anything yet.'

'You don't want us,' my mother whispered.

'Take this, buy the kids some sweets.'

'They shouldn't have any before lunch,' my mother said and went behind me into the room across the hall. 'Who scattered these pictures about? Pick them up right away. And you help him,' she said to my brother.

As we quietly picked up the Famous People pictures, my mother opened the old chests and looked at her childhood dresses, her ballet costumes, her angel costumes and everything else that was packed inside. The dust under the black skeleton of the pedal sewing machine filled my nostrils, making my eyes water.

As we washed our hands in the small closet, my grandmother said in her gentle imploring voice, 'Mebrure, why don't you take this teapot you're so fond of? It's rightfully yours. My grandfather—he was such a fine man—bought it for my mother when he was the governor of Damascus. It came all the way from China. Take it, please.'

'I don't want anything from you, Mother darling,' my mother said. 'Put it back in your cupboard, you'll break it. Come on, children, kiss your grandmother's hand.'

'But Mebrure, dearest, please don't even think of being angry at your poor mother,' my grandmother said as she held her hand out for us to kiss. 'Please, I beg of you, don't leave me here all alone without a visit.'

We quickly went down the stairs and the three of us pulled open the iron door. The glorious sunlight dazzled our eyes and the fresh air filled our lungs.

'Make sure you close the door properly!' my grandmother called out from the top of the stairs. 'Mebrure, stop by again this week, OK?'

We walked away in silence, holding our mother's hands. In the tram we sat quietly listening to the coughs of the other passengers until the tram left. When it set off, my brother and I moved up a row with the excuse that we wanted to sit in a seat where we could see the conductor, and began playing Tops or Bottoms. I won back some of the pictures I'd lost. In the confidence of winning, I upped the stakes and quickly began to lose again. At the Osmanbey stop, my brother changed the stakes, 'If I win I get the rest of your pile, if I lose, you get fifteen of your choice.'

We played. I lost. Secretly keeping two of the pictures, I gave the entire stack to him. I moved back a row and sat next to my mother. I didn't cry. Like my mother, I stared sadly out of the window as the tram gathered speed, moaning softly as it went, at the passing of all those people and places that no longer exist—the dressmakers' shops overflowing with spools of coloured thread and fabrics imported from Europe; the sun-faded, rain-tattered awnings of the pudding shops with their steamed-up windows, the bakeries with loaves of fresh bread neatly lining their shelves, the gloomy lobby of the Tan Film Theatre, where we saw films about ancient Rome full of slave girls more beautiful than goddesses, the street children selling used comic books in front of the cinema, the barber with the sharp moustache and scissors who always frightened me, and the half-naked local madman who always stood by the barber-shop door.

We left the tram at the Harbiye stop. As we walked home, my

brother's smug silence drove me mad. I took the Lindbergh picture out of my pocket where I'd hidden it.

It was the first time he'd ever seen it. 'Number 91, Lindbergh,' he read with awe. 'With the plane he flew across the Atlantic! Where did you get that?'

'I didn't have my jabs yesterday,' I said. 'I came home from school early and saw Dad before he left. Dad bought it for me.'

'That means half of it is mine,' he said. 'Besides, in the last round we played for *all* your pictures.' He tried to snatch the picture out of my hand, but he wasn't fast enough. He grabbed my wrist and twisted it. I kicked him in the leg. We began fighting.

'Stop it!' my mother shouted. 'Stop it, you two! We're in the middle of the street!'

We stopped. A man in a suit and tie and a woman wearing a gigantic hat went past. I was embarrassed that we'd fought in public. My brother took two steps forward and then stumbled to his knees. 'It really hurts,' he said, holding his leg.

'Get up,' hissed my mother. 'Get up right now. Everyone's staring.'

My brother stood up and began limping like a wounded hero in a war movie. I was worried that maybe he really was hurt, but I was also satisfied to see him in that condition. After walking on in silence for a while, he said, 'You're going to get it when we get home.' He turned to my mother and said, 'Mum, Ali didn't get his jabs.'

'I did too, Mum.'

'Hush!' she shouted.

We'd reached the point across from our apartment. We waited for the tram coming from Maçka to pass before crossing the road. Immediately afterwards, a truck followed by the Beshiktash bus and then a light purple DeSoto went by. That's when I realized my uncle was peering through the window into the street. He hadn't noticed us; he was staring at the passing cars. I watched him intently for a while.

The road had long since cleared of traffic. When I turned to my mother to see why she hadn't taken our hands and led us across the street, I noticed she was weeping quietly. □

GRANTA

FIT MOTHER

Peter Ho Davies

Fit Mother

The court had given me six months to prove I was a responsible adult and a fit mother. 'But how am I supposed to do that?' I wanted to know. 'How am I supposed to prove I'm any kind of mother if they take Luke away?' 'Catch-22,' Billy said, like that explained it. Billy was no help. Luke was two months old and we were twentywhatever, but his eyes when they took him away seemed older than anything.

When we got home, Bill said he was sad. He said he was going out to score, did I want to come? But I just sat there on the sofa and shook my head. Luke was supposed to be a new start for us. I'd cleaned myself up when he was inside me, but when I came home Bill wanted to do some celebrating. 'Yes!' He held Luke overhead like the Stanley Cup. 'I'm a dad!' He rolled himself a joint as fat as a cigar and when he passed it to me he called me Mama-mia and when I slid it back I called him Daddy-o. I'd been high on Luke when I was pregnant, but coming home all sore to our apartment in the converted motel on Ferry was a downer. I needed a little pick-me-up. I'd been clean as snow for nine months, but after all the Demerol and ephedrine they'd pumped into me during labour I figured a few tokes wouldn't much matter. I crashed pretty quick, but then I woke up to Luke crying. Billy told me to lay back down. 'Papa-san's got it covered.' He was so proud, he was grinning like a cartoon of himself. I heard Luke yelling and Bill walking up and down with him, talking softly, telling him in a deep voice, 'Luke, I am your father,' and laughing to himself until he set the baby off again. I must have fallen back asleep. Sometime after that's when Billy got the idea to blow smoke in Luke's face to mellow him out. It worked fine and Bill was smug as fuck in the morning. 'It's the crying cure,' he said. But Luke was still sleeping at lunchtime and when I put my head close his breathing was bad, whistly like a slow flat, and I screamed at Bill until he took us to the hospital. Luke was OK then, but the nurse called social services on us.

Luke's toys and shit were everywhere still. I hugged one of our old cushions to my stomach and stroked it. Ever since I was a kid I've had a habit of squeezing feather pillows, until one of the little quills pokes through the fabric and I can tease it out. There are always little wisps of feathers on our rug. I was working on another

ELI REED/MAGNUM PHOTOS

one in the pillow now, pressing the sharp point against my finger until it punctured the cover, strumming it back and forth, finally plucking it out. This pillow used to be plump and soft, now it's skinny and no good for sitting on. One corner was crusty from where Luke had chewed it. You could still smell his diapers, even though the social worker had taken him away a week ago. It made me think of the times I pressed my face to his belly when I changed him. He smelled so good. Sometimes, I'd just run my nose all over him, sniffing him up while he giggled and squirmed. I wondered who'd look after him now. A foster mother, they'd told us. 'A methadone mom,' Bill said when the lawyer explained it, and that started me crying because it made me the shit Luke was coming off. I tried to imagine her, this replacement mom, but all I could picture was my own mother. She was a fit mom. She was a responsible adult. And look how I ended up. Moms was all alone down there in Arizona. I hadn't seen her since I ran off in '86, but I kept a PO Box because she sent cheques sometimes. I still had the letter she wrote me when Dad died and another when she moved from Texas four years ago. And then it struck me. Maybe she could come up here to Eugene and help us get our shit together. If she lived with us maybe the court would change its mind.

Having Luke was so painful, I felt like I was being torn in two. I wasn't going to give him up now.

I thought of calling Moms up, but I hadn't done that for a long time and if I did it now with this news it might not be so good. The shock might kill her, I thought. The shame, most likely. We should go see her, drive down there. Sure, I thought. Drive down there and get her.

I told Bill when he got back and he looked at me like, 'Your Mom!?!'

'I do have one.'

Jeez.

He didn't want to, but I told him we had to. He knew that look. He'd seen it before when I was strung out. My gotta-score look. Besides he loved road trips, popping speed. They made him feel like Hunter S. Thompson, even in our two-tone '87 Voyager.

It took us eighteen hours and when we got there my back was aching but Billy was still wired. 'Howdy,' he said (he'd been talking like that since Flagstaff), giving Moms a big hug. 'Howdy, Ma'am.' But then he couldn't sit still. He had to stretch his legs, he said, walking about bow-legged like he'd got off a horse. That made her laugh. At least he broke the ice. But I couldn't watch him the whole time, and every so often he'd whistle and call out, 'You've got some right purty stuff here. My, my.' He was stealing. I knew it. I wouldn't have minded, but that old family stuff was Luke's, too, now. 'Whatever happened to that silver ashtray, Moms?' I asked her, when I saw him come back with his pockets bulging. 'And that nice table lighter?' But she couldn't remember. Then Bill said he had to go out, 'get me some smokes'. I told Mom he was shy but she said he had lovely manners. I watched her carry the teacup she'd set for Bill to the kitchen and it shook in its saucer like the DTs.

'Jesus, Moms,' I said. 'When d'you get so old?'

I guess she had me when she was thirty-six or seven, already. For a long time they didn't think they could have kids, my folks, and then there I was. Now Moms's hair was white and thin and she walked real slow and stooped. But she was pleased to see me, although it took her a minute to figure out who I was.

So we sat around and talked. We had some laughs. People dropped by. Friends of Moms. She called them all up to tell them she had a visitor, her daughter. She told them all I was in town on business and I thought she'd got it wrong, but then she winked at me and I said I was in—'Computers.' She was still sharp, Moms, I thought, and she could help me out with the courts, I was sure of it. She looked like the perfect grandma, even if she didn't know she was one yet. It wasn't until later, after the friends had gone and we were alone, that I told her, and then she just sat there very still and I had to tell her again—'A little boy,' I said. 'Called Walt.' Walter was my Dad's name. I'd thought of this in the van on the way down. I'd been saving it up. And then I saw the tears gleaming in her eyes and we held each other for a long time. I told her I'd wanted to bring the baby to see her, but that I was in a fix, that I needed her help and she nodded and said, yes; yes, yes, anything, of course. The thing is she didn't remember what had gone on before—all the shit I pulled.

Just didn't remember it one bit. 'Forgive and forget,' she said. 'And vice versa. That's my motto.' I was so relieved. So long as she remembered who I was and that she loved me.

Bill called that night. He wasn't doing John Wayne any more. The cops had picked him up. 'Buying?' I said. 'But you had a big stash.' I'd seen him going into the trunk at rest stops every time I went to the bathroom. I thought he'd just packed for the trip. 'Selling,' he told me. He wanted me to bail him, so I said sure and hung up. 'Who was that?' Moms wanted to know. I took a deep breath. 'Just some sales guy,' I said.

The thing about Bill is that I did love him, but then Luke came along and I really loved him. When Moms asked me what had happened to my friend, 'the cowboy', I told her he had to ride off into the sunset.

The next morning I started getting her packed. I went down to the condo office and told them she'd be away for a few months on vacation with me. They looked surprised. They asked me if I thought that was a good idea and I told them I thought it was a great idea.

On the road she was quiet the whole way. Kept turning her head to look at me and then out the window and then back at me. The radio was busted so I tried to talk to her about the old days, the house, Dad, but she didn't say anything. I just started talking about whatever came into my head, like this old game show we used to watch. My dad was with Exxon then and they wanted him in Scotland on account of the North Sea oil so we were living in Aberdeen for a year. It was called *The Generation Game*—just a dumb show, with cheesy sets and bad toupees really—and the gimmick was that the teams were mothers and sons, uncles and nieces, grandmas and grandsons. There was a bit at the end, a memory test, where the contestants sat in front of a conveyor belt and watched all these prizes slide by. Then they got to sit in a spotlight and everything they could remember in one minute they could keep. Toaster, blender, golf shoes, cuddly toy. There was always a cuddly toy. The prizes weren't much and it was corny, but we loved it, yelling at the TV, screaming at them what they forgot.

'That'll be us,' I told Moms. 'You and me, playing *The Generation Game*.'

We were real close that year, two Americans in Scotland. We went to all the castles together. I couldn't understand the accents of anyone at school and all they knew about Texas and oil was *Dallas*. Moms and I had more in common than anyone else we knew for the first time. But that was also the year I started getting high. On gas fumes first, then later sniffing glue, doing whip-its behind the cafeteria. It felt so dumb passing around a tube of glue; it was just a game. But then when we moved back to Houston, I got serious. Dope, coke, crack, smack. Finally, Moms told me I had to choose: my home or my habit; her or the heroin. It was no choice at sixteen. Not even close. I kept in touch with Dad for a few years after I left. He would meet me for coffee, take me for a big dinner, or if I was too fucked buy me boxes of groceries. He gave me money, too, though he always made me promise not to spend it on shit. He told me, after I left, she just stayed in her room for weeks. She never went out, didn't eat, kept the drapes pulled.

'She won't even answer the phone,' he said, meaning in case it was me.

'I'm not as strong as her,' he said, meaning he still had to see me, behind her back.

He was still hooked, I told him, but she was going cold turkey. In her first letter to me after seven years, when she told me he was gone, she said he'd made her promise to do what she could for me. I took the money she sent, but I knew enough not to get in touch. She didn't need me back in her life. Not after she'd kicked me. And yet, here I was again.

Outside, the road was rough, it sounded like static under the tyres, until we hit one of those patches of fresh tarmac when everything went quiet for a moment. It was like trying to tune a radio, except all I could hear in the good spots was Moms's breathing.

We stayed at a Snooz Inn just outside Salt Lake (I put it on Moms's Visa), shared a room for the first time in twenty years. When she came out of the bathroom to go to bed, she had her head caught in her nightgown and I had to get up and help her set it straight, but then when her head appeared she was all flustered. 'I can manage,' she said, and then I felt embarrassed in just my bra and panties—

stretch marks and tracks still showing.

It was raining when we got to Eugene which saved me giving Moms the tour. I wouldn't have known what to say anyway. Billy always liked to call it 'the town where the Sixties never died'. He liked to say he came to college here on account of Ken Kesey—that and the fact they filmed *Animal House* down the block—and stayed because Springfield was the crystal-meth capital of the west.

When we got to our apartment it was dark, which I thought would help, because the building looks better at night, although sometimes the johns from Seventh like to cruise you. She just took one look and said, 'Well!' and rolled her sleeves up and went right at it. She found all the crap under the sink—Windex, Mr Clean—from the last tenants, and I cut up an old maternity dress for a rag and left her to it while I fetched her stuff from the van and made up a bed for myself on the goodwill sofa. When I tried to help her she told me to sit down, like I was in the way. She was happy, I thought. Happy to be doing, to be needed, I guess. But just when she was going great I heard her give a little cry. She was in the kitchen and when I went in, it seemed so beautiful. It shone. She was mopping, there was water on the floor, but then I saw she was wet. 'An accident,' she said, and I could tell she wanted to run to the bathroom, she kept lifting her feet, but she couldn't because she didn't want to get pee everywhere and she was whimpering with the frustration. Well, I helped her out, of course. The mess wasn't much compared to crack houses I've seen, though I didn't tell her that. Got her changed—turns out there was a pack of diapers, big ones, in her case, but she'd forgotten to put one on—threw her dress in the laundry and cleaned up. 'You cleaned up after me,' I told her. 'Turn about's fair play.'

And that's how we went at it those first few weeks. Moms was great at cooking and cleaning, but she was also real good to me. I used to have a lot of trouble with the breast pump. It hurt and I didn't like to use it, but then my breasts would leak all over. The smell of my milk always made me cry for Luke. But Moms helped me with the pump, boiling up the plastic pieces in a saucepan on the stove before I used it. She wiped my breasts, caught a drop on the end of her finger and tasted it. 'That's good stuff,' she said, and she held out her finger to me and I licked it. She made me get little bottles to sterilize and store it in and we kept a stash of them in the fridge to supply the social worker when I saw her each week. Luke didn't like formula, she told me, and it made me glad to think of him still jonesing for me. Moms could still look after me and the house like the old days. But looking after herself, that's where I came in. The shower was tricky for her until we got her a plastic lawn chair in there, and afterwards I'd help dry her off, dust her with talc, and work in the lotion. At night I rubbed her back and her legs and feet. Her legs were knotted with veins, the muscles hard like wood, but I liked to rub on them until they loosened up and she purred with pleasure.

The only problem with all this cleaning was I could no longer smell Luke anywhere. I slept with his stuffed bear for a while, but soon it just smelled like me. At night I kept waking up thinking I heard him, but it was only the whining of neighbourhood dogs or the hooting and bleating of trains in the yards over by Fifth. I told Moms and she took my hand and made me get in with her. I still woke up, but it wasn't so bad as alone.

The apartment was looking in great shape when the social worker, Ms Ross, came for a visit. I'd met her before at the courthouse. She asked me to step outside to talk so she could smoke. She told me how it would go, and when we were done she stubbed out the butt before it was half gone. 'Trying to quit,' she told me. 'Yeah, it's tough,' I said and she blushed.

Now, she looked around her at the tidy living room, the swept floors, and she seemed surprised. She asked about Bill and I said he'd split, that I'd told him to go. 'If you're not part of the solution,' I told her firmly. 'So you're a single mom,' she said, making a note in her book. 'How'd you feel about raising a child alone?' Which was perfect really, because I got to go, 'I'd like you to meet someone.' It was like unveiling a statue. I'd told Moms to dress nice and wait in the bedroom before I called her, and now she came out and her make-up that I'd only helped her with a little was great and she had on a tweedy suit and her pearls, only she still had her hair in rollers. I didn't know what to say but the social worker didn't seem to mind. Moms just came on in and said, Hello, Pleased to meet you, and sat herself down. I tucked an afghan around her and we went on just as happy as you please. Afterwards Moms and I laughed about it. I took out her curlers and she patted her hair in the mirror and we both agreed it had come out fine.

When she left, the social worker told me she was pleased with my progress. She said she could see that family was important to me, and then she got back in her Saturn. When she waved I saw, under her sleeve, that she was wearing a patch. I went in and gave Moms a hug and she beamed like Mr Clean. We had visits then every two weeks and they went well. On the second visit Luke was allowed to come and play for a while. I fed him while Moms and the social worker (her name was Beth) watched and chatted. He was so greedy it made me laugh. The social worker kept talking about Luke, Luke this, Luke that, and Moms kept saying how Walt was a great baby, too, until I explained that his name was Walter Luke. Beth looked at her paperwork again and then at me, and I said, 'Yes,' and nodded at her and I saw her write it down. When Walt pooped I got out the baby works and changed him. His diapers seemed so small compared to Moms's; his skin, as I ran the wipe over it, so soft. Afterwards I just held him and held him and it was like the best fix in the world. When I gave him up at the end of the day, I was sweating, shaking, and Moms held me and told me, 'Oh, darling, I know it's hard.'

About a week later Bill showed up at the door. He'd left a few messages on Moms's machine back in Phoenix that I'd listened to and erased, but I'd been half expecting him. I guess he got a bailbondsman to get him out, but I was pretty sure he was breaking some law or other coming all the way to Oregon like that. I was taking a shower, but I heard his voice at the door when Moms opened it. She was very nice to him, but she made like she didn't know who the hell he was. Bill just stood there and whined about this being his place and Moms told him quietly that it couldn't be and he couldn't come in, and then she started shouting, 'Rape,' in her little old lady voice and Bill beat it after that. The last I heard of him was his footsteps twanging down the metal stairs outside. He took the van, which was his anyway, but I figured it was worth it to see the back of him. He likely lost it to the bondsman anyway, when I called in a tip that he'd left the state. He was a tattooist, Bill, so I knew he'd do OK inside.

Sometimes after a bath I'd look at the little lizard he did on my shoulder and I'd think, You were an artist, Bill, as well as an asshole. Moms and I laughed over it all night, and she kept it up the whole time saying she'd never seen him before in her life. 'Come on!' I said.

At the next visit Beth asked me to bring Walt down to the car with her. It had been a great visit. Moms had been playing with Walt, peekaboo, and when I said it was time for the baby to go, she'd held him for a second, kissed his hair. 'He smells just like you did,' she told me, handing him over. 'Takes me back.'

In the lot, Beth complimented me on the apartment, on turning my life around. 'I admire the way you care for your mother,' she said. I just beamed at her. 'I would like to recommend that Walt be returned to you,' she said, and I thought my smile would just break my mouth. 'Thank you,' I said, but quietly because the baby was sleeping. 'Thank you. Thank you. Thank you.' But Beth shook her head. 'I'd like to,' she said. 'You've proved yourself a responsible caregiver. You'd be a good mother. But I'm not sure the circumstances in your home are ideal for a child.'

'What do you mean?' I hissed. 'How clean do you need it to be?'

'I mean your mother,' she said. 'She's clearly senile and she represents a potential danger to herself and to the baby. While you and Walt were playing I saw her get up to make tea, put the kettle on the stove and turn the gas on, but forget to light it. I had to turn it off myself. Last visit I saw her put a foil package in the microwave.'

'Oh, that microwave hasn't worked for weeks,' I told her, but she just nodded and I wanted to bite my tongue. What I didn't tell her was that the milk in the tea Moms made the last visit had been mine.

'I have an older parent myself.' She paused to pop a piece of gum in her mouth. 'I don't know if I could do what you're doing. I'm sympathetic, really. But it's my duty to put Walt first. Can you tell me you can watch him and your Mom twenty-four hours a day?'

'Yes! Sure!'

She shook her head.

'So what you're saying is it's OK for me to be a single mom, but not a single daughter?'

Beth just chewed.

'Well, what am I supposed to do?'

She looked at me. 'I can't tell you that,' she said, holding out her hands for the baby.

I stood in the parking lot for a long time after she left. I watched a mother walk by with an empty stroller and a kid a little older than Walt walking alongside, pushing a toy stroller with a doll in it.

When I went back in I looked at Moms. She smiled at me and said, 'I like your friend Beth. What a lovely baby she's got.'

I took the bus with Moms back to Phoenix the next week. Her friends were pleased to see her. 'Everyone's so friendly here,' she said, beaming. She marched around the room like it was a hotel or something. She ran her finger over the shelves looking for dust. Finally, she said, 'I'll take it.'

'I'll visit,' I said. 'With Walt.' She nodded.

'You're the best, Moms,' I told her and she said, 'Not hardly. Look at the mess I made with you.'

That made me jump, but then I saw she was joking.

'No,' she said. 'You make me proud.'

I'd waited all my life to hear her say it, and when she said it I knew she meant it and she was wrong. Don't you remember, I wanted to yell. Don't you remember what I was like? The dope. The coke. The crack. The smack.

I started crying then, but she told me, 'Shh, shh, shh.'

'I like it here,' she said. She looked out of the window. 'You can see the world go by.' I stood with her and we watched a bunch of kids on rollerblades. Moms waved a little. I thought they'd give her the finger, but they didn't see her. A line of cars turned the corner, the sun flaring off each windshield in turn, like a flashbulb.

'I like it here,' she said again.

Later, on the street outside, I looked back up to her room and I waved. I couldn't see her, that desert sun was shining on the glass. I hoped she wasn't there, but I thought maybe she was. I got on the bus and rode down the street with my arm out of the window the whole way, and then we took the corner. I thought of her at her window, her eyes dazzled by the light, turning around, her arm gone sore from waving, her eyes adjusting to the dimness of her room. □

GRANTA

THEN AND NOW

Daniel Meadows

Daniel Meadows

In July 1973 I bought a 1948 double-decker Leyland Titan PDI bus for £360.20 from Barton Transport in Chilwell, Nottingham. (If you want to see it today, go to the Midland Bus and Transport Museum at Wythall near Birmingham where it has been fully restored.) I was twenty-one years old, fresh out of art school, and I wanted to photograph ordinary English people. I wasn't interested in celebrities.

My idea was to park my bus in different towns and cities round England and offer strangers a free portrait. They in turn would offer to take me into their homes, or to their places of work or leisure, where I could make the photographs that would eventually form my grand statement about British society. And while I was on the road, I could use the bus as a gallery—I could display my pictures in its windows—as well as a travelling darkroom and a home. I gave the whole enterprise a name: the Free Photographic Omnibus.

The project was financed with £3,500 (about £24,000 today) raised in sponsorship, personal donations and two grants from the Arts Council. The journey started in York on 22 September 1973 and ended 10,000 miles later in Barrow-in-Furness on 2 November 1974.

I operated portrait sessions in twenty-two different towns, from Southampton in the south to Newcastle-upon-Tyne in the north, and photographed 958 people. Every evening I would develop the pictures in my makeshift darkroom ready for the people in them to collect the next day. I was filmed for television and written up in newspapers. In August 1974, the *Daily Mirror*, then Britain's biggest circulation newspaper, called the bus project 'The Great Ordinary Show'.

In October 1975 some of the photographs were published as a book, *Living Like This*, and exhibited at the ICA in London. But a quarter of a century later it is not those photographs—the ones I then considered my 'serious' work—that have enjoyed a revival, but the free portraits, the ones I shot to give away.

In 1996, the oral historian Alan Dein, who had bought a dog-eared copy of *Living Like This* from a market stall in London's Brick Lane, invited me to make a documentary about the bus for BBC Radio 4. The following year the curator and writer Val Williams organized an exhibition called 'National Portraits'. It toured widely.

In September 1998, following a public viewing of the pictures at the international festival of photography at Arles in France, the *British Journal of Photography* reported that the Free Photographic Omnibus had acquired 'cult status'.

As the photographs were published and exhibited I began to worry about the people in the pictures. I was concerned to know how they felt about being rediscovered? What had happened in their lives? Since I had no addresses, I decided to solicit the help of local newspapers in towns where I thought enough of a community might have survived for the pictures to jog a memory or two. I went first to Barrow-in-Furness in Cumbria, then to Hartlepool in County Durham, then to Southampton. I was spurred on by something Val Williams had written. She had called the pictures 'realistic chronicles from the imagination', and she wrote: 'Daniel Meadows has traced many of the people he photographed then, but this is of little interest to us. It wouldn't even help to know their names.' But I couldn't agree. To me the people were real enough.

In the articles I asked readers to telephone in if they recognized themselves, or anyone in the pictures. It was hardly an exact science. It is one thing to identify people but something else altogether to find them again or persuade all of those who appeared in a particular picture to turn up at the same time on the same day and be re-photographed. In Hartlepool in 1998, when I published a set of bus photographs, all thirty-one of those shown were identified. But not all of them could be found. And a surprising number were dead—young people, too.

When I started doing these re-shoots I tried to match the poses as accurately as possible with the original. But in twenty-five years, people change shape and forcing them into an old pose is like asking them to dress in clothes they've grown out of. (When it came to clothes, what they wore for the new photograph was chosen with much more care than what they were wearing in the original. This time, because I had made an appointment, they were dressing to be photographed.) I soon realized it wasn't important to match the poses exactly. I wasn't recreating the photographs, I was re-recording the people in them. The original is always the more evocative, but the combination of the two, then and now, is the more instructive.

1. The Boot Boys: Brian Morgan, Martin Tebay, Paul McMillan, Phil Tickle and Mike Comish, 1974 and 1995

1. The Boot Boys.
In 1973 the Boot Boys were fifteen years old and in their final year at school. After school they became apprenticed tradesmen; four of them at Vickers Engineering in Barrow (where nuclear submarines are built: Polaris then, Trident now), and the fifth, Brian, at North West Gas. In 1995, they found themselves among the bus portraits published in the Barrow *Evening Mail*.

Brian Morgan: I'd nipped home on the Wednesday afternoon and my girlfriend said: 'Sit down. I've got something to tell you.' And I thought it was something really serious—which it turned out to be. Her hairdresser had phoned her up saying: 'Go and buy an *Evening Mail* and open the middle pages.' Then the phone started ringing. I was in too much of a state of shock to answer it. But the next day was the worst. Just like the other lads in the photograph—the amount of sarcasm they got was unreal. Suicidal. Every cupboard door, and locker door, every drinks machine, there was a photocopy on it, and sarcastic comments underneath.

Martin Tebay: A lot of lads the same age as me are jealous of the picture because lads aged fourteen or fifteen don't often get photographs taken like that. You know, when they're young, their parents take a lot, but as you get older you want to go somewhere on your own and you don't get so many photographs taken.

Paul McMillan: I was in Lanzarote on holiday when it was printed. When I landed, my mate's wife said: 'There was a picture of you in the *Evening Mail*. It was you and four of your friends.' And as soon as she said 'four of your friends' I knew which ones she was talking about. And it all came back. My mother's got the original picture in an album.

Phil Tickle: That is the worst picture I have ever seen of myself! A lot of people would back me up on that. It's some bad gear isn't it, really?

We all wanted to be Boot Boys. It was the fashion at the time. But we didn't all have the gear. Obviously it was what you could afford. Instead of Doctor Martens I had what we called Major Domos. They had the same effect. The reason Mike isn't in that gear is because he went to a school that required a uniform whereas we didn't. And Brian liked flares. But he still had his Doctor Martens on. Our pants were 'parallels'.

We all read the book *Boot Boy* [by Richard Allen]. It was obviously meant to appeal to people our age and almost told you how to behave. Fighting all the time, and looking cool and being in trouble. It related so well to the things we knew. We used to get in the odd fight. Martin looks the most threatening but he was probably the softest out of us all. But he had the best gear. Whereas I had to wear what my brother wasn't wearing that day.

I was a vandal. Not a great vandal. But you felt like you had to do your bit. I don't think I did anything particularly bad. Snapped the odd car aerial perhaps. You look back and you think, 'God, if anyone snaps my car aerial I'll kill them.' But that's part of growing up. We weren't such bad kids, to be honest. I mean there was no such thing as drugs. We tried the odd fag and that was it really.

We met because we were in the Army Cadets. Paul was the sergeant and Mike was a corporal. We used to go down the rifle range and shoot a two-two. You can imagine, the discipline down there was nil. [I remember] we went on a camp to Glencorse Barracks in Edinburgh. It was an all-important part of growing up and kids these days don't get it. They're thrust into adulthood so soon that they don't go through all these little traumas and adventures that we used to go through. They are starting to act like adults when they're fourteen and it's such a shame.

I've got a boy of fourteen now. I live his life for him every day. I might have a rough exterior but my outlook is so different from my father's. My dad was a disciplinarian, but I see myself as being on a par with my children. I take them everywhere. I play with them. I don't do it as much as I should but I do it nine hundred per cent more than my father did. I've never been on a holiday with my parents in my life. But that's the way things were then. I still kiss my son. He can't go without kissing me, although he doesn't want to.

I'd still like to see him [go into] a trade. If he got to university I would be proud of him but, tell you the truth—it's probably a working-class concept—I sometimes think to myself: 'If he ever did that, would he be really happy?' Because I know what happy is at my own level. Being a working-class person, it doesn't take a lot to make me happy, to be honest. You want enough money to have a good life. Maybe a holiday every year. Whereas I think sometimes when people go to university they are searching for something they never actually find. They come back overqualified, they've gone into a different class system. I want him to have a good life and be comfortable. And I want it for all my children. I've got a lot of worries about them and you can only hope things turn out right.

2. Karen and her mother Barbara, 1974

Karen Cubin and Barbara Taylor, 1995

2. Karen Cubin and Barbara Taylor (previous page).

In November 1974, Karen, on the arm of her mother Barbara, was fifteen and recovering from an appendix operation. It was either that, she told me in 1995 when I went back to photograph her with her mother, or playing truant from school—which she did a lot. 'Jigging school, hiding in multi-storey car parks, sitting in cafés with mates.' It must have been a Friday, she said, because they only took the big plastic shopping bag Barbara is carrying when they went to the Friday market in Barrow. Her own small canvas school bag was 'full of Smartie tubes'.

In 1974 Barbara was wearing a wig. She explained in 1995 that she'd been ill, and her hair had begun to fall out. On the morning of the photograph the hairdresser had tried to inject some body into what was left of her hair with a perm. But the perm had gone wrong. More hair had fallen out and he'd given up trying. He said there was nothing for it, she'd have to wear a wig. So she'd put on the wig and walked home. There she collected Karen and the shopping bag and, somewhere between Dalton Road and the new covered market, she came across a young man standing next to a double-decker bus offering to take her picture for free. She agreed to have it done, she said, because she wanted to know what she looked like in the wig.

But Karen remembered it differently. 'She said it was a perm gone wrong. It wasn't. She just had this thing for wigs. I don't know why, but she had lots of different wigs. All kinds, ginger ones. And she used to have these stands [for them] and we used to bite the noses off them or pull the [bits of] polystyrene out. There were six of us. I have two half-brothers. And we used to put the wigs on when she went up town and pull 'em to bits and wreck 'em more or less.'

Karen runs a pet shop and is married to Barry, with whom she was going out at the time of the first photograph. They married when she was nineteen. 'I was very young, very naive. My mother never taught me anything, you see, not about anything that should be talked about like the facts of life. My girls know all about that, and they can come to talk to me about anything as well, anything. Whereas I could never do that with my mother. [I tell them to] Do what they feel happy in doing. And try to be good at it. Which I know they will. They've got a good teacher.'

3. Angela, Dot and Kim (following page).
In 1974 all three of them were fifteen and playing truant. Angela was a brunette, now she's a blonde. Her cousin Kim, on the right, was a blonde and now she's a brunette. Kim hated having to wear a skirt for school. She thought her legs were too skinny. So she took trousers in her school bag and changed into them for the walk home.

After school, Kim and Angela left Barrow for London where they tried to make a living working in hotels. But they came home again and went to work in the local wool factory. They were nineteen. Kim lives in Preston now. She has three children. A fourth, the eldest, was brain damaged at birth and died last year. He was fifteen.

Angela is a carer—she used to call it 'home help' but there's no cleaning with the job any more. She also takes in foster children. She gets a pound an hour. She does it because she likes it. One day, she says, she'll become a proper foster mother, but she's not in a hurry. 'If you take them in for a pound an hour, you prove that you aren't in it for the money,' she said, 'so when you apply to be a foster mother, they believe you.'

On the day they'd all three agreed to be photographed again, Dot (the tall girl in the middle) never turned up. She had promised to only the day before, and since we'd all come quite a distance, we were disappointed. But Angela and Kim were not quick to blame her. Things have been difficult for Dot, they said. She doesn't have much to celebrate at the moment.

We waited all morning to see if she would change her mind. There were hushed, urgent phone calls, but there was still no sign of her. Kim's mother made us sandwiches and the kids played outside climbing a big sycamore in the churchyard while we talked.

Kim's mother remembered being hauled up to the school once to be told that Kim and Angela had missed school for a whole month. 'We were terrible tearaways,' Angela said. 'Always lagging off.' 'We went with fellers,' Kim said. 'And to your dad's,' said Angela.

In the end I decided to photograph Angela and Kim on their own. The missing figure in the photograph seemed to stand for something more than just Dot's absence—for the way people's lives change, the way things don't always go the way we'd like.

3. Angela, Dot and Kim, 1974

Angela Hendley and Kim Hillman, 1995

Following pages:
4. Michael and Peter McParland.
The twins were two years old and out in the double buggy with their mother, Theresa, when they were photographed in 1974. Her immediate concern was that if she agreed to have their photograph taken, she would have to rouse Peter (the one on the right) who was asleep. Today, the original photograph is pasted in the family album.

In August 1995, when I went back to Barrow to photograph the twins, they were twenty-three. After school they had been apprenticed in the local shipyards. Michael is a sheet metal worker and Peter is a plumber. But after the downturn in the nuclear submarine business there were no more jobs in Barrow and they began working away on contract. At the time of the new photograph, Michael had returned from a job in Sweden and Peter was home from Wales for the weekend.

5. David and Maureen Wade.
David Wade was setting off to collect his degree in Business Studies from Salford University when I went to photograph him with his mother in July 1995, and he had several job interviews lined up. His mother, Maureen, still runs the Bath Street Post Office in Barrow with her husband. When I photographed her in 1974, she had two children—her daughter was out of the frame in a pushchair—later she had two more. 'I'd just nipped out to do some shopping when you popped up and asked me if I'd like to have my picture taken. I said: "Yes, but you'll have to be quick."'

6. Robin Jones with Leslie Fothergill, 1974, and his wife, Bernadette, 1998.
In 1974 Robin Jones was seventeen, an apprentice insulation engineer at Teespoint oil refinery, and going out with Leslie Fothergill. In 1998, he was married to Bernadette. Knowing he'd recently got married, the local newsagent stuck the picture from the *Hartlepool Mail* in the window and wrote on it: *'Hey, hey, hey, Mr Jones. You've got a thing going on. Sing it.'* Nobody knew where to find Leslie Fothergill.

7. David and Mary Ingram.
In 1974, David was two, and had to be picked up to have his picture taken. In November 1998, David was the parent and Mary the grandparent. He had a son of three, and twin four-month-old daughters, but he and his wife, who's a hairdresser, still lived at home with his parents.

8. Martin and Debbie Pout.

In May 1999 I drove to Tonbridge in Kent, taking Martin Pout with me. He hadn't seen his sister for three years. 'We're not the closest of families,' Debbie had written to me when I organized the reunion, 'so I don't really talk to him that often, but only due to apathy and laziness and not bad feeling.' She works as a graphic designer in Tonbridge. Martin is a postgraduate sports scientist. Debbie remembered being photographed in 1974, when she was nine and Martin was two.

'I was a very shy person and it was a very alien thing, that sort of thing didn't happen in Hartlepool. And I remember holding on to Martin, I was very frightened as you can tell from the photograph.

'It must have been a school day because I wouldn't have been wearing a skirt if it wasn't. I was at primary school so we didn't have school uniform. But my brother Kevin and I had the same jumpers. The one in the picture was blue and he had a red one. We had our school photos taken in them. And it was a horrible brown crimplene skirt. I hated wearing skirts, I was such a tomboy.

'In Hartlepool we lived in a nice little pocket on a pretty horrible council estate surrounded by thugs and criminals. My mum moved from there only recently. She was twenty-five years in the same house. It came as a bit of a blow when she suddenly sold it because we didn't get to say goodbye. It was number fifty-seven Dryden Road.'

'They were all poets round that area,' said Martin. 'Dryden, Thackeray, Chaucer, Swinburne...' 'Macaulay, Marlowe, Shakespeare,' Debbie continued, 'proper names. Not like round here. There's a firm called Sunburst Commodity Trading and the bloke persuaded the council to have all the streets named after him. So there's a Sunburst Close, and a Roundel Way, which is his logo; Merchant Place, because he was an import-export merchant; Stella Close, which is named after his wife; and Napoleon Drive, which is his dog.'

Martin didn't remember the picture being taken at all. 'But I do remember the photograph because it was one which was always in the photograph drawer at home and periodically I would go through it and look at them. I kept seeing that picture and I just made up my own story of it. Forever I've always thought it was taken in front of a garage which belonged to my auntie and uncle who live in an area of Hartlepool called the Fens. I always thought it was taken there. You tell me it's not, but I still think it is.'

4. Michael and Peter McParland, 1974 and 1995

RUSSELL
ATHLETIC

5. David and Maureen Wade, 1974 and 1995

6. Robin Jones and Leslie Fothergill, 1974

obin and Bernadette Jones, 1998

7. David and Mary Ingram, 1974 and 1998

8. Martin and Debbie Pout, 1974 and 1999

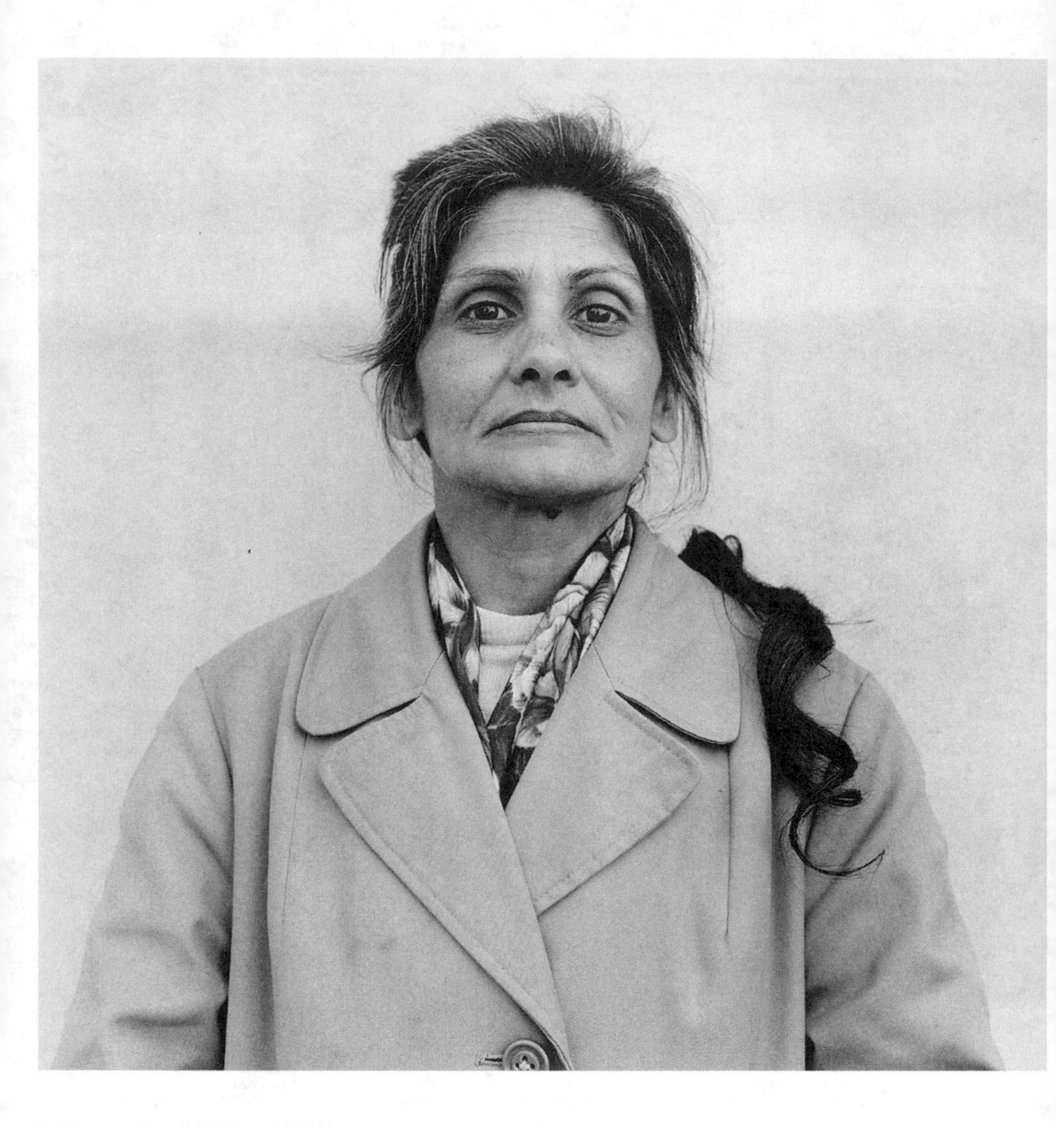

9. Florence Snoad, 1974 and 1999

9. Florence Snoad.
Florence—'Floss'—was forty-eight in May 1974 when I first photographed her and seventy-three when I photographed her again in September 1999. She was born in 1926 in Rajputana, northern India, into a large Anglo-Indian family called Franklin and went to live with an uncle and aunt at the age of three. She was, she says, the 'odd one out', a phrase she uses a lot when describing herself. In due course her aunt and uncle adopted her. They brought her to England in 1936 and they settled in Southampton. During the war, as a teenager, she met and married a sailor from London, Frederick William Snoad, by whom she had two daughters, now both in their fifties. They have moved away and have careers and families of their own, but they keep in touch and Florence visits them often.

I asked what she might have been doing in Guildhall Square on that May morning in 1974.

'I had probably just finished one of my mop-and-bucket jobs and was hanging around "being a yob",' she said, laughing. 'I used to sit about just waiting for them all to come out of the offices so that I could go back in and get on with the cleaning. Sometimes I'd do a bit of painting and drawing.' She showed me some of her brightly coloured paintings done in a pointillist style, landscapes mostly, with horses and windmills.

'I worked for an agency that sent you out on different cleaning jobs. Offices, hotels. An early shift and a late shift. I used to work on my own. Always a loner. I knew very well that whatever job I went for I would be hopeless, but they have to give you a chance, don't they? I knew I would be fired, or there'd be an excuse to get rid of me. It wasn't a race thing. It wasn't discrimination. It was just that I was always pig-in-the-middle.

'Right from the start I was one of life's losers. At school the teachers would tell the other children to ask their families if they would like to befriend Florence, take her home, and the hands would go up yes, yes, yes, and I'd be so hopeful. And then, a week later, they'd all say no. I'm ever so sorry, mother doesn't like her, father doesn't like her, the cat doesn't like her, the dog, there was always some excuse. I got used to it.

'People are always offering to pray for me, I don't know why, but I never felt I belonged to a particular god, Jesus Christ or anything like that.

'When I became a mother, I wasn't conventional. My daughters brought me up, I think! The other mothers all worked in shops or in factories and they had their own circle of friends. If you couldn't get work then you were supposed to stay at home and do your cooking and your cleaning but

I didn't have any need for that because my husband worked away a lot and never came home at a fixed time. He could do his own cooking anyway. And my daughters, once they were teenagers, they lived independent lives.

'Of course, I might have been on my way to a modelling job that day. Life modelling. Just rag and bone and a hank of hair, isn't it? My husband said it was OK so I did it. They would send me a little telegram from the art school in Winchester telling me when they wanted me. So perhaps that's where I was going after you took that picture.

'Or dancing. I used to go off on my own dancing. I didn't often get a partner. So I used to do my own thing, my 'fan and feather' as I call it. Down at the Guildhall. They'd have someone playing the keyboards, or a tape, and I would dance. Towards the end I would remove my skirt and I would just have on my black stockings like the old-fashioned Victorian naughty girls, and a few strands of coloured grass instead of a skirt and feathers sticking in my hair and a garland of flowers round my bosom. I did a combination of all the ethereal dances, the dying swans. But now I don't go any more. I stopped four or five years ago. After my husband died I lost all incentive.'

Frederick Snoad died in 1996 when the council were in the middle of renovating Florence's house. She used the word 'confloption' to describe the chaos of that time—nursing her dying husband while all around her builders were refitting fireplaces and installing double glazing. The stress of it was too much for her and she collapsed. Afterwards, fed up with moving his ashes from room to room, she sent the workmen away, then decided it was time to find her husband's ashes a last resting place.

'We got on to one of those big pleasure boats showing day trippers the sights of London, and we managed to find a sheltered bit at the back of the top deck and, on the way back up the river, we emptied the container and all his ashes just blew out and landed on the water to be carried away on the tide out to sea. He was with us in spirit there because he loved London.

'He's a nice ghost but it is very lonely without him. His garden does what it likes, it dies with the seasons and the birds do the same thing, nesting and escaping the cats. I live in my ghost home and drift through each day from one void into another. I have no close friends, only officialdom. I'm used to their forms. Now I'm compost to be scattered over wild mountains and flowers, my hair to form frost and icicles over cherry and fruit blossom. There is no earthly place—my husband is there waiting for me. Maybe I'll have some friends some day. I think all our lives are different, I don't think you can put everybody in a category, ever.'

10. May and Molly Gower, 1974

Molly Gower, 1997

10. Molly Gower and her mother, May.
On Wednesday 15 May 1974, Molly and May posed against the wall of C&A's in Guildhall Square, Southampton. Molly was eighteen. Twenty-two years later she still has the original picture. In a letter to me about it, sent on 14 May 1995 shortly after I tracked her down, she wrote: 'You must give me advice as I have tried to lift the photo off a sticky-backed page of a photo album. The writing on the back, the date etc., has torn away! But the shiny top picture remains intact. But I dare not detach it.'

We arranged to meet at Butlin's Holiday Camp in Minehead, Devon, where she was taking a Christian retreat, a Spring Harvest Holiday. When we talked in her chalet, number K2 Redwood, I had with me another copy of the picture.

'That's it!' said Molly. 'There's Mum. There's me. I'm wearing a yellow mac and a pink fluffy hat. I've still got the hat but I haven't got the mac. We shared the hat, mother and I, you see, whoever felt like wearing it. We got on very well. She was a very intelligent, interesting lady. I'd come back from work and she'd said: "I think we'll go down and have our photographs taken so that we can get into the records." That's what she said: "We want to go down in the records."

'At that time she was looking after me, doing all the housework, cooking my meals for me. And of course then there was a big reverse and I had to look after her and cook all the meals for her and do all the housework.

'She had a stroke and I didn't quite know what it was; what had made her look the way she did. And we didn't have a telephone and I just ran screaming out into the street asking for help. And a neighbour phoned an ambulance immediately because I didn't know why she had a twisted face on one side and couldn't get out of her chair. I didn't even know what strokes were. And I depended on her a great deal for things and so it was a terrible shock to me.

'But I wouldn't let her go into a home so I just learned to cope and struggle through. And I dressed and washed her and I learned to get very strong and to push a wheelchair over great distances.'

When did your father die? I asked her.

'Oh, father's still alive. Yes. [At the time of the picture] I think the divorce might just have taken place. We had a disagreement. That was all it was really. You know the slightest thing seemed to upset one or other of them and, you know, the rows would start. So it was inevitable really.

Mother was struggling on her own. And it was very hard for her not to have a husband [because] she'd been brought up in a family with lots of brothers around. All of a sudden she was responsible for the house, the finances, the bills and...and for me. It was hard on her and she worried about it.'

Then after the stroke you had to look after her? I said.

'Yes, the roles were reversed [until] last year, February twenty-third, 1995. She only seemed to have a head cold and they kept pumping her full of antibiotics. I asked the nurse to try to pump her lungs out. She was a very strong lady apart from the stroke, you see. And the nurse told me she didn't have time. So I don't think they put enough time and care into her because they could have saved her. I think I could have got her better so I feel very, very bitter about it 'cause she was my best person, my best person in all the world and I've lost her.

'When I was looking after my mother I had something like fifty-nine pounds as a carer and mother had a hundred pounds—something like that or just over—for her disability. The Social Security took that whole lot away from me and I had to support myself and my home on forty-six pounds a week. Forty-six pounds a week! I couldn't do it. I went down to the Social Security, I said: "I'm really crying now."

'People started giving me odd tins of food. I got by on that. This country is very, very tough on carers, you know. After all I'm one of England's heroes. I worked eight years to keep a mother from going into a nursing home and yet they hardly want to give me any money now. They kept me for six months on forty-six pounds a week. I've been terribly emotionally upset over that, apart from the bereavement.

'I've managed to get my mother buried out in the countryside. She came from the parish of Netley Marsh. And as I walked into this very pretty place with the fields round, and this lovely old church, I knew she'd gone home and I felt better about that. It's a double grave so I can rest there too. And I know it might seem rather morbid but I'm very pleased about that because I intend to live until I'm a good ninety, otherwise I will be cheated. She was cheated of a few years.

'And there's spring flowers growing around, and a hedgerow. She's very near the hedge. There's a beautiful mature tree. I can sit there, you know, and... So I'm very pleased that there's a plot waiting for me.'

11. Mary Clarke, 1974 and 1998

11. Mary Clarke.

Mary was married with five children in 1974, but she broke up with her husband soon after the first picture was taken. When I photographed her again in Hartlepool last year she told me that she had lost touch with all five of her children since then.

All of them?

'Yes, all of them,' she said. But in the next breath she was telling me that the second one—she never used any of their names—lived in Bradford and had sent her a card from Turkey in the summer. 'He might show up before Christmas with the grandchild.'

Did she really think so?

'They'll need me before I need them, tell you the truth.'

Does she miss them?

'Not really.'

What had her husband done for a job?

'He worked on the railway as a goods guard and he got made redundant because he had an accident. He lost his thumb between the vans. And he gets a pension every week now. He's sixty-nine, he's still alive, I see him every week down the town but I don't speak to him. Because I call him names behind his back! I won't mention the names. If he sees us [me], he, like, looks at us or he'll say to somebody else: "Seen her!" And I always say to my son: "Don't tell him nowt!" I know he goes to see his father, and I told him: "Don't you ever mention my name to him 'cause if I find out I will be down there and I will hit you."

'I'm not one for mixing with people. That's why I always go drinking in The Engineers because I've mixed in up there. Thursday night and Friday night we play bingo. I've won a bottle of wine, I've won whisky. I've won all sorts. I've got two good friends in The Engineers. She's seventy-two and her husband is sixty-five and he's blind. We were both drunk last night. I went to the bar, there was a couple of blokes there who said: "Seen your photo in the paper, Mary. Can we have your autograph?" I said: "Yeah," and I signed it for them. The next thing I knew was they sent a pint across and my friend said: "Put it underneath the table," because I already had one on the table. Then all of a sudden there was a tray brought in to us with a big round paper plate full of food on it. I said: "What's all this?" It was a treat for us because they'd seen my photo in the *Mail*. They asked me: "Are you going to have your picture taken again?" And I thought: "I'll have to keep myself sober for tomorrow." But I got drunk anyway.'

What were you doing at the time I took the photograph?

'I was working in the canteen at GEC where they made the televisions. I worked from seven o'clock in the morning until half past ten. Part-time. But then my husband stopped working because of his heart trouble and the manageress offered to take me on full-time. It was smashing. The bairns being at school an' all. It worked out. I worked from seven o'clock in the morning until three o'clock in the afternoon. I did the meals in the kitchen—fish, chips, peas—and then I went in the canteen to serve it out. I really enjoyed it. On a Friday afternoon I used to get the buffer out and clean the canteen floor.

'Then all the trouble started [at home]. When I went in one day the manageress asked me if I was all right and I just broke down crying and I told her that I'd left my husband. She told me to go home and get it all sorted out. "No," I said, "I'm leaving." She said: "What are you going to do?" Because, with the factory about to close down, I wouldn't get any redundancy money if I just left. And I said: "Oh, I'll get some work. But first I'm going to a jeweller's to get my ring cut off." And that's the best thing I did. I never did get any redundancy money.

'But so long as I lived on my own I was all right. I used to just go to the bingo. I never used to drink then. I had a good reason for getting into drinking but I wouldn't tell nobody what it is. But I had a good reason for it. I just went on the drink. My husband used to say, "How much money have you got? What are you doing with this? What are you doing with that?" And in the finish I just said: "I'm going drinking." That's how I started the drinking and I've been drinking ever since. I had a reason for drinking and I wouldn't mention it to anybody, even to the one I'm living with. He doesn't even know.

'I've got a lot of friends in The Engineers. I used to go in The Boilermakers but I got barred out because I hit one of the committee men with my handbag. I got barred out for three months and then I was allowed back in again. Then me and my partner went to a funeral, [with] his sisters and his brothers and his brother-in-laws, and we ended up in The Boilermakers. It was his auntie's funeral. And we went there and were playing bingo when one of the committee men told our lad to tell us all to shut up. I said: "We aren't doing owt. I'm playing bingo." And I got up and hit him with my handbag. And we were barred out. Shortly after that it caught on fire and I got the blame for it. It's been set on fire twice. The second time, it was my birthday on the fourth of April. Me and my sister-in-laws went off for a drink. We went to Rio's in York Road. From there to The Jackson's Arms and from The Jackson's Arms to The Engineers. We were just pulling out when we saw the fire engines again. "Mary's set fire to The Boilermakers," they said. And I said: "Oh, I wish I had done." In the end I got the blame for it so I might as well have done it. I am awkward, but I'm not one to go out and cause trouble.

'I don't belong in Hartlepool. I belong in Durham. I never liked Hartlepool since the day I put my foot in it. I was bred and born in Durham. My dad worked for the gas board. My mum had eight of us to fetch up. Me, Jean, Pauline, Valerie, Iris, that's the girls. The boys were Denis, Edward and Benny. We were brought up to respect our elders. If we were in someone's house and they were talking privately, they used to say to us: "Kids should be seen and not heard." And we used to get a clip around the earlobe and get out. I lost my mum when she was forty-two. I was twenty-one. I left Durham the following year, when my husband came to work in Hartlepool. I looked after my mum and I used to do the neighbour's housework as well. I used to stop in a lot and watch the kids. They are all still around. If they want me, they know where to find me. If I want them, I know where they are. I know the phone number, it's all down in the book.

'I've got kidney trouble. I went into hospital in May for a heart operation. I told the doctor: "I'll give up the drinking but don't tell me to give the cigarettes up. No. I like the tabs too much." I phoned up my son and let him know. I left a message with his wife Janice. He never phoned up to see how I was or sent a card. But I don't mind. I had two operations in one. They took so much of my bowel away. I've got a touch of cancer. So I'm just hoping. I've lost weight. I've gone down to six stone. I'm not bothered because my mother had it and she lived till she was forty-two. Well I've lived a few years longer, haven't I? I'm sixty. It runs in the family. I don't know if any of my sisters have got it because they don't even know that I've been in hospital. I just kept it to myself. But I'm going to phone them up and break it to them gently. And then they'll come across for us.' □

With thanks to Mark Burman at BBC Radio 4

GRANTA

EXCHANGE OF PLEASANT WORDS

Aleksandar Hemon

1.

What year was it? We have chosen to believe it was 1811. Therefore: in the autumn of 1811, Alexandre Hemon got up from his slothful bed in Quimper, Brittany; sold, unbeknownst to his widowed mother, their only horse—a perennially exhausted nag—for thirty silver coins; and joined, after some adventurous drifting, Napoleon's army on its way to Russia, heading for yet another glorious victory. He was, we believe, twenty-one at the time. We imagine him marching through Prussia, still stunned by the greatness of the world; crossing the Nieman River in June of 1812, the river washing off a gossamer coat of dust and cooling his sore, blistering feet. Then we can see him charging at the ferocious Russians at Smolensk. At Borodino, he leads the infantry attack armed with a sabre; he single-handedly captures a battery of begging-for-mercy Russians. ('No, Tolstoy, that was not a victory!' my father might exclaim when narrating this particular stretch of the family history.) We watch with him the flames of Moscow scalding the sky's belly. But there's no joy any longer in his extinguished heart: the victories don't seem so wholesome any more, and his sore feet have changed state—now they're frozen solid. Then comes the humiliating, murderous retreat. The officers are nowhere in sight, the soldier next to him just soundlessly drops in the snow like an icicle, then never gets up, and the Russians keep mauling the mutilated body of the great army. He stumbles and falls through the snow-laden steppe and when he raises his head he's in the midst of a thick forest.

We know very well that the route of the army's retreat went through what is today Belorussia, and there's no plausible explanation for Alexandre ending up in western Ukraine, near Lvov. Certain factions in the family suggested that higher forces had had a hand in the miraculous (mis)placement of Alexandre. My father—who deems himself the foremost authority on the family history and one of its main narrators—dismisses the implausibility with a derisive frown, providing as evidence a map of Ukraine, dating from 1932, on which Smolensk (for example) is just inches away from Lvov.

Be that as it may, Alexandre went astray from the straight road of defeat and found himself, unconscious, in the midst of a pitch-dark forest. He had drifted to the edge of the eternal black hole, when someone pulled him out of it, tugging his benumbed leg. There's hardly any doubt that that was the tribe's great-great-grandmother Marija. Alexandre opened his eyes and saw the angelic smile of a seventeen-year-old girl who was trying to take off his decrepit, yet still precious, boots. Let me confess that a blasphemous thought has occurred to me: the angelic smile might have been seriously deficient in a considerable number of teeth, due to the then-common winter scurvy. She, naturally, decided to take him home, unloading the firewood and mounting him on the tired nag (somehow, that was the epoch of tired nags). Her parents, surprised and scared, could not resist her determination, so she made him a bed near the hearth and then nursed him out of his glacial numbness, patiently rubbing his limbs to get the blood started. (Uncle Teodor sometimes likes to add a touch of gangrene at this point.) She fed him honey and lard, and spoke to him mellifluously. Yes, she rekindled his heart and they did get married. Yes, they're considered to be the Adam and Eve of the Hemon universe.

My mother, who proudly descends from a sturdy stock of Bosnian peasantry, considered all this to be the typical 'Hemon propaganda'. And she may well have been right, I'm afraid to say. For we have no well-established facts from which the unquestionable existence of Alexandre Hemon would necessarily follow. There is, however, some circumstantial evidence:

a) At the time of the Winter Olympics in Sarajevo, my sister held in her hand a credit card in the name of a certain Lucien Hemon. Lucien was the rifle manager for the French biathlon team. He told my sister, not hesitating to flirt with her, that Hemon was a rather common family name in Brittany and suggested, after she had told him the highlights of the family history, that a Napoleonic soldier could well have carried it over to Ukraine. That was the germ from which Alexandre sprang, and the previously dominant theory that 'Hemon' was a Ukrainian variation on 'demon' was indefinitely suspended.

b) In 1990, a busload of excited Bosnian Ukrainians went to Ukraine in order to perform a set of old songs and dances, long forgotten in the oppressed ex-homeland. While they were staying in a waterless hotel in Lvov, the Hemons decided to venture into the village (Ostanyevichy) that my great-grandfather's family had left to move to Bosnia. I should point out that a widespread belief in the family was that we had no kin in Ukraine. As they snooped around the depressed village, mainly populated by bored-to-senility elderly folks, they aroused plenty of suspicion among the villagers, who must have believed that the KGB was on to them again. In antique Ukrainian, just for the hell of it, they questioned toothless men leaning on their canes and fences about Hemons in the village, until one of them pointed peevishly at the house across the dirt road. The man in the house told them that, yes, he was a Hemon, but had no knowledge of any kin in Bosnia. He told them outright that he was no fool and that he knew they worked for the police. They tried to dissuade him from throwing them out, pointing out that police agents and spies do not move around in such large and compact groups—there were fourteen of them, all vaguely resembling one another and scaring the wits out of their poor distant cousin. Next day, the man (his name was, not surprisingly, Ivan) visited them in their dismal hotel, considerately bringing a bottle of water as a present. They told him, trying to outshout each other, about the exodus to Bosnia, about the family bee-keeping, about the legendary Alexandre Hemon. Yes, he told them, he might have heard about a Frenchman being related to the family a long time ago.

Thus it was definitely established by the family that our tree was rooted in glorious Brittany, which clearly distinguished us from other Ukrainians—a people of priests and peasants—let alone Bosnian Ukrainians. Once Alexandre Hemon was officially admitted to the family, the interest for things Gallic surged, and no one much cared for the nuanced differences between the Bretons and the French. My father would unblinkingly and determinedly sit through an entire French movie—French movies used to bore him out of his mind—and then would claim some sort of genetic understanding of the intricate relations between characters in, say, *A Bout de Souffle*. He went so far as to claim that my cousin Vlado was the spitting image of Jean-Paul Belmondo, which consequently made Vlado (a handsome blond young man) begin referring to himself as 'Belmondo'. 'Belmondo is hungry,' he would announce to his mother upon returning from work in a leather-goods factory.

Further developments in the Hemon family-name history were propelled—I'm proud to say—by my literary exploits. In the course of attaining my useless comparative literature degree at the University of Sarajevo, I read *The Iliad* and found a lightning reference to 'Hemon the Mighty'. Then I read *Antigone* where I discovered that Antigone's suicidal fiancé was named Hemon—Hemon pronounced as Haemon, just like our family name. In the *agon* with Creon, Hemon at first looks like a suck-up:

> My father, I am yours. You keep me straight
> with your good judgement, which I shall ever follow.
> Nor shall a marriage count for more with me
> than your kind leading.

But then they get into a real argument, and Hemon tells Creon off: 'No city is the property of a single man,' and 'You'd rule a desert beautifully alone,' and 'If you weren't a father, I should call you mad.'

My father dutifully copied the one page from *The Iliad* that, towards the bottom, had 'Hemon the Mighty' and the handful of pages in *Antigone* where the unfortunate Hemon agonizes with the cocky Creon. He highlighted every sighting of the Hemon name with a blindingly yellow marker. He kept showing the copies to his co-workers, poor creatures with generic Slavic surnames, which—at best!—might have signified a minor character in a socialist-realist novel, someone, say, whose life is saved by the fearless protagonist or who simply and insignificantly dies. My father didn't bother to read *Antigone*, never mind tens of thousands of lines of *The Iliad*, and I failed to mention to him that 'Hemon the Mighty' is absolutely irrelevant in the great epic, or that Antigone's illustrious fiancé committed not-so-illustrious suicide by hanging.

The following semester, I found a Hemon in *The Aeneid* who makes a fleeting appearance as the chief of a savage tribe. Sure enough, my father added the promptly highlighted photocopy to his little Hemon-archive. Finally, in *Gargantua and Pantagruel* I stumbled upon 'Hemon and his four sons' involved in an outrageous Rabelaisian orgy. The Rabelais reference, however, provided the missing link with the French chapter of the family history, which now could be swiftly reconstructed all the way back to 2000 BC.

There is, unfortunately, a shadow stretching over this respectable history, a trace of murky, Biblical past that no one dared to follow but that the designated, though inept, historian feels obliged to mention: My cousin Aleksandra still remembers the timor and terror she felt when, in church, she heard the priest utter—clearly and loudly—our name. The priest, she says, described a man who stood in the murderous crowd under the cross on which Our Saviour was expiring in incomprehensible pain, his eyes (the man's, of course) bulging with evil, bloodthirsty saliva running down his inhuman chin, laughing away Our Saviour's suffering. 'What kind of man is he?' thundered the priest. 'What kind of man could laugh at the Lamb's slaughter? *Hemon* was his name, and we know that his seed was winnowed and scattered all over this doomed earth, eternally miserable, alone and deprived of God's love.' Stricken with horror (she was nine), she retched and ran out, while her father, my uncle Roman, who was not paying attention, kept saying 'Amen!'

Later investigations found no Hemons in the Bible, although it is entirely unclear who the researcher was and how exactly the research was conducted. The official explanation, accepted by the entire family, was that the priest was performing an act of vicious revenge, probably because my aunt Amalija called him 'a pig in the vestment' while the wrong ears were listening, or because my father married a communist.

In any case, few thought that we carried the mortifying burden of the ancient sin on our shoulders, or that we would have a family reunion in hell. 'We have always been honest, hard-working people,' my father announced to the priest who replaced the hostile one (who had moved to Canada), pointing his finger towards the ceiling, beyond which, presumably, there was the supreme judge and avenger. The priest amicably nodded and accepted a bottle of home-made slivovitz and a jar of first-class honey, with which the potentially eternal dispute between the Hemons and God (regarding his Son) was settled, it seemed then, satisfactorily for both parties.

I have had doubts, however, along with some of my younger cousins and a very close relative. I have had doubts and fears that indeed we could have committed the terrible sin of sniggering at someone else's suffering. Perhaps that's why we emigrated, again, in the 1990s, from Bosnia to the United States. Perhaps this is the punishment: to live half-lives, unable to forget what we used to be, afraid to be addressed in a foreign language, no longer able to utter anything truly meaningful. I have seen my parents, mute, in an elevator, in Schaumburg, Illinois, staring at their uncomfortable toes, stowed in foreign shoes, as a breezy English-speaking neighbour entered the elevator and attempted to commence a conversation about the unkind Midwestern weather. My father kept pressing the buttons '11' and '18' (where the verbose American was heading), as if they would terminate the fucking multilingual world and take us all back to the time before the Tower of Babel was unwisely built and history began to unwind in the wrong, inhuman direction. My mother occasionally grinned painfully at the confounded neighbour, as the elevator rose arduously, through the molasses of silence, to the eleventh floor.

2.

Inspired by the success of the Sarajevo Olympiad and the newly established ancient family history, the family council, righteously headed by my father, decided to have an epic get-together, which was to be held only once, and was to be recorded as the Hemoniad. The minutes from that family-council meeting (taken by me) can scarcely convey the excitement and joyous awareness of the event's future importance. Allow me to step out of my historian's shoes (one size too small) and become a witness for an instant: I can attest that there was a moment of comprehensive silence—a fly was heard buzzing stubbornly against the windowpane; fire was cracking in the stove; someone's bowels disrespectfully grumbled—a moment when everyone looked into the future marked by the Hemoniad, the event that would make our Homeric cousins envious. Even Grandfather, in one of his precious lucid moments, seemed to recognize everyone and did not ask: 'Where am I?' The magic was dispelled when the milk-pot boiled over, and a swarm of aunts flew towards the stove to repair the damage.

Thus it was decided that the Hemoniad was to be held in June 1991, at our grandparent's estate, which was falling apart because of my grandfather's dotage, but was, nevertheless, 'the place where our roots still hold the land together, fighting cadaverous worms'. It was also decided that the Hemons should reach out to the Hemuns, the family branch that grew out of the tree trunk of Uncle Ilyko, my grandfather's brother.

This is their history: Uncle Ilyko went from Bosnia to Ukraine to fight for Ukrainian independence in 1917. After the humiliating defeat, in 1921, he walked to the newly formed border between Romania and Yugoslavia, where they arrested him and put him on the train back to Kiev. He jumped off the train, somewhere in Bukovina, and then roamed, as the first snow of the year, ominously abundant, was smothering the earth. He almost froze to death, but was found and saved by a young war-widow, who nursed him out of glacial darkness all winter, asking for nothing from him, but to warm her cold feet and dilute her loneliness. In the spring, he got up from the shaky bed, took from her trembling hands a bundle containing knitted socks, a brick of cheese, and her daguerreotype. He kissed her tearful cheeks, including a hirsute wart, and walked, only at night, back to the Romanian–Yugoslav border. Sometime in the spring of 1922, he swam across the Danube, whose murky, cold waters dissolved the daguerreotype.

Well, we never liked him. He was a violent, impetuous man. The day Ilyko returned home—where everyone thought he was long dead—he got into a fight with Grandfather, because my grandfather had married the girl Ilyko had had a crush on. Infuriated, he went to Indjija, Serbia, married a native, and let a drunken clerk change his name to Hemun, which became the original sin of the Hemun branch. Indeed, the Hemuns avoided contact with the descendants of my grandparents, barely spoke Ukrainian, sang no Ukrainian songs, danced no Ukrainian dances, and thought of themselves as Serbs. The Hemuns, then, were to be saved from 'the weed of otherness', and come back to 'the forest of flesh and bone growing out of the ancient Hemon roots'. When they told Grandfather that the Hemuns were to come back to their historic home, he—God bless him—asked, 'And who are they?'

In the weeks after the family-council meeting, the invitation was forged in the Olympic minds of my blind Uncle Teodor and my father. Uncle Teodor made suggestions, and my father rejected them as he typed. Let me submit an image: Uncle Teodor running different formulations by my father: '...the branch that was unjustly severed...the branch that fell off and broke the tree's heart...the branch that shrivelled, detached from its roots...' My father's index fingers leaping up and down the typing keyboard, like virgins dancing for gods—Father occasionally using a virgin to pick his nose, and saying: 'No...no...no...no...' Like all the great documents of history, the Hemoniad invitation went through many drafts and finally attained the form of exceptional grace and power.

It clearly stated the purpose: '...to reattach the most formidable branch to its just place...';

the place: '...the Hemon family estate, where thousands of years of history are told by bees and birds and chickens...';

the logistics: '...we shall feast on spit-roast piglets and mixed salad, and if you need cakes and pastry, you are advised to make them yourselves...';

the structure: '...spare time will be spent in the house, in the courtyard, in the backyard, in the field, in the orchard, in the apiary, in the garden, in the cow shed, by the creek, in the forest, in conversation and exchange of pleasant words...'

The invitation was gladly received by many, and responses from all corners of the family began pouring in. The participation of many Hemuns was heralded by a phone call from the oldest Hemun, Andrija, and a tide of elation advanced through the family. Oh, those days when planning a piglet slaughter over the phone had mythological proportions; when old stories were excavated from the basements of memory, and then polished and embellished; when sleepless, warm nights were wasted in trying to make sleeping arrangements, until Uncle Teodor suggested the hay under the cow-shed roof, where 'the youth' could sleep; when my mother kept rolling her eyes, suspicious of any mass-meeting of people of the same ethnicity; when aunts independently met to organize the cake and pastry production, lest we have a surfeit of *balabushki*.

I'm afraid this sentence was inescapable: the day of the Hemoniad arrived. A huge tent had been put up, above a long table. The stage for 'the orchestra' had been built under the walnut tree in the centre of the courtyard. Uncle Teodor, they say, was up at dawn, sitting on the porch and rehearsing the stories for the last time. I woke up (allow me to interpolate a personal memory) to the incessant warbling of birds nesting under the roof. When I descended the stairs, I saw a pair of dancing headless chickens, trying to run away from something (but they couldn't because it was everywhere), their wings arrhythmically flapping, blood spurting out of their necks in decreasing streams. We had breakfast sitting around the big table, passing panfuls of fried chicken livers and hearts, and platefuls of sliced tomatoes and pickles. 'This,' said Uncle Teodor, 'is the greatest day of my life.'

The Hemuns arrived all at once, with a fleet of shining new cars, like a colonizing army. They were uniformly overweight and spoke with a northern-Serbian drawl, which implied a life of affluent leisure. Nonetheless, everyone hugged each other, cheeks were smacked with kisses, hands were shaken ardently, and backs were slapped to the point of bruising. Uncle Teodor hollered, 'Welcome, Hemuns!', and then proceeded from Hemun to Hemun, offering them his stump. He turned his ear to each of them, asking, 'And who are you?' and then memorized their voices.

The day went on in an agreeable atmosphere of general merriment and pleasant conversing. We have pictures, recorded on tape, of the crowd in the tent, milling in a perpetual attempt to get closer to each other, like atoms forced to form a molecule, merging into one big body, with moist armpits and indestructible vocal cords. The band played all day, on and off, sovereignly led by my cousin Ivan, who kept winking, over his heavy-breathing accordion, at every woman under forty not directly related to him. When the band played old Ukrainian songs, the Hemuns sat grinning, confounded and embarrassed, for they could not understand a word. But everyone danced in whatever way they could, waltzing clumsily, their hands adhering to their partner's bobbing sides and sweaty palms; or, their stage fright temporarily cured by an infusion of a helpful beverage (beer was my choice), they would dance *kolomiyka*, spinning at different speeds, from neck-breaking to mere circular trotting.

Around one o'clock, as the sun like a stage light got stuck right above the walnut tree top, my six aunts ascended the stage, having been introduced by Uncle Teodor, who recited their hypocoristic names like a poem: 'Halyka, Malyka, Natalyka, Marenyka, Julyka, Filyka.' They sang a song about a young Ukrainian soldier being sent off to die in yet another battle for the freedom of Ukraine, who was doing what most soldiers in most of the Ukrainian songs did all the time—he was saying goodbye to his inconsolable mother and his faithful bride-to-be. They sang (my aunts) with their arms akimbo, serenely swaying and rubbing each other's elbows. They looked like six variations of the same woman. Grandfather suddenly pricked up his ears, as if recognizing the song, but then he was retaken by the demons of slumber and succumbed with a grunt. Meanwhile, the soldier died (as we had all expected) and his faithful bride-to-be was about to be ravished by the same force that was to enslave Ukraine. 'This song,' explained Uncle Teodor, after my aunts bowed, blushed and scuttled off the stage, 'is about the value of freedom and independence.'

Then lunch was served, and everyone sat around the long table, with Grandfather floating on the Lethe at its head. The table was creaking under heaps of pork and chicken limbs. There were big-eared soup bowls, which were reverently passed around the table, steam enthusiastically gushing out of them like smoke from a snoozy volcano. There were plates of green onions, stacked like timber, and tomato slices sunk in their own slobber. After lunch, everyone became drowsy, descending from the mountains of meat to the lowlands of sleep. Snippets of conversation died off within seconds, for no one's blood was capable of reaching the brain. Grandfather was fast asleep and snoring, leaning on his sagely stick. He burped in his sleep and moved his tongue over his upper lip, touching the bottom of the moustache, and then in the opposite direction along the lower lip, for a whiff of pleasant taste had escaped the inferno of slow digestion and reached his palate. Finally, everyone yielded to the stupor, and excited flies could land, after a long journey, on the continent abundant with meat and salad. They would comfortably sit on a slice of bread, greasing themselves to dazzling summer-fly glitter. Abruptly they would ascend, as if to check whether they could still fly, and then descend again, buzzing messages of festive pleasure to each other. Watching them, it occurred to me that they were our flies—Hemon flies—and therefore better than other flies, oblivious to their historical role.

On the videotape of the Hemoniad, the only document of the glorious festivity that reached the United States, this transcendental torpor is contained within three or four intense minutes of silence, the hum of the breeze in the microphone notwithstanding. It is important to note, however, that the flies disappeared in the process of converting the tape from PAL-SECAM to NTSC.

Then Uncle Teodor was snatched out of his wheezing tranquillity and led to the stage, where he was ushered into a chair. The level of consciousness abruptly rose around the table. Uncle Teodor said, 'I will tell you stories now, because it is important to know one's own history. If you know the stories, just sit quiet and listen—we have people who don't know them.' The Hemuns—people who didn't know the stories—fidgeted and glanced at each other, for they suspected that the stories would present them as treacherous and weak people. But Uncle Teodor had different intentions. He began with the Hemons of *The Iliad*, their doughty feats and their contribution to the burning of Troy. Then he talked about the Hemon who almost married Antigone, the most beautiful woman of the ancient world. He barely touched on the Hemon who was Aeneas' sidekick and who founded the Roman Empire with him. He talked about Hemons defending European civilization from a deluge of barbarian Slavic marauders. Then he skipped a number of centuries and nearly brought tears to everyone's eyes talking about the murderous retreat and Alexandre's travails and the horrors of the Russian winter. He told us of Alexandre's hallucinations: armies of headless men, marching in circles, and of trying to escape a gigantic axe that strove to decapitate him, until he fell down. 'He didn't feel the snap, but he felt blood spurting and the cold slowly gnawing his limbs.' And then he was saved by our Ur-Mother Marija. As Uncle Teodor was narrating their budding love and Alexandre's recovery, Grandfather burst to the surface of the day, looked around in genuine astonishment and asked me, since I was sitting next to him:

'Who are these people?'

I said, 'They're your tribe, Grandpa.'

'I've never seen them in my life.'

'Yes, you have, Grandpa.'

'And who are you?'

'I'm one of your grandchildren.'

'I've never seen you in my life.'

'Well, now you can see me.'

'Where are we?'

'We're home, Grandpa.'

That seemed to satisfy him, so he dropped his head to his chest, and was back in the boat crossing the Lethe. In the meantime, Uncle Teodor got to Alexandre and Marija's progeny. The Hemons of the mid-nineteenth century were all invariably bright and dexterous and hard-working, but they seemed to have perennially suffered from Polish and Russian injustice, plus tuberculosis and scurvy. Moreover, women kept miscarrying, while men kept falling from trees and being gored by disobedient cattle. 'And yet we survived!' exclaimed Uncle Teodor. He went on to tell a story I had never heard before, a story about the ancestor who had gone to America to become a rich man, and when he became a rich man he returned to his village. He built a beautiful house and did nothing but court rural virgins, receive guests, and drink with them. One of his guests, probably the devil incarnate, dared him to spend a night at the local graveyard, which was known to be haunted by the village Jews massacred in a pogrom. He bet his whole estate that he would spend the night and he did, but he met the rosy-fingered dawn with his hair completely white and his hands unstoppably shaking. He never told anyone what he had heard or seen, but the next day he gave all he had to the rabbi of the few remaining Jews so he could build a home for the wandering spirits. He was deemed insane after that by his relatives, who had just got used to being members of a wealthy family, and who claimed that it was Jewish magic that had cast a spell on their dear cousin. One day he disappeared, and no one ever saw him again. Uncle Teodor claimed that he had gone back to America, and that we probably have some American cousins. As we imagined our half-mad hoary cousin sailing towards the Statue of Liberty, coffee was served. We sipped strong tarrish liquid from demitasses, without really noticing that Uncle Teodor had omitted the second half of the nineteenth century (probably because some of our forefathers were prone to pogrom fever) and begun telling the well-known narrative about the exodus to Bosnia.

Imagine the crushing poverty, the year-long drought and cattle plague, the bone-cracking cold of the 1914 winter, the widespread banditry of hungry, destitute ex-peasants—we all writhed in our seats, fretting over the unforeseeable future with our ancestors. Great-grandparents Teodor and Marija, the story went, packed all they had: a few bundles of poorly patched clothing; a beehive, sealed to make the trip; some clay pots and a coal iron; a roll of money they had saved up, which spent the trip in my great-grandmother's bosom absorbing sweat and entertaining lice. Grandfather, presently dozing off next to me, and Ilyko fought throughout the journey. He told us how they had been given a piece of uncultivated land—'this very land'—which was now 'the best piece of land in Bosnia', although, to tell the truth, it produced nothing but retarded corn and shrivelled apples. Great-grandfather went to Sarajevo to get the papers for the land on the day Archduke Franz Ferdinand was killed. He bought an accordion there, 'this very accordion', which was not true, for Uncle Teodor himself had crushed the accordion some years ago. Oh, the years of struggling and working from sunup to sundown. And then Ilyko went to fight the Bolsheviks—'We all know what happened then, and that is why we are all here now.'

It was the Hemuns who got impatient first, and their impatience quickly became contagious. As Uncle Teodor, entirely carried away, continued talking about Uncle Julius and his twenty-five years in Stalin's camps, both the Hemuns and the Hemons kept rising, hastening towards the outhouse, pouring slivovitz down their throats, chit-chatting, anything but listen to the blind narrator. By the time Uncle Julius got to the Arkhangelsk camp, where he was to be sentenced to death, no one—except me—was listening. My father stood up and said, 'Enough, Teodor. You'll continue later.' But he never did, for the band started playing again and everybody was imbibing elating beverages. Again, shoulders were slapped, crushing hugs and smacking kisses generously exchanged; some trance-like dancing began. Some of it can be seen on the videotape, but not without effort, because I had one drink too many, and the camera was held by my tremulous hands. Thus the image is shaking and tilting like the giddy people in it. As the camera was taken away from me to be shut off, so was my clear-mindedness, and everything became dizzy and dim. Allow me to submit several discontinuous memories—images and sensations that flashed before the helpless mind's eye, as my mind capsized and sank to the sandy bottom of complete oblivion: the noxious, sour manure stench coming from the pigsty; the howling of the only piglet left alive; the fluttering of chickens; pungent smoke, coming from moribund pig-roast fires; relentless crunching of the gravel on which many feet danced; my aunts and other auntly women treading the *kolomiyka* on the gravel, their ankles universally swollen, and their skin-hued stockings descending down their varicose calves; the scent of a pine plank and the prickly coarseness of its surface as I laid my cheek on it and everything spun, as if I were in a washing machine; my cousin Ivan's sandalled left foot tap-tap-tapping on the stage, headed by its stocky big toe; the cakes and pastries arrayed on the bed (on which my grandmother had expired), sorted meticulously into chocolate and non-chocolate phalanxes; the intense, chewy taste of green onions and pork that washed off my palate, immediately followed by a billow of gastric acid; greasy itchiness around my mouth, adumbrating numerous, putrid pimples; the hysterical, aroused, chained dog leaping at me, nearly choking himself and coating my hands and face with his drool; the seething warmth of the concrete steps, in the proximity of the dog, where I attempted to regain my seasick consciousness; the needly hay under the revolving roof of the cow shed; my hand holding a long, crooked stick (a Napoleonic sword), beating a nettle throng (Russian soldiers), and my forearms burning and rubicund; truckloads of helmeted soldiers, passing by the house, shooting in the air, and showing us the three-fingered sign, shouting and throwing bottles at the chickens; trucks dragging erected cannons, and dark jeeps following them; an unfamiliar cat, caught as it was stealthily jumping on to the table strewn with gnawed bones and splinters of meat, staring at me, the pupils stretched to the edges in utter feline disbelief, as if I were not supposed to be there, as if my vomitous existence had not been approved by the potent being whose approval the cat clearly had.

Then I was sitting down on the grass, leaning against the walnut tree, then closing my eyes and carefully searching for the position in which my head would stop gyrating. I put the tips of my index fingers against my temples, and thus fixed my head, not daring to blink, let alone to move. I heard the din of voices, the garrulous babel, the uproar of guttural excitement, which all eventually ebbed. Then I could hear (although I'm not sure I did) my father's voice, 'wishing to conclude this epic festival of Hemonhood, with words that could not possibly match the greatness of the occasion'. He talked about our ancient roots and 'thousands of years of Hemonian diligence', which helped us survive the biggest catastrophes in human memory. 'Do you think it is an accident that our ancestor Alexandre was one of the few to survive the unfathomable defeat of Napoleon's army? Do you think it is just luck that he progressed through several heart-chilling blizzards to meet the woman of his life, the Eve of the Hemon universe?' No one dared to answer these questions, so he went on and on, and talked about the courage it took to move to Bosnia, 'the wild frontier of the Austro-Hungarian Empire'. He dwelt for some time, as I was successfully resisting retching, on 'the progress that we brought to these parts' with 'civilized bee-keeping, iron plough and carpentry skills'. We built 'our empire out of nothing', and it was 'no accident that our grandfather met with the Archduke before he was assassinated—our stock is heroic and royal'. He told us (although I was barely there) that we should 'read the Greeks, the founders of the Western civilization' if we didn't believe—'We're all over the history of literature.' So he proliferated thoughts about the family history, mentioning names that I could not attach to faces any more—they all merged into my grandfather who was presently and perpetually passing in and out of nothingness. I do not know where our greatness ended—if indeed it ever ended—for I passed out. Then I heard energetic applause, a choir of hands clapping and clapping, and someone was slapping my face. As I opened my eyes, everything rushed away from me, except the face of my mother, who said, 'It seems that the history wore you out. Do you want to vomit?'

My mother led me away, while I mismanaged my steps, from the tumultuous tribal space, holding my right arm above the elbow, and I felt her swollen, arthritic knuckles squeezing my muscle. 'The trouble with the Hemons,' she said, 'is that they always get much too excited about things they imagine to be real.' I was wobbling, looking at the prows of my feet, imagining the straight line that I had to follow so as not to appear drunk. But then I simply closed my eyes and let my mother steer me around chairs and chickens and buckets and tree stumps and flower beds. 'I made a terrible fool of myself,' I said. 'You're almost a man now,' she said. 'And that is a man's privilege.'

She made me sit under a shrivelled apple tree. Small, wizened apples—not unlike my brain at that moment—hung like earrings from crooked, exhausted branches. My mother sat down by my side and put her arm around me. I wanted to put my head on her lap, but she said, 'No, you'll just get dizzier.' We could hear the Hemons-Hemuns hollering against the music, which from a distance sounded discordant. We could still hear the trucks, and I realized that they had been passing by all day. 'I wish these trucks would stop,' I said. 'They probably won't for a while,' my mother said. Her hands smelled of coffee and vanilla sugar. She told me about the time her father gave their only horse away.

'It was in '43 or '44, a young man came running out of the corn. Mother and Father knew him, he was lank and had blue eyes, a Muslim from a nearby village. He said that the Chetniks had killed his whole family, that he escaped, leaping through a window, and now they were after him. He had a bruise on his cheek, as if someone had kissed him with plum-lips. He asked my father for the horse so he could get away and join the partisans. Father glanced at my mother; she said nothing, but he knew and he went to get the horse, cursing all along, "Fuck this world and the bloody sun and this country when everyone needs my horse." The young man, his name was Zaim, kissed both of my father's cheeks and promised he would return the horse once the evil had blown over. So he rode off, waving at us. But then the Chetniks came, riding their horses like cowboys. "Where is he?" they yelled. "Where's the circumcised dog?" And my father said, "What's the trouble, brothers?" They all had beards and rifles and knives. They shouted, "Did you see the Turkish bastard?" Father said, "I don't know who you're talking about." "You're lying!" they yelled. "You're a traitor!" Then they beat him with rifle butts, they threw him on the ground and kicked him with their boots. "What's wrong with you, motherfucker, you're one of us? Where's the Turk? Who's he to you?" I thought they would slit our throats, no problem. My brother was in the partisans, but we spread the word that he was in Srem, working.'

'You've never told me this,' I said.

She continued: 'They kept beating him until he was bleeding and unconscious. My mother wept and begged them to spare him. Then one of them, beardless, came to me and said, "There's a little Serbian girl who is going to tell us where the Turk is." Oh, I couldn't say a word, and then I saw my mother's frightened eyes, and her hands squeezing the strength out of each other. I told them I hadn't seen anyone and that I would tell them if I had. So they left, and the beardless one told us that he would personally judge us if he found out we were lying. That was our only horse, you know, all we had.'

I resisted falling asleep, trying to keep my eyes open, but then I succumbed, leaning on my mother's shoulder, even in my dreams aware of the possibility of disgorging myself. I slept for hours, thinking in my troublesome sleep that I was leaning on my mother, but then I woke up, with my cheek on a molehill, sprawled on the ground covered with rotting apples. I went back to the yard and all the Hemuns were gone, as if I had dreamed them; and everyone else was cleaning up, storing away the food or taking the tent and the stage apart. I did not need to have been there to know what happened at the end. It can all be seen on the tape, which we occasionally watch when I visit my parents in Schaumburg, Illinois. We rewind and fast-forward to get to the moment we most cherish. We freeze the frame to remember a name, we fill in the gaps, caused by unwarranted cuts and blanks thanks to a ten-dollar conversion in a Pakistani store on Devon and Mozart. Frequently, there's a little tide of fractious dots rising from the bottom of a trembling picture, always trying to reach the centre. Finally, the last image is of my mother, just about to say something—something irreverent about 'the Hemon propaganda', perhaps. That is all too clear from her clever eyes and the lingering, undeveloped grin. She never says it, forever on the verge of saying something. She can never remember what she was going to say, and the screen suddenly turns blindingly blue, and we turn it off and rewind the tape to the beginning. □

GRANTA

UNCLE ED

Keith Fleming

Edmund White and Keith Fleming, Central Park reservoir, 1976

Back in 1976 when I was sixteen, my uncle, the novelist Edmund White, rescued me from the messy aftermath of my parents' divorce and brought me to live with him in New York. It was, and still is, the defining moment of my life, yet my experience as the heterosexual teenage ward of a young gay uncle was even weirder than one might imagine. For though it has now become more common for gay men to adopt children, when my uncle assumed responsibility for me in the hedonistic 1970s it was still so rare that no one else among his large circle of gay Manhattan friends had a child living under his roof. And while today's gay parents make an effort to provide stable, conventional homes, Uncle Ed continued to lead the life of a dandy, equally at home with leather bars and Lincoln Center. Many a school night would find me doing my homework at the kitchen table at ten in the evening and my uncle, freshly showered and dressed in leather jacket and jeans, saying Good Night as he headed out the door for a wild night downtown at the Mineshaft or the Toilet.

Taking me in was a favour Uncle Ed had granted my mother, his older sister, on the spur of the moment. She'd called him up one night to say that she couldn't stand to see me rotting away in the adolescent psycho ward my father and stepmother had put me in after I'd started cutting classes, leaving my room in a mess, and telling them Fuck You too much.

Uncle Ed's willingness to take me in was all the more extraordinary given how poor he was. When I arrived in New York in January 1976 he had just turned thirty-six and was the author of a single published book, *Forgetting Elena*, a novel that had sold only a few hundred copies but had miraculously managed to be singled out for praise by Vladimir Nabokov. Though Uncle Ed would soon be at work on *The Joy of Gay Sex* and *Nocturnes for the King of Naples*, two books that would make his name, when I first came to live with him he was making ends meet by ghost-writing a US history textbook.

Uncle Ed was living on the Upper West Side with another Keith, a blond, boyish actor named Keith McDermott (faced with the dilemma of two Keiths now living with her son, Ed's mother, my grandmother, solved the problem by designating Keith McDermott

'Keith number one' and me 'Keith number two'). A month after I moved into their large apartment at Eighty-sixth and Columbus, Keith number one landed the role of the disturbed teenage boy in the Broadway production of *Equus*, in which he would star opposite Richard Burton. As he prepared for his role Keith couldn't resist regarding me—a real-life teenager fresh from the bughouse—as a sort of model, and his portrayal of the boy in *Equus* ended up incorporating two odd mannerisms I had in my earliest days in New York: a robotic way of walking without swinging my arms and a tendency to peer at people with a furtive, sidelong glance.

My uncle blamed these mannerisms on my confinement in the psycho ward. There, I'd been deprived of fresh air and exercise and been tormented by my psychiatrist, Dr Schwarz, who was always threatening to send me off to a 'long-term treatment facility' in the Maine woods where the inmates were made to scream at one another and clear paths in the snow using teaspoons. Twenty years earlier, in the 1950s, while growing up in the same Chicago suburb as I did, Uncle Ed had nearly been institutionalized aged fifteen after rashly telling his divorced mother that he wanted to marry the son of a man that she was thinking of marrying. She'd sent my uncle to be evaluated by a local psychiatrist who pronounced Ed 'unsalvageable' and recommended he be locked away for good. My uncle ended up going off to boarding school instead, where he saw a psychoanalyst twice a week who treated homosexuality as the symptom of an underlying but curable neurosis.

The rage Uncle Ed still felt towards this analyst must have been what fuelled the fervour I heard in his voice whenever he'd start berating 'that monster'—as he'd taken to calling my Dr Schwarz. And it is remarkable how similar our two shrinks were. Each man had a love of holding forth and a lack of curiosity unbecoming in a psychiatrist. And each saw so many patients that he was often half asleep or falling asleep and had trouble remembering people's names—though each would no doubt have dismissed this as a minor, even irrelevant quibble, since both doctors administered their therapy as though a patient's personal details, whatever they might be, would merely have turned out to confirm their general theories.

But the worst thing about our psychiatrists was that they failed to grasp what truly bothered my uncle and me even as they were egocentric enough to insist that they alone knew how to 'cure' us. My uncle's real problem was simply that he happened to be a sensitive boy unfortunate enough to be struggling to come to terms with his homosexuality in the repressive 1950s. In my case, what most haunted me was the severe, pustular acne I had developed—a condition that had gone untreated and apparently unconsidered by Dr Schwarz and his staff as a possible cause for all my miserable, defiant behaviour. This horrible acne, which my parents had also never thought to do anything about, was the first thing my uncle noticed when I arrived. The next day an appointment was made for me with a dermatologist and soon the stinky sulphur potion prescribed was working wonders on my face.

Over the next few weeks I was also sent off to the barber and the dentist. One morning I discovered that the pair of plaid pants I'd brought to New York had disappeared from my dresser in the tiny maid's room off the kitchen that I'd been given as a bedroom; eventually I realized my uncle must have thrown them discreetly in the trash. But good taste is as easily acquired as bad by a teenager, and I was soon very attached to the old jean jacket and blue Italian shirt my uncle had given me (we were the same size) as well as the tweed jacket and other clothes he bought me at the discount men's store, Barney's Basement. And I soon came to appreciate the unfussy, entirely practical emphasis Uncle Ed placed on the importance of appearance. When I asked him why he bothered conforming to the reigning gay clone look of short hair, flannel shirt unbuttoned at the top to expose chest hair, and leather jacket, he'd charmed me by answering simply, 'Because if I didn't, I'd never get laid.'

I had assumed I'd be attending the local public school but my uncle surprised me by saying he wanted me to go to an expensive private one. My mother agreed to help out with a monthly cheque, but my father not only refused to contribute towards my expenses but even baulked at sending us my school record, which we needed to get me admitted into any new school. Only after Uncle Ed had called up my father and stepmother in a cold fury was the record finally sent.

Over the next few months, whenever the burden of meeting all my expenses seemed overwhelming, my uncle began suggesting that

I sue my father. Children suing their parents had just come into vogue and Ed said he'd been inspired by a magazine article about a Maryland teen who had won damages *and* a divorce from his parents. But after thinking it over I told Ed that I just didn't think I was up to suing my father, that I'd rather go to a public high school if prep school was something we couldn't afford. In retrospect, I see that I probably should have tried to get a court to order my father to contribute to my welfare. At the time, however, my still considerable self-hatred (Am I really worthy of a prep school?) mingled with feelings of timidity and shyness (Do I really have a case? Am I really ready for the 'spotlight' of playing, in a courtroom, the role of avenging son?). I should have focused more on my poor uncle's feelings and less on my own.

As it turned out, thanks in part to the advance Ed received to co-write *The Joy of Gay Sex*, I was able to remain at prep school.

On my father's list of objections to my moving to New York, number one must have been that I might turn gay in Uncle Ed's care. But my sexuality turned out to be one of the few things about me that I didn't and couldn't change and gay sex one of the few things about gay men I wasn't interested in imitating. Never before had I met men in their thirties and forties who looked so young and acted so lively, light-hearted and curious. If I was the only teenager in my uncle's world, there was no lack of 'kids', for that's what my uncle and his friends all called one another ('Drink up, kids'; 'Well, kids, it's been fun'). Before long I'd accepted my uncle's ways as being quite normal, even exemplary (my mother and grandmother were saying I sounded more and more like Ed on the phone, sometimes even mistaking me for him).

But then one day I brought a classmate home for lunch and saw my uncle anew. The lunch had been Ed's idea; he'd heard me speak of Richard, a good-looking but rather ordinary boy who'd become my first New York friend mostly because he happened to live in a building near ours and, unlike other classmates who hailed cabs or disappeared down subway stairs when class let out, made the same walk I did down Eighty-sixth Street. As I set out for school that morning my uncle told me, 'Don't worry, I promise not to act too gay,' but the moment Richard and I arrived for lunch I found myself embarrassed to be *feeling* embarrassed. 'Hi Richard, let me take your coat,' my uncle sang out, extending a hand instead of giving Richard the peck on the cheek a young gay visitor and I myself could usually expect.

'My nephew's told me all about how great you are,' my uncle went on, gesturing for Richard to sit down in one of the green metal kitchen chairs. Uncle Ed had apparently decided that lunch in the humble kitchen would be more comfy—more *straight*, I guess—than the kind of luncheon he'd serve his own friends in the dining room, all flowers and ratatouille and ice water in crystal pitchers. But as my uncle whisked the batter for our cheese soufflé I saw how hopelessly awkward the situation was, how despite all efforts to rein himself in, his face and voice would always be too animated for someone like Richard, the compliments too over-the-top. I realized then how theatrical my uncle was; how he and his friends had evolved a manner that could be very much like being on stage, with every sentence uttered a potential 'line' and every facial expression a clear, even exaggerated, register of what was being felt.

My uncle's relationship with his room-mate Keith McDermott (who was now playing the boy in *Equus* each night yet had mischievously taken to referring to himself as 'Mom' at home around me during the day) was something I came only gradually to understand. Although they slept in separate bedrooms, I'd assumed at first they were 'a couple' in the way that everyone I'd ever known defined the concept. But as I heard them talk in each other's presence about their outside sexual escapades (they both joked, for instance, about knowing the number of the payphone down below our windows so that they would be ready to ring it if a cute 'trick' happened to be walking past), I began to think things between them were merely merry and casual.

Only one night when Uncle Ed explained to me that taking me in had helped to distract him from how miserably in love he'd fallen with Keith, did I finally understand how painful their relationship could often be for him. But then anyone might have been confused after having listened to Edmund White espouse, as I had, a gleefully modern philosophy involving the compartmentalization of love and sex and friendship as practised by him and his fellow gay New Yorkers. As he put it a few years later in his book, *States of Desire*: 'Sex is performed with strangers, romance is captured in brief affairs, friendship is assigned to friends.'

And yet what Uncle Ed seems to have longed for with Keith was precisely the kind of long-term romance unmentioned in this philosophy—a romance, it's true, that would allow both partners the freedom to supplement their sex life with anonymous sex with others, but that would nonetheless remain an arrangement based on the primacy of home life (bringing tricks home, that is, would be forbidden). In Ed's actual relationship with Keith the problem was simply that Keith, while loving my uncle as a friend, did not feel physically attracted to him.

Despite the demands of his night life, which often kept him out till two in the morning or later, my uncle had decided he should make an effort to be present at breakfast before I went off to school. One morning, however, I failed to rise from my bed in the maid's room. I had developed insomnia while in the psycho ward, tossing and turning with worry each night about being sent to that frightening place in the Maine woods, and on this particular morning my uncle ended up carrying my breakfast in on a tray that he placed beside my bed. Even so, I was so groggy that morning that when he looked in a moment later I still hadn't raised my head from the pillow.

Seating himself on the edge of my bed, he cooed sweetly, 'Wake up, Nephew, wake up.'

Then: 'Or maybe I should join you under the covers, mmm?'

Followed by: 'No? Of course not. How about some scrambled eggs with your toast?'

If my uncle was an experienced seducer, he was equally experienced at rejection. For there was no aftermath to this gentle, entirely verbal little come-on from him. And I think of it as having been a verbal thing. If decades before he had experienced his crazily inappropriate remark to his mother (given the context of the 1950s) that he wanted to marry her boyfriend's son as something that just popped out of him, his remark to me was again, I think, something that just somehow popped out of his mouth. Whatever it was, it had all happened in the wink of an eye, and was just as quickly gone forever from the realm of possibilities. It had been an intensely awkward passing instant, it's true, but it was also something I promptly forgot about, as did he, like a crazy dream dreamed just before waking. All that mattered to me was that there would be no lingering awkwardness and that our relationship would continue unchanged; which is exactly what happened.

My uncle's spur-of-the-moment remark to me should probably also be seen against the backdrop of mid-Seventies Manhattan. Those were the days, after all, when one could enter an apartment building on a hot summer day, as I did once, and see through an open door the young super, dressed only in his underpants, lying on a bed in his studio apartment and beckoning one to join him. Then, too, as an 'acne survivor', what most haunted me was that I was still ugly; any passing nod to my attractiveness was thus something that, if not always exactly welcome, was never altogether displeasing. In fact, when a famous gay poet visited the apartment one day I discovered that I felt only flattered to learn that he had been interested enough to ask Ed later, when they were alone, whether I too 'shared the family taint'.

Spring break rolled around and Uncle Ed decided that he and I needed to escape slushy March Manhattan for a few days and fly down to Puerto Rico. Ed wanted us to take this trip despite having told me that he had $500 to his name and that the plane tickets we were using weren't quite kosher: 'Not to worry, though. We'll just make sure we're very casual as we go through boarding.' We arrived without a hitch in San Juan late in the afternoon and by sunset, which my uncle pointed out occurred with sinful speed in the tropics, we were sauntering barefoot on the beach, each sampling a rum punch from a plastic cup. After dinner Ed guided us into a four-star hotel, through its lobby, and out the other side, saying that all his life he'd taken pride in trespassing through expensive places and being taken for someone who belonged there. At a palm tree in front of our modest guest house he told me gently, 'OK Kiddo, I'm going to go cruising for a couple hours. Here's twenty dollars to do whatever you're going to do.'

It was on this little vacation, the only days that I've ever had my busy, sociable uncle more or less to myself, that I realized there would always be limits to our communion. The next night we happened to be walking around Old San Juan together when he pointed out a circular stone bench that was invitingly shadowy under dreamy, overhanging trees: 'When I was your age I was always wanting to sit in places like that and talk all night about life and love and what it all means. Now of course I couldn't be less interested.'

I'd heard him say similar things before. When a dinner guest would make the mistake of staying on too deep into the evening and unburdening himself too extensively, the guest was sure to be criticized as 'juvenile' afterwards by my uncle and Keith McDermott as they washed and dried the dinner plates. Ed and Keith would agree that they no longer had any patience for heart-to-heart talks, which were pointless as well as exhausting; they'd then go on to declare, in the spirit of Oscar Wilde, that everything of interest could be found on the surface of things and that deeper probing almost guaranteed a tedious conversation.

It could be hard to know what my uncle genuinely believed since he was capable of declaring contrary opinions over the course of a single dinner party. He'd launch into a pet topic such as the 'provincialism' of Midwesterners, for instance, the way they had of dithering over everything, including saying Goodbye, which irritated him no end when he was visiting out there because he didn't want another hug, didn't want to say 'Well, you take care now,' and longed instead to get away with a simple, crisp Goodbye the way New Yorkers do. But an hour later he'd be praising Midwesterners and attacking New Yorkers. Now he'd be describing himself as 'a good, public-library Midwestern intellectual' who was sick of meeting Princeton-educated New Yorkers who'd 'majored in Cocktail 101 and have opinions about everything but never really read anything'.

If the opinions that Uncle Ed was inspired to declare could be unpredictable and, as he admitted to me once, 'so wrapped up in irony that I sometimes don't know what I really think', what remained constant was his sensibility, particularly his notions of social etiquette. He disliked party games; he disliked jokes, especially long ones; he disliked wit for its own sake, particularly wit that left the witty feeling self-satisfied and the listener mute. What he liked was warm, table-wide chattering that never splintered off into five separate tête-à-têtes and which left everyone free to chip in because no one went on too long or got too pompous. Helping everything along was my uncle's rule of thumb that one charmed beautiful people by treating them as though they were smart, and brilliant people as though they were sexy.

Uncle Ed may have indulged himself in his busy social and sexual lives but the code he lived by put more emphasis on self-discipline than hedonism. More than anything he seemed to have styled himself after an eighteenth-century man of the world. The first book he'd suggested I read had been Lord Chesterfield's *Letters to his Son* and I instantly recognized my uncle in Chesterfield's dictum that a gentleman never rises later than ten in the morning, no matter when he might have gone to bed, and that his day should be divided evenly between study and pleasure, which mutually refresh each other. From time to time my uncle would feel obliged to tell me that it was probably difficult for a young person such as myself to grasp the hard work going on beneath what must look like a life devoted to fun, but I knew how hard he worked. After school, as I lay reading on the living-room sofa, I'd hear him hammering out *The Joy of Gay Sex* on his typewriter in the den dominated by a framed picture of a dead-serious Nabokov staring out with formidable, piercing eyes.

My uncle had also started writing his novel *Nocturnes for the King of Naples*, but this was something he preferred to 'compose', the word he always used, by hand on thick sheets of paper using a beautiful fountain pen. As he wrote, his telephone would keep ringing with yet another call from yet another friend checking in or making plans for the evening, and I came to know the glamour of such a busy, popular telephone (and consequently, the shame of the quieter phones I'd known in the Midwest). Yet my uncle imposed discipline on his love of conversation, limiting each phone chat, however amusing and punctuated by his deep, wonderfully wicked laughter, to a brisk five minutes. The real secret to his being able to have so much fun *and* get so much done, I realized, resided in his energy. As I lay on the sofa staring into space with *Letters to his Son* on my chest, I'd find myself thinking that were a movie to be made of his life the cameras would hardly ever need to stop rolling, so much did he seem to be perpetually 'on', socializing and writing and throwing himself into every minute of the day.

If there was glamour to the regularly ringing phone, there was magic in the music continuously playing on Uncle Ed's dishevelled record player. One after another the discs of Handel's concerto grosso would plop down from where they hung stacked above the turntable—a mechanism that my uncle reminded me actually fell within the robot category. It was easy to see why he used the word *compose* to refer to his novel-writing because music was obviously his favourite art. Just as had happened with Keith McDermott when he first moved in with Ed, I too was learning from my uncle to love 'serious music' and to discover how a perpetual Brahms and Bruckner background gave an ordinary afternoon a much-needed boost, supplying it with soaring heroism and sadness and making me feel that my own emotions were being deepened and improved. When Ed had been a teenager reading novels while his father worked at his desk, the Brahms and Mahler records his father continually played had been the only thing they had in common, something my uncle had even hoped might constitute a 'shared rapture' between him and his impassive father. I myself saw the music we listened to while my uncle worked at his desk not so much as our shared rapture (he gave of himself enough that I didn't need to grasp at such a lonely consolation) but rather as the outward presence of the magic contained in the writing he was doing.

Ed also enjoyed foisting his taste in literature on his two Keiths. Along with liking some of the usual giants (Nabokov for his eye, Proust for his mind, Tolstoy for his worlds), my uncle was also crazy about the Norwegian novelist Knut Hamsun who, as he put it, 'might be dumb but he's always so sensual and inspired'. Fran Lebowitz with her New York cynicism was another favourite, and her remark that children are a bore because they have no fashion sense and are incapable of offering one a truly interesting *loan* was something he loved to repeat.

As I got to know him better, I saw that concealed behind my uncle's warm, all-purpose sympathy was an extremely opinionated, even astringent mind. Thus while I'd learned from his example to hear out even the most crashing bore at a party with nodding encouragement, I also learned to ridicule self-indulgent 1970s pop therapy for devoting so much energy to making people feel better that it was being forgotten that such a thing existed as *'actual guilt'*. I learned from him to scorn the notion of the artist as too beautiful for this world—as too exquisite to keep practical affairs in order or remain emotionally stable. More than once I was advised never to become a writer, to become a businessman instead, because writers were so poorly paid. If I must be a writer, he suggested I satirize flaky creative types instead of the usual bourgeois targets.

Uncle Ed believed in an old-fashioned education. When I'd had to choose between a progressive school in the East Village and the stodgy one with the English faculty on the Upper West Side that I did end up attending, what most influenced me was Ed's stinging characterization of the East Village school as being 'the kind of place where if you show up late for class they say you're being "creative"'. But while it might seem that my uncle was simply pouring his opinions into my impressionable Midwestern mind, this would leave out my own feeling that dormant within me was something now answering, awakening, to his sensibility. For I was not simply a passive audience but someone who constantly egged him on, quizzing him so much that once he grew exasperated enough to tell me, 'You think I have all the answers.'

In our daily talks in the kitchen Uncle Ed and I together had come up with something we called 'the icky system', a system that rated the quality of Ed's sex with various people based on the idea that all sex is to some degree icky. The icky system awarded only negative scores and the highest rating that could be bestowed on his sex with someone was 'minus one icky' (the rating he gave Keith McDermott), though more par for the course was, 'Oh, I think the guy last night must have been minus four or maybe even minus five ickies.'

Uncle Ed's candour with me, which some could see as hardly appropriate fare for a sixteen-year-old nephew, is something I see as being an inescapable part of his style: he treated everyone he spent a lot of time with as a confidant, an adult. This candour with me was actually something I took as a sign of respect and stability, I who'd suffered at the hands of my father and all his secret plotting against me. The truly icky system was Dad's. Because were it not for my uncle's intercession, I'm convinced I would have continued to rot away in the 'units' or 'facilities' my father had been determined I stay in till I was eighteen, my horrible acne getting even worse—a fate I don't want to begin to contemplate.

In my earliest days in New York nearly everyone we met seemed charmed by the idea of such a young, unlikely uncle having adopted his nephew. Uncle Ed didn't look like a father figure, he didn't look much older than I did, really. Today, a quarter of a century later, he finally does look like a father, except I don't see him as one any more. Nor would he want me to. Just the other day he was complaining that a young friend had blurted out to him, 'You're my father figure, Ed'—something my uncle so hated hearing that he immediately told the young man, 'Oh. Well you're *my* father figure.' □

GRANTA

GOING ABROAD

W. G. Sebald

TRANSLATION BY MICHAEL HULSE

Farbe der Augen
Colour of eyes
Couleur des yeux

BRAUN

Größe / Height / Taille

184 cm

Unterschrift des Paßinhabers / Signature of bearer / Signature du titulaire

Länder, für die dieser Paß gilt / Countries for which this passport is valid
Pays pour lesquels ce passeport est valable

Für alle Länder / For all countries / Pour tous pays

Paßausstellende Behörde / Issuing authority / Autorité ayant délivré le passeport

Ausgestellt (Ort) / Issued at / Délivré à

GENERALKONSULAT
DER BUNDESREPUBLIK DEUTSCHLAND
MAILAND

Datum / Date / Date

04. AUGUST 1987

Unterschrift / Signature / Signature

Nr. H 3560586

Going Abroad

In October 1980 I travelled from England, where I had then been living for nearly twenty-five years in a county which was almost always under grey skies, to Vienna, hoping that a change of place would help me get over a particularly difficult period in my life. In Vienna, however, I found that the days proved inordinately long, now they were not taken up by my customary routine of writing and gardening tasks, and I literally did not know where to turn. Early every morning I would set out and walk without aim or purpose through the streets of the inner city, through the Leopoldstadt and the Josefstadt. Later, when I looked at the map, I saw to my astonishment that none of my journeys had taken me beyond a precisely defined sickle- or crescent-shaped area, the outermost points of which were the Venediger Au by the Praterstern and the great hospital precincts of the Alsergrund. If the paths I had followed had been inked in, it would have seemed as though a man had kept trying out new tracks and connections over and over, only to be thwarted each time by the limitations of his reason, imagination or will power, and obliged to turn back again. My quartering of the city, often continuing for hours, thus had very clear bounds, and yet at no point did my incomprehensible behaviour become apparent to me: that is to say, my continual walking and my reluctance to cross certain lines which were both invisible and, I presume, wholly arbitrary. All I know is that I found it impossible even to use public transport and, say, simply take the 41 tram out to Pötzleinsdorf or the 58 to Schönbrunn and take a stroll in the Pötzleinsdorf Park, the Dorotheerwald or the Fasangarten, as I had frequently done in the past. Turning in to a coffee house or bar, on the other hand, presented no particular problem. Indeed, whenever I was somewhat fortified and refreshed I regained a sense of normality for a while and, buoyed up by a touch of confidence, there were moments when I supposed that I could put an end to the muted condition I had been in for days, and make a telephone call. As it happened, however, the three or four people I might have cared to talk to were never there, and could not be induced to pick up the receiver no matter how long I let the phone ring. There is something peculiarly dispiriting about the emptiness that wells up when, in a strange city, one dials the same telephone numbers in vain. If no one answers, it is a disappointment of huge significance, quite as if these few random ciphers were a matter of life or death. So what else could I do, when I had put the coins that jingled out of the box back into my pocket, but wander aimlessly around until well into the night. Often, probably because I was so very tired, I believed I saw someone I knew walking ahead of me. Those who appeared in these hallucinations, for that is what they were, were always people I had not thought of for years, or who had long since departed, such as Mathild Seelos or the one-armed village clerk Fürgut. On one occasion, in Gonzagagasse, I even thought I recognized the poet Dante, banished from his home town on pain of burning at the stake. For some considerable time he walked a short distance ahead of me, with the familiar cowl on his head, distinctly taller than the people in the street, yet he passed by them unnoticed. When I walked faster in order to catch him up he went down Heinrichgasse, but when I reached the corner he was nowhere to be seen.

After one or two turns of this kind I began to feel a vague apprehension, which manifested itself as a feeling of vertigo. The outlines on which I tried to focus dissolved, and my thoughts disintegrated before I could fully grasp them. Although at times, when obliged to lean against a wall or seek refuge in the doorway of a building, fearing that mental paralysis was beginning to take a hold of me, I could think of no way of resisting it but to walk until late into the night, till I was utterly worn out. In the ten days or so that I spent in Vienna I visited none of the sights and spoke not a word to a soul except for waiters and waitresses. The only creatures I talked to, if I remember correctly, were the jackdaws in the gardens by the city hall, and a white-headed blackbird that shared the jackdaws' interest in my grapes. Sitting for long periods on park benches and aimlessly wandering about the city, tending increasingly to avoid coffee houses and restaurants and take a snack at a stand wherever I happened to be, or simply eat something out of paper—all of this had already begun to change me without my being aware of it. The fact that I still lived in a hotel was at ever greater variance with the woeful state I was now in. I began to carry all kinds of useless things around with me in a plastic bag I had brought with me from England, things I found it more impossible to part with as every day went by.

Returning from my excursions at a late hour, I felt the eyes of the night porter at my back subjecting me to a long and questioning scrutiny as I stood in the hotel lobby waiting for the lift, hugging the bag to my chest. I no longer dared switch on the television in my room, and I cannot say whether I would ever have come out of this decline if one night as I slowly undressed, sitting on the edge of the bed, I had not been shocked by the sight of my shoes, which were literally falling apart. I felt queasy, and my eyes dimmed as they had once before on that day, when I reached the Ruprechtplatz after a long trail round the Leopoldstadt that had finally brought me through Ferdinandstrasse and over the Schwedenbrücke into the first district. The windows of the Jewish community centre, on the first floor of the building which also houses the synagogue and a kosher restaurant, were wide open, it being an unusually fine, indeed summery autumn day, and there were children within singing, unaccountably, 'Jingle Bells' and 'Silent Night' in English. The voices of singing children, and now in front of me my tattered and, as it seemed, ownerless shoes. Heaps of shoes and snow piled high—with these words in my head I lay down. When I awoke the next morning from a deep and dreamless sleep, which not even the surging roar of traffic on the Ring had been able to disturb, I felt as if I had crossed a wide stretch of water during the hours of my nocturnal absence. Before I opened my eyes I could see myself descending the gangway of a large ferry, and hardly had I stepped ashore but I resolved to take the evening train to Venice, and before that to spend the day with Ernst Herbeck in Klosterneuburg.

Ernst Herbeck has been afflicted with mental disorders ever since his twentieth year. He was first committed to an institution in 1940. At that time he was employed as an unskilled worker in a munitions factory. Suddenly he could hardly eat or sleep any more. He lay awake at night, counting aloud. His body was racked with cramps. Life in the family, and especially his father's incisive thinking, were corroding his nerves, as he put it. In the end he lost control of himself, knocked his plate away at meal times or tipped his soup under the bed. Occasionally his condition would improve for a while. In October 1944 he was even called up, only to be discharged in March 1945. One year after the war was over he was committed for the fourth and final time. He had been wandering the streets of Vienna at night, attracting attention by his behaviour, and had made incoherent and confused statements to the police. In the autumn of 1980, after thirty-four years in an institution, tormented for most of that time by the smallness of his own thoughts and perceiving everything as though through a veil drawn over his eyes, Ernst Herbeck was, so to speak, discharged from his illness and allowed to move into a pensioners' home in the town, among the inmates of which he was scarcely conspicuous. When I arrived at the home shortly before half past nine he was already standing waiting at the top of the steps that ran up to the entrance. I waved to him from the other side of the street, whereupon he raised his arm in welcome and, keeping it outstretched, came down the steps. He was wearing a glencheck suit with a hiking badge on the lapel. On his head he wore a narrow-brimmed hat, a kind of trilby, which he later took off when it grew too warm for him and carried beside him, just as my grandfather often used to do on summer walks.

At my suggestion we took the train to Altenberg, a few kilometres up the Danube. We were the only passengers in the carriage. Outside in the flood plain there were willows, poplars, alders and ash trees, allotment gardens and occasionally a little house raised on pillars against the water. Now and then we caught a glimpse of the river. Ernst let it all go by without venturing a word. The breeze that came in at the open window played about his forehead. His lids were half closed over his large eyes. When we arrived in Altenberg we walked back along the road a little in the direction we had come and then, turning off to the right, climbed the shady path to Burg Greifenstein, a medieval fortress that plays a significant part not only in my own

imagination but also, to this day, in that of the people of Greifenstein who live at the foot of the cliff. I had first visited the castle in the late 1960s, and from the terrace of the restaurant had looked down across the gleaming river and the waterlands, on which the shadows of evening were falling.

Now, on that bright October day when Ernst and I, sitting beside each other, savoured that wonderful view, a blue haze lay upon the sea of foliage that reaches right up to the walls of the castle. Currents of air were stirring the tops of the trees, and stray leaves were riding the breeze so high that little by little they vanished from sight. At times, Ernst was very far away. For minutes on end he left his fork sticking upright in his pastry. In the old days, he observed at one point, he had collected postage stamps, from Austria, Switzerland and the Argentine. Then he smoked another cigarette in silence, and when he stubbed it out he repeated, as if in amazement at his entire past life, that single word 'Argentine', which possibly struck him as far too outlandish. That morning, I think, we were both within an inch of learning to fly, or at least I might have managed as much as is required for a decent crash. But we never catch the propitious moment. — I only know that the view from Burg Greifenstein is no longer the same. A dam has been built below the

castle. The course of the river was straightened, and the sad sight of it now will soon extinguish the memory of what it once was.

We made our way back on foot. For both of us the walk proved too long. Downcast we strode on in the autumn sunshine, side by side. The houses of Kritzendorf seemed to go on forever. Of the people who lived there not a sign was to be seen. They were all having lunch, clattering the cutlery and plates. A dog leaped at a green-painted iron gate, quite beside itself, as if it had taken leave of its senses. It was a large black Newfoundland, its natural gentleness broken by ill-treatment, long confinement or even the crystal clarity of the autumn day. In the villa behind the iron fence nothing stirred. Nobody came to the window, not even a curtain moved. Again and again the animal ran up and hurled itself at the gate, only occasionally pausing to eye us where we stood as if transfixed. As we walked on I could feel the chill of terror in my limbs. Ernst turned to look back once more at the black dog, which had now stopped barking and was standing motionless in the midday sun. Perhaps we should have let it out. It would probably have ambled along beside us, like a good beast, while its evil spirit might have stalked among the people of Kritzendorf in search of another host, and indeed might have entered them all simultaneously, so not one of them would have been able to lift a spoon or fork again.

We finally reached Klosterneuburg by way of Albrechtstrasse at the upper end of which there is a gruesome building banged together out of breeze-blocks and prefab panels. The ground-floor windows are boarded up. Where the roof should be, only a rusty array of iron bars protrude into the sky. Looking at it was like witnessing a hideous crime. Ernst put his best foot forward, averting his eyes from this fearful monument. A little further on, the children inside the primary school were singing, the most appealing sounds coming from those who could not quite manage to hit the right notes. Ernst stood still, turned to me as though we were both actors on a stage, and in a theatrical manner uttered a statement which appeared to me as if he had committed it to memory a long time ago: That is a very fine sound, borne upon the air, and uplifts one's heart. — Some two years previously I had stood once before outside that school. I had gone to Klosterneuburg with Clara to visit her grandmother, who had been taken into the old people's home in Martinsstrasse. On the way back we went down Albrechtstrasse and Clara gave in to the temptation to visit the school she had attended as a child. In one of the classrooms, the very one where she had been taught in the early 1950s, the selfsame schoolmistress was still teaching, almost thirty years later, her voice quite unchanged—still warning the children to keep at their work, as she had done then, and also not to chatter.

Alone in the entrance hall, surrounded by closed doors that had seemed at one time like mighty portals, Clara was overcome by tears, as she later told me. At all events, when she came out she was in such a state of distress as I had never seen her in before. We returned to her grandmother's flat in Ottakring, and neither on the way there nor that entire evening did she regain her composure following this unexpected encounter with her past.

The St Martin's home is a large, rectangular building with massive stone walls dating from the seventeenth or eighteenth century. Clara's grandmother, Anna Goldsteiner, who was afflicted with that extreme kind of forgetfulness which soon renders even the simplest of everyday tasks impossible to perform, shared a dormitory on the fourth floor. Through the barred, deeply recessed windows there was a view down on to the tops of the trees on the steeply sloping ground to the rear of the house. It was like looking upon a heaving sea. The mainland, it seemed to me, had already sunk below the horizon. A foghorn droned. Further and further out the ship plied its passage upon the waters. From the engine room came the steady throb of the turbines. Out in the corridor, stray passengers went past, some of them on the arm of a nurse. It took an eternity, on these slow-motion walks, for them to cross from one side of the doorway to the other. How strange it is, to be standing leaning against the current of time. The parquet floor shifted beneath my feet. A low murmuring, rustling, dragging, praying and moaning filled the room. Clara was sitting beside her grandmother, stroking her hand. The semolina was doled out. The foghorn sounded again. A little way further out in the green and hilly water landscape, another steamer passed. On the bridge, his legs astride and the ribbons on his cap flying, stood a mariner, signalling in semaphore with two colourful flags. Clara held her grandmother close as they parted, and promised to come again soon. But barely three weeks later Anna Goldsteiner, who in the end, to her own amazement, could no longer even remember the names of the three husbands she had survived, died of a slight cold. At times it does not take much. For weeks after we learned of her death I could not put out of my mind the blue, half-empty pack of Bad Ischl salt under the sink in her council flat in Lorenz Mandl Gasse which she would never now be able to use up.

Footsore from our walk, Ernst and I emerged from Albrechtstrasse on to the town square, which sloped slightly to one side. For a while we stood irresolute on the kerb in the dazzling midday sun before trying, like two strangers, to cross the road amid the infernal traffic, almost being run down by a gravel truck. Once we were on the shady side of the street we dived into a bar. At first the dark that enveloped us as we entered was so impenetrable for eyes accustomed to the midday glare that we were obliged to sit down at the first table we came to. Only gradually and partially did our sight return and other people become apparent in the gloom, some of them bent low over their plates, others sitting curiously upright or leaning back, but all of them without exception on their own, a silent gathering, the shadow of the waitress threading among them, as if she were the bearer of secret messages between the several guests and the corpulent landlord. Ernst declined to eat anything, and instead took one of the cigarettes I offered him. A time or two he appreciatively turned the packet with its English wording in his hands. He inhaled the smoke deeply, with the air of a connoisseur. The cigarette, he had written in one of his poems,

is a monopoly and must
be smoked. So that it
goes up in flames.

And, putting down his beer glass after taking a first draught, he observed that he had dreamed about English Boy Scouts last night. What I then told him about England, about the county in East Anglia where I live, the great wheatfields which in the autumn are transformed into a barren brown expanse stretching further than the eye can see, the rivers up which the incoming tide drives the sea water, and the times when the land is flooded and one can cross the fields in boats, as the Egyptians once did—all of this Ernst listened to with the patient lack of interest of a man who has long been familiar with every detail he is being told. I then asked if he would write something in my notebook, and this he did without the slightest hesitation with the ballpoint which he took from his jacket pocket, resting his left hand on the open page. His head to one side, his brow furrowed in concentration, his eyelids half-closed, he wrote:

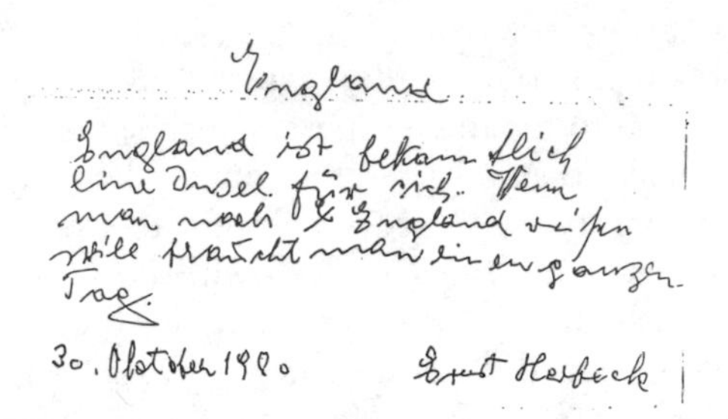
England
England ist bekanntlich eine Insel für sich. Wenn man nach England reisen will braucht man einen ganzen Tag.
30. Oktober 1980 Ernst Herbeck

England. England, as is well known, is an island unto itself. Travelling to England takes an entire day. 30 October 1980. Ernst Herbeck. — We left. It was not far now to the St Agnes home. When we parted, Ernst, standing on tiptoe and bowing slightly, took his hat from his head and with it, as he turned away, executed a sweeping motion which ended with him putting the hat back on; a performance which seemed to be, at the same time, both childishly easy and an astonishing feat of artistry. This gesture, like the manner in which he had greeted me that morning, put me in mind of someone who had travelled with a circus for many years.

The train journey from Vienna to Venice has left scarcely any trace in my memory. For what may have been an hour I watched the lights of the southwestern metropolitan sprawl pass by, till at length, lulled by the speed of the train, which was like an analgesic after the never-ending tramping through Vienna, I fell asleep. And it was in that sleep, with everything outside long since plunged into darkness, that I beheld a landscape that I have never forgotten. The lower portion of the scene was well-nigh immersed in the approaching night. A woman was pushing a pram along a field track towards a group of buildings, on one of which, a dilapidated pub, the name Josef Jelinek was painted in large letters over the gabled entrance. Mountains dark with forests rose above the rooftops, the jagged black summits silhouetted against the evening light. Higher than them all, though, was the tip of the Schneeberg, glowing, translucent, throwing out fire and sparks, towering into the dying brightness of a sky across which the strangest of greyish-pink cloud formations were moving, while visible between them were the winter planets and a crescent moon. In my dream I was in no doubt that the volcano was the Schneeberg, any more than I doubted that the countryside, above which I presently rose through a glittering shower of rain, was Argentina, an infinitely vast and deep green pastureland with clumps of trees and countless herds of horses. I awoke only as the train, which for so long had been threading the valleys at a steady pace, was racing out of the mountains and down to the plains below. I pulled down the window. Swathes of mist were ripping past me. We were hurtling onwards at breakneck speed. Pointed wedges of blue-black rock thrust up against the train. I leaned out and looked upward, trying in vain to make out the tops of the fearful formations. Dark, narrow, ragged valleys opened up, mountain streams and waterfalls threw up white spray in a night on the edge of dawn, so close that their cold breath against my face made me shiver. It occurred to me that this was the Friaul, and with that thought came naturally the memory of the destruction which that region had suffered some few months before. Gradually the daybreak revealed landslides, great boulders, collapsed buildings, mounds of rubble and piles of stones, and here and there encampments of people living in tents. Scarcely a light was burning anywhere in the entire area. The low-lying cloud drifting in from the Alpine valleys and across that desolated country was conjoined in my mind's eye with a Tiepolo painting which I have often looked at for hours. It shows the plague-ravaged town of Este on the plain, seemingly unscathed. In the background are mountains, and a smoking summit. The light diffused through the picture seems to have been painted as if through a veil of ash. One could almost suppose it was this light that drove the people out of the town into the open fields, where, after reeling about for some time, they were finally laid low by the scourge they carried within them. In the centre foreground of the painting lies a mother dead of the plague, her child still alive in her arms. Kneeling to the left is St Thecla, interceding for the inhabitants of the town, her face upturned to where the heavenly hosts are traversing the aether. Holy Thecla, pray for us, that we may be safely delivered from all contagion and sudden death and most mercifully saved from perdition. Amen.

When the train had arrived in Venice, I first went to the station barber's for a shave, and then stepped out into the forecourt of Ferrovia Santa Lucia. The dampness of the autumn morning still hung thick among the houses and over the Grand Canal. Heavily laden, the boats went by, sitting low in the water. With a surging rush they came from out of the mist, pushing ahead of them the aspic-green waves, and disappearing again in the white swathes of the air. The helmsmen stood erect and motionless at the stern. Their hands on the tiller, they gazed fixedly ahead. I walked from the Fondamenta across the broad square, up Rio Terrà Lista di Spagna and across the Canale di Cannaregio. As you enter into the heart of that city, you cannot tell what you will see next or indeed who will see you the very next moment. Scarcely has someone made an appearance but he has quit the stage again by another exit. These brief exhibitions are of an almost theatrical obscenity and at the same time have an air of conspiracy about them, into which one is drawn against one's will. If you walk behind someone in a deserted alleyway, you have only to quicken your step slightly to instil a little fear into the person you are following. And equally, you can feel like a quarry yourself. Confusion and ice-cold terror alternate. It was with a certain feeling of liberation, therefore, that I came upon the Grand Canal once again, near San Marcuola, after wandering about for the best part of an hour below the tall houses of the ghetto. Hurriedly, like the native Venetians on their way to work, I boarded a vaporetto. The mist had now dispersed. Not far from me, on one of the rear benches, there sat, and in fact very nearly lay, a man in a worn green loden coat whom I immediately recognized as King Ludwig II of Bavaria. He had grown somewhat older and rather gaunt, and curiously he was talking to a dwarfish lady in the strongly nasal English of the upper classes, but otherwise everything about him was right: the sickly pallor of the face, the wide-open childlike eyes, the wavy hair, the carious teeth. *Il re Lodovico* to the life. In all likelihood, I thought to myself, he had come by water to the *città inquinata Venezia merda*. After we had alighted I watched him walk away down the Riva degli Schiavoni in his billowing Tyrolean cloak, becoming smaller and smaller not only on account of the increasing distance but also because, as he went on talking incessantly, he bent down deeper and deeper to his diminutive companion. I did not follow them, but instead took my morning coffee in one of the bars on the Riva, reading the *Gazzettino*, making notes for a treatise on King Ludwig in Venice, and leafing through Grillparzer's *Italian Diary*, written in 1819. I had bought it in Vienna, because when I am travelling I often feel as Grillparzer did on his journeys. Nothing pleases me, any more than it did him; the sights I find infinitely disappointing, one and all; and I sometimes think that I would have done far better to stay at home with my maps and timetables. Grillparzer paid even the Doge's Palace no more than a distinctly grudging respect. Despite its delicately crafted arcades and turrets, he wrote, the Doge's Palace was inelegant and reminded him of a crocodile. What put this comparison into his head he did not know. The resolutions passed here by the Council of State must surely be mysterious, immutable and harsh, he observed, calling the palace an enigma in stone. The nature of that enigma was apparently dread, and for as long as he was in Venice Grillparzer could not shake off a sense of the uncanny. Trained in the law himself, he dwelt on that palace where the legal authorities resided and in the inmost cavern of which, as he put it, the Invisible Principle brooded. And those who had faded away, the persecutors and the persecuted, the murderers and the victims, rose up before him with their heads enshrouded. Shivers of fever beset the poor hypersensitive man.

One of the victims of Venetian justice was Giacomo Casanova. His *Histoire de ma fuite des prisons de la République de Venise qu'on appelle Les Plombs écrite à Dux en Bohème l'année 1787*, first published in Prague in 1788, affords an excellent insight into the inventiveness of penal justice at the time. For example, Casanova describes a type of garrotte. The victim is positioned with his back to a wall on which a horseshoe-shaped brace is mounted, and his head is jammed into this brace in such a way that it half encloses the neck. A silken band is passed around the neck and secured to a spool which a henchman turns slowly till at length the last throes of the condemned man are over. This strangulating apparatus is in the prison chambers below the lead roofs of the Doge's Palace. Casanova was in his thirtieth year when he was taken there. On the morning of 26 July 1755, the Messergrande entered his room. Casanova was ordered to surrender any writings by himself or others that he possessed, to get dressed and to follow the Master of the Keys. The word 'tribunal', he writes, completely paralysed me and left me only such physical strength as was essential if I were to obey. Mechanically he performed his ablutions and donned his best shirt and a new coat that had only just left the tailor's hands, as if he were off to a wedding. Shortly after he found himself in the loft space of the palace, in a cell measuring twelve feet by twelve. The ceiling was so low that he could not stand, and there was not a stick of furniture. A plank no more than a foot wide was fixed to the wall, to serve as both table and bed, and on it he laid his elegant silk mantle, the coat, inaugurated on so inauspicious an occasion, and his hat adorned with Spanish lace and an egret's plume. The heat was appalling. Through the bars, Casanova could see rats as big as hares scuttling about. He crossed to the window sill, from which he could see but a patch of sky. There he remained motionless for a full eight hours. Never in his life, he recorded, had the taste in his mouth been as bitter. Melancholy had him in its grip and would not let go. The dog days came. The sweat ran down him. For two weeks he did not move his bowels. When at last the stone-hard excrement was passed, he thought the pain would kill him. Casanova considered the limits of human reason. He established that, while it might be rare for a man to be driven insane, little was required to tip the balance. All that was needed was a slight shift, and nothing would be as it formerly was. In these deliberations, Casanova likened a lucid mind to a glass, which does not break of its own accord. Yet how easily it is shattered. One wrong move is all that it takes. This being so, he resolved to regain his composure and find a way of comprehending his situation. It was soon apparent that the condemned in that gaol were honourable persons to a man, but for reasons which were known only to their Excellencies, and were not disclosed to the detainees, they had had to be removed from society. When the tribunal seized a criminal, it was already convinced of his guilt. After all, the rules by which the tribunal proceeded were underwritten by senators elected from among the most capable and virtuous of men. Casanova realized that he would have to come to terms with the fact that the standards which now applied were those of the legal system of the Republic rather than of his own sense of justice. Fantasies of revenge of the kind he had entertained in the early days of his detention—such as rousing the people and, with himself at their head, slaughtering the government and the aristocracy—were out of the question. Soon he was prepared to forgive the injustice done to him, always providing he would some day be released. He found that, within certain limits, he was able to reach an accommodation with the powers who had confined him in that place. Everyday necessities, food and a few books were brought to his cell, at his own expense. In early November the great earthquake hit Lisbon, raising tidal waves as far away as Holland. One of the sturdiest roof joists visible through the window of Casanova's gaol began to turn, only to move back to its former position. After this, with no means of knowing whether his sentence might not be life, he abandoned all hope of release. All his thinking was now directed to preparing his escape from prison, and this occupied him for a full year. He was now permitted to take a daily walk around the attics, where a good deal of lumber lay about, and contrived to obtain a number of things that could serve his purpose. He came across piles of old ledgers with records of trials held in the previous century. They contained charges brought against confessors who had extorted penances for improper ends of their own, described in detail the habits of schoolmasters convicted of pederasty, and were full of the most extraordinary accounts of transgressions, evidently detailed for the delectation solely of the legal profession. Casanova observed that one kind of case that occurred with particular frequency in those old pages concerned the deflowering of virgins in the city's orphanages, among them the very one whose young ladies were heard every day in Santa Maria della Visitazione, on the Riva degli Schiavoni, uplifting their voices to the ceiling fresco of the three cardinal virtues, to which Tiepolo had put the finishing touches shortly after Casanova was arrested. No doubt the dispensation of justice in those days, as also in later times, was largely concerned with regulating the libidinous instinct, and presumably not a few of the prisoners slowly perishing beneath the leaden roof of the palace will have been of that irrepressible species whose desires drive them on, time after time, to the very same point.

In the autumn of his second year of imprisonment, Casanova's preparations had reached a point at which he could contemplate an escape. The moment was propitious, since the inquisitors were to cross to the *terra firma* at that time, and Lorenzo, the warder, always got drunk when his superiors were away. In order to decide on the precise day and hour, Casanova consulted Ariosto's *Orlando Furioso*, using a system comparable to the *sortes Virgilianae*. First he wrote down his question, then he derived numbers from the words and arranged these in an inverse pyramid, and finally, in a threefold procedure that involved subtracting nine from every pair of figures, he arrived at the first line of the seventh stanza of the ninth canto of *Orlando Furioso*, which runs: *Tra il fin d'ottobre e il capo di novembre*. This instruction, pinpointing the very hour, was the all-decisive sign Casanova had wanted, for he believed that a law was at work in so extraordinary a coincidence, inaccessible to even the most incisive thought, to which he must therefore defer. For my part, Casanova's attempt to plumb the unknown by means of a seemingly random operation of words and numbers later caused me to leaf back through my own diary for that year, whereupon I discovered to my amazement, and indeed to my considerable alarm, that the day in 1980 on which I was reading Grillparzer's journal in a bar on the

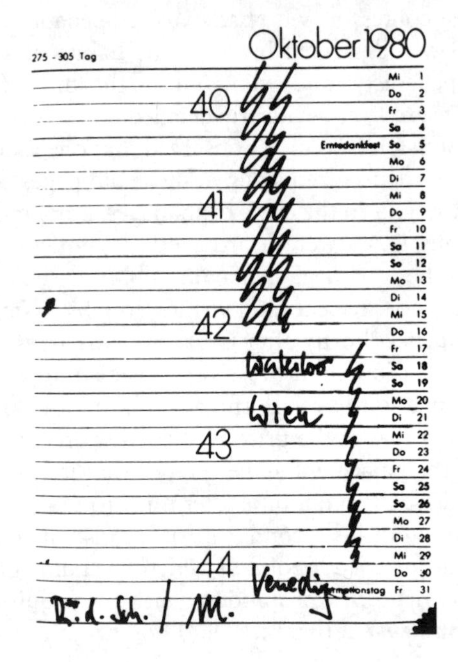

Riva degli Schiavoni between the Danieli and Santa Maria della Visitazione, in other words near the Doge's Palace, was the very last day of October, and thus the anniversary of the day (or rather, night) on which Casanova, with the words *E quindi uscimmo a rimirar le stelle* on his lips, broke out of the lead-plated crocodile. Later that evening I returned to the bar on the Riva and fell into conversation with a Venetian by the name of Malachio, who had studied astrophysics at Cambridge and, as shortly transpired, saw everything from a great distance, not only the stars. Towards midnight we took his boat, which was moored outside, up the dragon's tail of the Grand Canal, past the Ferrovia and the Tronchetto, and out on to the open water, from where one has a view of the lights of the Mestre refineries stretching for miles along the coast. Malachio turned off the engine. The boat rose and fell with the waves, and it seemed to me that a long time passed. Before us lay the fading lustre of our world, at which we never tire of looking, as though it were a celestial city. The miracle of life born of carbon, I heard Malachio say, going up in flames. The engine started up once more, the bow of the boat lifted in the water, and we entered the Canale della Giudecca in a wide arc. Without a word, my guide pointed out the Inceneritore Comunale on the nameless island westward of the Giudecca. A deathly silent concrete shell beneath a white swathe of smoke. I asked whether the burning went on throughout the night, and Malachio replied: *Sí, di continuo. Brucia continuamente.* The fires never go out. The Stucky flour mill entered our line of vision, built in the nineteenth century from millions of bricks, its blind windows staring across from the Giudecca to the Stazione Marittima. The structure is so enormous that the Doge's Palace would fit into it many times over, which leaves one wondering if it was really only grain that was milled in there. As we were passing by the facade, looming above us in the dark, the moon came out from behind the clouds and struck a gleam from the golden mosaic under the left gable, which shows the female figure of a reaper holding a sheaf of wheat, a most disconcerting image in this landscape of water and stone. Malachio told me that he had been giving a great deal of thought to the resurrection, and was pondering what the Book of Ezekiel could mean by saying that our bones and flesh would be carried into the domain of the prophet. He had no answers, but believed the questions were quite sufficient for him. The flour mill dissolved into the darkness, and ahead of us appeared the tower of San Giorgio and the dome of Santa Maria della Salute. Malachio steered the boat back to my hotel. There was nothing more to be said. The boat berthed. We shook hands. I stepped ashore. The waves slapped against the stones, which were overgrown with shaggy moss. The boat set about in the water. Malachio waved one more time and called out: *Ci vediamo a Gerusalemme.* And, a little further out, he repeated somewhat louder: Next year in Jerusalem! I crossed the forecourt of the hotel. There was not a soul about. Even the night porter had abandoned his post and was lying on a narrow bed in a kind of doorless den behind the reception, looking as if his body had been laid out. The test card was flickering softly on the television. Machines alone have realized that sleep is no longer permitted, I thought as I ascended to my room, where tiredness soon overcame me too.

Waking up in Venice is unlike waking up in any other place. The day begins quietly. Only a stray shout here and there may break the calm, or the sound of a shutter being raised, or the wing-beat of the pigeons. How often, I thought to myself, had I lain thus in a hotel room, in Vienna or Frankfurt or Brussels, with my hands clasped under my head, listening not to the stillness, as in Venice, but to the roar of the traffic, with a mounting sense of panic. That, then, I thought on such occasions, is the new ocean. Ceaselessly, in great surges, the waves roll in over the length and breadth of our cities, rising higher and higher, breaking in a kind of frenzy when the roar reaches its peak and then discharging across the stones and the asphalt even as the next onrush is being released from where it was held by the traffic lights. For some time now I have been convinced that it is out of this din that the life is being born which will come after us and will spell our gradual destruction, just as we have been gradually destroying what was there long before us. Thus it was that the silence which hung over the city of Venice that All Saints' morning seemed wholly unreal, as if it were about to be shattered, while I lay submerged in the white air that drifted in at my half-open window. The village of W., where I spent the first nine years of my life, I now remember, was always shrouded in the densest fog on All Saints' Day and on All Souls'. And the villagers, without exception, wore their black clothes and went out to the graves which they had put in order the day before, removing the summer planting, pulling up the weeds, raking the gravel paths, and mixing soot in with the soil. Nothing in my childhood seemed to possess more meaning than those two days of remembrance devoted to the suffering of the sainted martyrs and poor unredeemed souls, days on which the dark shapes of the villagers moved about in the mist, strangely bent over, as if they had been banished from their houses. What particularly affected me every year was eating the *Seelenwecken*, the special rolls that Mayrbeck baked on those commemorative days only, precisely one apiece, for every man, woman and child in the village. These *Seelenwecken* were made of white bread dough and were so tiny that they could easily be hidden in the fist. There were four to a row on the baking tray. They were dusted with flour, and I remember one occasion when the flour dust that remained on my fingers after I had eaten one of these *Seelenwecken* seemed like a revelation. That evening, I spent a long time digging in the flour barrel in my grandparents' bedroom with a wooden spoon, hoping to fathom the mystery which I supposed to be hidden there.

On that first day of November in 1980, preoccupied as I was with my notes and the ever widening and contracting circles of my thoughts, I became enveloped by a sense of utter emptiness and never once left my room. It seemed to me then that one could well end one's life simply through thinking and retreating into one's mind, for, although I had closed the windows and the room was warm, my limbs were growing progressively colder and stiffer with my lack of movement, so that when at length the waiter arrived with the red wine and sandwiches I had ordered, I felt as if I had already been interred or laid out for burial, silently grateful for the proffered libation, but no longer capable of consuming it. I imagined how it would be if I crossed the grey lagoon to the island of the departed, to Murano or further still to San Erasmo or to the Isola San Francesco del Deserto, among the marshes of St Catherine. With these thoughts, I drifted into a light sleep. The fog lifted and I beheld the green lagoon outspread in the May sunshine and the green islets like clumps of herbage surfacing from out of the placid expanse of water. I saw the hospital island of La Grazia with its circular panoptic building, from the windows of which thousands of madmen were waving, as though they were aboard a great ship sailing away. St Francis lay face down in the water of a trembling reed-bed, and across the swamps St Catherine came walking, in her hand a model of the wheel on which she had been broken. It was mounted on a stick and went round in the wind with a humming sound. The crimson dusk gathered above the lagoon, and when I awoke I lay in deep darkness. I thought about what Malachio had meant by *Ci vediamo a Gerusalemme*, tried in vain to recall his face or his eyes, and wondered whether I should go back to the bar on the Riva, but the more I deliberated, the less was I able to make any move at all. The second night in Venice went by, then All Souls' Day, and a third night, and not until the Monday morning did I come round, in a curious condition of weightlessness. A hot bath, yesterday's sandwiches and red wine, and a newspaper I had asked for, restored me sufficiently to be able to pack my bag and be on my way again.

The buffet at St Lucia station was surrounded by an infernal upheaval. A steadfast island, it held out against a crowd of people swaying like a field of corn in the wind, passing in and out of the doors, pushing against the food counter, and surging on to the cashiers who sat some way off at their elevated posts. If one did not have a ticket, one had to shout up to these enthroned women, who, clad only in the thinnest of overalls, with curled-up hair and half-lowered gaze, appeared to float, quite unaffected by the general commotion, above the heads of the supplicants and would pick out at random one of the pleas emerging from this crossfire of voices, repeat it over the uproar with a loud assurance that denied all possibility of doubt, and then, bending down a little, indulgent and at the same time disdainful, hand over the ticket together with the change. Once in possession of this scrap of paper, which had by now come to seem a matter of life and death, one had to fight one's way out of the crowd and across to the middle of the cafeteria, where the male employees of this awesome gastronomic establishment, positioned behind a circular food counter, faced the jostling masses with withering contempt, performing their duties in an unperturbed manner which, given the prevailing panic, gave an impression of a film in slow motion. In their freshly starched white linen jackets, this impassive corps of attendants, like their sisters, mothers and daughters at the cash registers, resembled some strange company of higher beings sitting in judgement, under the rules of an obscure system, on the endemic greed of a corrupted species, an impression that was reinforced by the fact that the buffet reached only to the waists of these earnest, white-aproned men, who were evidently standing on a raised platform inside the circle, whereas the clients on the outside could barely see over the counter. The staff, remarkably restrained as they appeared, had a way of setting down the glasses, saucers and ashtrays on the marble surface with such vehemence, it seemed they were determined to all but shatter them. My cappuccino was served, and for a moment I felt that having achieved this distinction constituted the supreme victory of my life. I surveyed the scene and immediately saw my mistake, for the people around me now looked like a circle of severed heads. I should not have been surprised, and indeed it would have seemed justified, even as I expired, if one of the white-breasted waiters had swept those severed heads, my own not excepted, off the smooth marble top into a knacker's pit, since every single one of them was intent on gorging itself to the last. A prey to unpleasant observations and far-fetched notions of this sort, I suddenly had a feeling that, amid this circle of spectres consuming their *colazione*, I had attracted somebody's attention. And indeed it transpired that the eyes of two young men were on me. They were leaning on the bar across from me, the one with his chin propped in his right hand, the other in his left. Just as the shadow of a cloud passes across a field, so the fear passed across my mind that these two men who were looking at me now had already crossed my path more than once since my arrival in Venice. They had also been in the bar on the Riva where I had met Malachio. The hands of the clock moved towards half past ten. I finished my cappuccino, went out to the platform, glancing back over my shoulder now and then, and boarded the train for Milan as I had intended.

I travelled as far as Verona, and there, having taken a room at the Golden Dove, went immediately to the Giardino Giusti, a long-standing habit of mine. There I spent the early hours of the afternoon lying on a stone bench below a cedar tree. I heard the soughing of

GIARDINO GIUSTI
VERONA

BIGLIETTO D'INGRESSO

№ 52314

the breeze among the branches and the delicate sound of the gardener raking the gravel paths between the low box hedges, the subtle scent of which still filled the air even in autumn. I had not experienced such a sense of well-being for a long time. Nonetheless, I got up after a while. As I left the gardens I paused to watch a pair of white Turkish doves soaring again and again into the sky above the tree tops with only a few brisk beatings of their wings, remaining at those blue heights for a small eternity, and then, dropping with a barely audible gurgling call, gliding down on the air in sweeping arcs around the lovely cypresses, some of which had been growing there for as

long as 200 years. The everlasting green of the trees put me in mind of the yews in the churchyards of the county where I live. Yews grow more slowly even than cypresses. One inch of yew wood will often have upwards of a hundred annual growth rings, and there are said to be trees that have outlasted a full millennium and seem to have quite forgotten about dying. I went out into the forecourt, washed my face and hands at the fountain set in the ivy-covered garden wall, as I had done before going in, cast a last glance back at the garden and, at the exit, waved a greeting to the keeper of the gate, who nodded to me from her gloomy cabin. Across the Ponte Nuovo and by way of the Via Nizza and the Via Stelle I walked down to the Piazza Bra. Entering the arena, I suddenly had a sense of being entangled in some dark web of intrigue. The arena was deserted but for a group of late-season excursionists to whom an aged cicerone was describing the unique qualities of this monumental theatre in a voice grown thin and cracked. I climbed to the topmost tiers and looked down at the group, which now appeared very small. The old man, who could not have been more than four feet, was wearing a jacket far too big for him, and, since he was hunchbacked and walked with a stoop, the front hem hung down to the ground. With a remarkable clarity, I heard him say, more clearly perhaps than those who stood around him, that in the arena one could discern, *grazie a un'acustica perfetta, l'assolo più impalpabile di un violino, la mezza voce più eterea di un soprano, il gemito più intimo di una Mimi morente sulla scena*. The excursionists were not greatly impressed by the enthusiasm for architecture and opera evinced by their misshapen guide, who continued to add this or that point to his account as he moved towards the exit, pausing every now and then as he turned to the group, which had also stopped, and raising his right forefinger like a tiny schoolmaster confronting a pack of children taller by a head than himself. By now the evening light came in very low over the arena, and for a while after the old man and his flock had left the stage I sat on alone, surrounded by the reddish shimmer of the marble. At least I thought I was alone, but as time went on I became aware of two figures in the deep shadow on the other side of the arena. They were without a doubt the same two young men who had kept their eyes on me that morning at the station in Venice. Like two watchmen they remained motionless at their posts until the sunlight had all but faded. Then they stood up, and I had the impression that they bowed to each other before descending from the tiers and vanishing in the darkness of the exit. At first I could not move from the spot, so ominous did these probably quite coincidental encounters appear to me. I could already see myself sitting in the arena all night, paralysed by fear and the cold. I had to muster all my rational powers before at length I was able to get up and make my way to the exit. When I was almost there I had a compulsive vision of an arrow whistling through the grey air, about to pierce my left shoulder blade and, with a distinctive, sickening sound, penetrate my heart.

On the third day of my stay in Verona, I took my evening meal in a pizzeria in the Via Roma. I do not know how I go about choosing the restaurants where I should eat in unfamiliar cities. On the one hand I am too fastidious and wander the streets broad and narrow for hours on end before I make up my mind; on the other hand I generally finish up turning in simply anywhere, and then, in dreary surroundings and with a sense of discontent, select some dish that does not in the least appeal. That was how it was on that evening of 5 November. If I had heeded my first inclination, I would never have crossed the threshold of that establishment, which even from the outside made a disreputable impression. But now there I sat, on a kitchen chair with a cover of red marbled plastic, at a rickety table, in a grotto festooned with fishing nets. The decor of the floor and walls was a hideous marine blue which put an end to all hope I might have entertained of ever seeing dry land again. The sense of being wholly surrounded by water was rendered complete by a sea piece that hung right below the ceiling opposite me, in a frame painted a golden bronze. As is commonly the case with such sea pieces, it showed a ship, on the crest of a turquoise wave crowned with snow-white foam, about to plunge into the yawning depths that gaped beneath her bows. Plainly this was the moment immediately before a disaster. A mounting sense of unease took possession of me. I was obliged to push aside the plate, barely half of the pizza eaten, and grip the table edge, as a seasick man might grip a ship's rail. I sensed my brow running cold with fear, but was quite unable to call the waiter over and ask for the bill. Instead, in order to focus on reality once more, I pulled the newspaper I had bought that afternoon, the Venice *Gazzettino*, out of my jacket pocket and unfolded it on the table as best I could. The first article that caught my attention was an editorial report to the effect that yesterday, 4 November, a letter in strange runic writing had been received by the newspaper, in which a hitherto unknown group by the name of

ORGANIZZAZIONE LUDWIG

claimed responsibility for a number of murders that had been committed in Verona and other northern Italian cities since 1977. The article brought these as yet unsolved cases back to the memories of its readers. In late August 1977, a Romany named Guerrino Spinelli had died in a Verona hospital of severe burns sustained when the old Alfa in which he customarily spent the night on the outskirts of the city was set on fire by persons unknown. A good year later, a waiter, Luciano Stefanato, was found dead in Padua with two 2.5-centimetre stab wounds in the neck, and another year after that a twenty-two-year-old heroin addict, Claudio Costa, was found dead with thirty-nine knife wounds. It was now the late autumn of 1980. The waiter brought me the bill. It was folded and I opened it out. The letters and numbers blurred before my eyes. 5 November 1980. Via Roma. Pizzeria Verona. Di Cadavero Carlo e Patierno Vittorio. Patierno and Cadavero. — The telephone rang. The waiter wiped a glass dry and held it up to the light. Not until I felt I could stand the ringing no

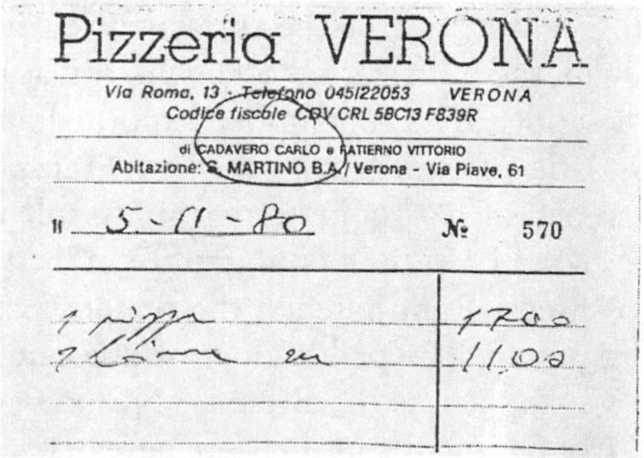

Pizzeria VERONA
Via Roma, 13 - Telefono 045/22053 VERONA
Codice fiscale CDV CRL 58C13 F839R
di CADAVERO CARLO e PATIERNO VITTORIO
Abitazione: S. MARTINO B.A. / Verona - Via Piave, 61
li 5-11-80 № 570
1 pizza 1700
1 [illegible] 1100

longer did he pick up the receiver. Then, jamming it between his shoulder and his chin, he paced to and fro behind the bar as far as the cable would let him. Only when he was speaking himself did he stop, and at these times he would lift his eyes to the ceiling. No, he said, Vittorio wasn't there. He was hunting. Yes, that was right, it was him, Carlo. Who else would it be? Who else would be in the restaurant? No, nobody. Not a soul all day. And now there was only one diner. *Un inglese*, he said, and looked across at me with what I took to be a touch of contempt. No wonder, he said, the days were getting shorter. The lean times were on the way. *L'inverno è alle porte. Sí, sí, l'inverno,* he shouted once more, looking over at me again. My heart missed a beat. I left 10,000 lire on the plate, folded up the paper, hurried out into the street and across the piazza, went into a brightly lit bar and had them call a taxi, returned to my hotel, packed my things in a rush, and fled by the night train to Innsbruck. Prepared for the very worst, I sat in my compartment unable to read and unable to close my eyes, listening to the rhythm of the wheels. At Rovereto an old Tyrolean woman carrying a shopping bag made of leather patches sewn together joined me, accompanied by her son, who might have been forty. I was immeasurably grateful to them when they came in and sat down. The son leaned his head back against the seat. Eyelids lowered, he smiled blissfully most of the time. At intervals, though, he would be seized by a spasm, and his mother would then make signs in the palm of his left hand, which lay in her lap, open, like an unwritten page. The train hauled onwards, uphill. Gradually I began to feel better. I went out into the corridor. We were in Bolzano. The Tyrolean woman and her son got out. Hand in hand the two of them headed towards the subway. Even before they had vanished from sight, the train started off again. It was now beginning to feel distinctly colder. The train moved more slowly, there were fewer lights, and the darkness was thicker. Franzensfeste station passed. I saw scenes of a bygone war: the assault on the pass—Vall'Inferno—26 May 1915. Bursts of gunfire in the mountains and a forest shot to shreds. Rain hatched the windowpanes. The train changed track at points. The pallid glow of arc lamps suffused the compartment. We stopped at the Brenner. No one got out and no one got in. The frontier guards in their grey greatcoats paced to and fro on the platform. We remained there for at least a quarter of an hour. Across on the other side were the silver ribbons of the rails. The rain turned to snow. And a heavy silence lay upon the place, broken only by the bellowing of some nameless animals waiting in a siding to be transported onward. □

GRANTA

THE FURNACE

Lydia Davis

My father has trouble with his hearing and does not like to talk on the phone, so I talk on the phone mainly to my mother. Sometimes she abruptly stops what she is saying to me, I hear a noise in the background, she says my name, and waits. Then I know my father has come into the room during her conversation and asked who she is talking to. Sometimes, at that point, he interjects a question for me, but often he asks her something that has nothing to do with me, while I wait at the other end of the phone. After she and I have gone on talking, he may come into the room again, having thought of something else he wants to say. When I hear his voice in the background I stop whatever I am saying to my mother and wait.

Sometimes she forces him to get on the phone. 'Tell her yourself,' she says. He gets on the phone and without saying hello tells me what it is he wants me to know and then gets off without saying goodbye. Back on the phone, she says, 'He's gone.'

Although he has never liked to talk on the phone, he has always liked to write letters. He usually prefers to write a letter that includes some kind of instruction, or at least a transmission of what he thinks will be new information. For a while, we carried on a correspondence whose regularity was unusual for my family, in which very little has ever been regular or systematic. Then I didn't hear from him for some weeks. Maybe I was the one who did not answer his last letter. I told my mother to tell him I would like to hear from him, and he then sent me some clippings from the Crime Beat section of their local paper. In the top margin he had written: 'The underside of Cambridge life.' Some entries he had marked with a dark line of ink down the side margin.

> ... A Jefferson Park man entered the dispute, slashing the teen just below the right eye with an unidentified weapon. While this happened, the Jackson Circle man stole the bike. Later, police found a Jackson Street man riding the bike. Police arrested the Jackson Circle man, Jackson Street man and Jefferson Park man and charged them with assault with a dangerous weapon (knife) and armed robbery.

On another clipping he had underlined certain sentences:

> Police officers recovered two martial arts swords and a meat cleaver. At 10 p.m. an employee of the Cantab Lounge reported that a suspect

> who had been shut off at the bar assaulted her by throwing a glass at her.
>
> A Cambridge resident reported that he was assaulted with a fingernail clipper by a suspect who was throwing trash around the doorway at Eddy's Place.
>
> A Rindge Avenue resident reported that her daughter hit her over the head with a glass.
>
> A Rindge Avenue resident reported that she was assaulted with a large pin by two other neighbourhood residents.

In the top margin of this clipping he had written: 'Strange weapons dept.'

After this he sent me an article he had written. He occasionally wrote an article or a letter to a newspaper about something that had come up in connection with the Bible or some other religious topic. The articles and letters were clever, and by now I was interested in the Bible and religious topics myself.

This one, on circumcision, was called 'The Unkindest Cut' and opened with a sentence about the 'male organ'. In his thin, shaky handwriting, he had noted in the margin at the top of the article that I shouldn't feel I had to read this, nor should my husband feel he had to read it. The note read sincerely, but he often attached disclaimers to the articles and letters he sent and I generally disregarded them.

Yet when I started the article, I found it hard to read so much about the male organ written by my father. I asked my husband if he would read it and tell me the gist of it but he did not really want to read it either. I did not know what to do about this situation, since it would have been awkward even to mention it to my father, but in time, as I took no action, I began to forget it. My father had probably forgotten it long before, since his memory has become more and more undependable, as he and my mother both point out.

But the letters he was sending me for a while were about the household he grew up in: besides his mother and father, there were two grandmothers and a grandfather who was slightly mad, maids, cooks and cleaning women who came and went, and his grandmothers' female nurse-companions and his grandfather's male nurse-companions, who also came and went. His father's mother owned the house and dominated it, to his mother's annoyance. I have seen this house, which still stands in a street not far from where they live, and it looks to me surprisingly modest to have held such a number and variety of people. The last time it was sold, my father read about the sale in the paper and wrote to the new owners, explaining that he had been born in the upstairs front room and had played in the hayloft of the small barn. The new owners were pleased to hear from him and sent him photographs of the house.

He would write to me in some detail and in the midst of it apologize, saying that what lay immediately ahead would be tedious and that I could read fast or skim if I liked. He said he was trying to recover facts that he had not thought of for most of a century. But I would write back asking for even more detail, because I wanted to come as close as I could to a way of life that seemed to me precious for several reasons, one being simply that even the memory of it was slipping away, because fewer and fewer people were alive who had experienced it.

Most recently we had gotten into a correspondence about the furnace in the house where he grew up. He said that while he lived there, changes had occurred, but they were all additions, and what was there to begin with remained. For instance, a gas stove was installed in the kitchen alongside the coal stove. His grandmother felt that for certain things the coal stove was more economical. A new oil furnace was added in the basement, but the huge old coal furnace remained. At some point electricity was added to gas for lighting. His grandmother kept both because in a storm, she warned them, the electricity might fail.

He remembered how one of the cleaning women used to comb her long hair in the kitchen at the end of the day, so that she could go forth suitably neat. She would then extract the hairs from the comb and put them, not in the stove, which required the effort of lifting one of the iron covers, but on top of the stove, where they burned to an ash that remained visible until someone thought to remove it.

In the early days, he said, a 'furnace man' would come at about seven in the morning to shake down the big furnace, remove ashes and clinkers, and shovel more coal in from one of the two big bins whose board sides projected into the cellar, resting on the cellar floor. An early furnace man was named Frank and his grandmother continued to call subsequent ones 'Frank' as her memory for names weakened. The furnace was a matter of constant concern in very cold weather. Even when his father was home, his grandmother would go down to investigate, and then, in order to force his father to act, would do something deliberately noisy to it. He would shout 'Mother, Mother,' pounding on the floor with his foot, and rush down the cellar stairs. She was not supposed to go down them, for they had no banisters, and there was a drop on either side to the cellar floor below. The only lighting came from the open door of the kitchen, from tiny dirty outdoor windows at ground level, and from a gas pipe that came down from the ceiling and supplied the same kind of feeble, naked flame that his mother used in her room to heat her curling iron.

On ash collection days the furnace man lifted the barrels up the steps of the bulkhead. In winter, a boardwalk was put down from the street in front of the bulkhead. Along this, or in the soft gravel when the walk was not in place, the furnace man, on the days of the city collection, rotated the tilted ash barrels. To bring the coal in, along the same boardwalk, required a two-man team: one man would shovel the coal into a container on the back of the second man, who would carry it into the yard, unshoulder it with a twist of his body, and dump it down the chute. Coal delivery was by horse and wagon when my father was a child. He said on a normal working day there would be at least three horses and wagons on his street, delivering ice, coal, milk, groceries, fruit and vegetables, or express packages, or peddling, or buying old newspapers or old iron. There was also a horse-drawn hurdy-gurdy.

What he said about his furnace and all the trappings of the furnace made me go down and look more carefully at our own furnace. Our house is either a hundred years old or a hundred and fifty, depending on which town historical document we believe. This furnace was converted to gas from coal probably forty years ago. The trappings were still there, a coal hod on the floor of the coal bin and, hanging on the wall, pronged iron bars for opening the hatches. I looked up and saw two long, stout boards stowed above the coal bin. Now that I had read what my father wrote about the men bringing the coal in across the snow, I had no doubt these boards were put down for the coal delivery here too. I was excited to discover this.

I wrote back to my father about what I had discovered, knowing that for several reasons he would be less interested in my coal furnace than his memories of his own. It is natural for an old man to be more engrossed in his memories than the present. But he has also always been more interested in his own ideas than anyone else's.

Although he likes to have conversations with other people and hear what they say, he does not know what to do with an idea of someone else's except to use it as a starting point from which to produce an even better idea of his own. His own ideas are certainly interesting, often the most interesting in a given situation. He has always been good company at a dinner party, even though as he aged, a time came when he would have to leave the table part of the way through and go lie down for a while.

Dinner parties were an important part of the life my mother and father had together from the very beginning. There was a skill to taking part in a dinner party, and a technique to giving one, especially to guiding the conversation at the table. There was an art to encouraging a shy guest, or subduing a noisy one. My mother and father are still sociable, but they are handicapped by their age now and limit what they do. Now they have people in for tea more often than dinner, and at a certain point during the tea, also, my father leaves the room to go lie down.

Though my mother still goes out to concerts and lectures, my father rarely does. One of the last events they went to together was a grand birthday party held in a public library. Four hundred guests were invited from around the world. My mother told me about it, including the fact that during the party my father fell down. He was not hurt. She was not in the same room with him when he fell.

He is unsteady on his feet, and has fallen or come close to falling quite often in the last few years. I was present when a health technician came to give advice about rearranging the apartment so that it would be safer for the two of them. The health technician observed my father there in the apartment for a while. My father's head is large and heavy and his body is thin and frail. The technician said he noticed that my father tended to toss his head back, and this threw him off balance. The technician said he should try to change that habit and also use his walker in the house. Although the technician was friendly and helpful, he was very energetic and spoke in a loud voice, and toward the end of the visit my father became too agitated to stay in his company any longer and left to go lie down. After that visit, my mother told me, my father tried to remember to use his walker but tended to leave it here and there in the apartment and then had to walk around without it to find it again.

If I ask my mother, on the telephone, how my father is, she often lowers her voice to answer. She frequently says she is worried about him. She has been worried for years. She is always worried about some recent or new behaviour of his. She often does not seem to realize that some of the behaviour is not recent or new, or that she is always worried about something. Sometimes she is worried because he is depressed. For a while she worried because he so often became hysterically angry. Not long ago it was because he seemed unnaturally interested in their Scrabble games. After that she said he was losing his memory, did not remember incidents from their life together, kept referring to one family member by the name of another, and sometimes did not recognize a name at all.

He had to stay in a rehabilitation hospital for a while after his last fall, to have some physical therapy. To my mother's astonishment, he did not mind playing catch with the other patients in the physical therapy group, or tossing a beanbag in a contest. She said this was not like him: she wondered if he was regressing to a childish state. She suspected that he had enjoyed the attention there, and the food. Since his return home, she told me, he had not been eating very well. She was upset because he did not seem to like her cooking any more. On the other hand he did finish a piece of writing he was working on.

A year ago, when my mother herself was in hospital with a serious illness, he and I went out to look for a restaurant where we could have supper before going back to sit with my mother. It was a cold, windy night in May. We were downtown in the city, in a neighbourhood of hospitals, tall well-lit buildings all around us.

There were walkways over our heads, and underground garages on all sides, but no restaurants that I could see. Stores were closed, not many cars went by on the streets and there was hardly anyone on the sidewalk. My father was unsteady on his feet and I was watching for every kerb and uneven piece of pavement. He was determined to find a restaurant where he could have an alcoholic drink. At last, we entered a passageway in one of the tall buildings, walking into what looked from the outside to be a deserted mall. Going down an empty corridor and past some empty store windows and up some steps, we found a restaurant with a bar and an amount of good cheer and number of lively customers that was surprising after the empty streets outside. We sat down at a table and talked a little, but my father's mind was on his drink and he kept looking for the waiter, who was too busy to come to our table. I was thinking that this dinner was likely to be the last one I would have in a restaurant with my father, and certainly the least festive.

In a ward on an upper floor of one of the tall buildings nearby, my mother lay suffering from a rare blood disorder and all the other ills that came one after another because of the treatment itself. We thought she might be dying, though my father seemed to forget this at times, or rather, if she seemed better one day, he cheered up completely and began making jokes again, as though she would certainly get well. The next day he might arrive at the hospital to find one of us crying and his face would fall.

My father grew so impatient for his drink that he stood up on his unsteady legs, bracing himself with his cane. The waiter came. My father ordered his drink. What he wanted so much was a Perfect Rob Roy.

His hearing is not good, and his eyesight is not very good either, and for a while, if I asked him how he was, he would say that except for his eyes and his ears, his balance, his memory, and his teeth, he was doing reasonably well. In order to read certain sizes of print he has to take off his glasses and hold the text within an inch or two of his nose. It used to be that sometimes, when I asked my mother how my father was, she would answer: 'He was well enough to go to the Theological Library today.' Then he stopped going to any library because it was so hard for him to see the titles of the books and to bend down to the lower shelves. Then his balance became so bad it was very risky for him to go out by himself at all. Once he fell in the street and hit the back of his head. A stranger passing in a car called an ambulance on his cellular phone. It was after that fall that he went into the hospital for physical therapy, and after he returned home he did not go out by himself any more. On one of my last visits, at Christmas, he said he needed a magnifying light for the large dictionary in the living room.

He has always enjoyed looking things up in the dictionary, particularly word histories. Now my mother says she is worried about him because he is no longer merely interested in word histories but obsessed by them. He will get up from a conversation with a guest at tea and go look up a word she has used. He will interrupt the conversation to report the etymology. He has always preferred an illustrated dictionary. He likes to study the pictures, particularly the pictures of handsome women. At Christmas, he showed me one of his favourites, the President of Iceland.

I have gone down to look at the furnace again because in a few days it will be removed and a new one put in its place. The dust is deep and grey in the old coal bin. The wooden planks that form the sides are rich in colour and smoothly fitted together. Tossed in the dust and half buried are an old coal hod and some metal parts of the coal chute. I ask my husband if the men who come to install the new furnace will have to remove the walls of the coal bin and he says he thinks they will not.

After I wrote to my father about my discovery of the boards, he answered my letter with another about his childhood and also another memory of coalmen, this one dating from when he was grown-up. He said he was out driving with my sister next to him in the car when he happened upon an accident that had just occurred. He said that two men had been delivering coal. The delivery truck had been parked at an angle in a driveway. The driver was talking to the owner of the house, presumably about the delivery. The second man, his assistant, was standing at the end of the driveway with his back to the truck, looking out at the street. The truck's brakes were apparently faulty and the truck rolled backward down the driveway.

Either no one saw this or no one cried out in time. The coalman's assistant was struck by the truck and run over, and his head was crushed. My father said he drove some distance past the accident, parked his car and, instructing my sister to stay where she was, went back to look. A short way beyond the man's crushed head, he saw the man's brains on the pavement.

My father said he knew he was wrong to go and look, he should have driven on. Then he began to talk about the anatomy of the brain; he said that the incident dramatized a conviction he had always had. He had always believed that consciousness was so dependent on the physical brain that the continuation of consciousness and one's identity after death was inconceivable. He admitted that this conviction was probably metaphysically naive, but that it had been strengthened by a lifetime's observation of many insane and manic-depressive types, some in his own family. Among the manic-depressive types, he said, he included himself. Then he went on to talk about the mind of God, whom he described as a Being with presumably no neurones.

Now the new furnace is installed and working but the house does not seem any warmer. The rooms that were always chilly before are still chilly. There is still a perceptible change in temperature as we go up to the second floor. The only difference is that because this new furnace works with fans, we can hear it when it is on. It is much smaller than the old one, and shiny. It makes a better impression on anyone visiting the house, which was one reason to get it, I realize now, since we may one day want to sell this house. I have cleaned out the coal bin, at last, preserving the coal hod and the sections of chute and storing them in another wooden stall in a part of the cellar we haven't touched yet.

My correspondence with my father about the furnace seems to have ended, as has our correspondence about his family. His letters, in fact, have shrunk to small scrawled notes attached to more clippings from the local paper.

He has sent my husband and me, twice, the same 'Ask Marjorie' column, one that discusses the shape of the earth and points out that the ancients knew perfectly well that the earth was round. Both times he wrote a message on the back of the envelope asking my husband and me if we were taught that in ancient times people believed the earth was flat.

He has also sent me more items from the Crime Beat section.

> At 10:30 p.m. a Putnam Avenue resident said an unknown person broke into the home by pushing in the rear door. A dollar bill was taken.
>
> At 9:12 a.m. a North Cambridge man from Mass. Ave. said someone had broken in but nothing was missing.
>
> A Belmont resident working at a Mass. Ave. address stated that another employee told her that she had been fired and then proceeded to scratch the victim in the neck.

By this one he wrote in the margin: 'Why? What is the connection?'

> Friday, March 11. At 11:30 p.m., a Concord Avenue woman was walking down Garden Street near Mass. Ave. when a man asked her 'Are you smiling?' The woman said yes, so the man punched her in the mouth, causing her lip to bleed and swell. No arrests were made.
>
> Three men were arrested for assault and battery on Third Street near Gore Street at 2:50 a.m. Two men are Cambridge residents, both charged with assault and battery with a dangerous weapon, a shod foot. A Billerica man received the same charge, but with a hammer.

My father put an X in the margin beside the grammar mistake.

> Tuesday, June 13. A Rhode Island resident reported that between 8:45 a.m. and 10 a.m., at an address on Garden St., an unknown person took her purse with $180 and credit cards. A male was witnessed under the table but the victim believed that it was someone from the power company.

On my last visit, my father seemed in worse condition than I had seen him before. When I asked him if he was working on anything in particular now, he said, 'No,' and then turned his head slowly to my mother and looked at her in bewilderment, his mouth hanging open. There was an expression of pain or agony on his face that seemed habitual. She looked back at him, waited a moment, impassive, and then said: 'Yes, you are. You're writing about the Bible and anti-Semitism.' He continued to stare at her.

Later that evening, before he went to bed, he said: 'This is symptomatic of my condition: you're my daughter, and I'm proud of you, but I have nothing to say to you.'

He left to get ready for bed, and then came back into the room wearing dazzling white pyjamas. My mother asked me to admire his pyjamas, and he stood quietly while I did. Then, he said: 'I don't know what I will be like in the morning.'

After he went to bed, my mother showed me a picture of him forty years before sitting at a seminar table surrounded by students. 'Just look at him there!' she said, as though what he had become now were some sort of a moral failing—an old man with a beaked profile like a nutcracker.

Saying goodbye, I held his hand longer than usual. He may not have liked it. It is impossible to tell what he is feeling, often, but physical contact has always been difficult for him, and he has always been awkward about it. Whether out of embarrassment or absent-mindedness, he kept shaking his hand and mine up and down slightly, as though palsied.

Recently, my mother said he was still worse. He had fallen again, and he was having trouble with his bladder. Can he still work? I asked her. To me, it seemed that if he could still work, then he was all right, no matter what else was going wrong with him. Not really, she said. 'He has been writing letters, but there are odd things in some of them. It may not matter, since they're mostly to old friends.' She said maybe she should be checking them, though, before he sent them.

It was a phone conversation with another old woman that reminded me of a name for this time of life I had forgotten. After telling me about her angioplasty and her diabetes, she said, 'Well, this is what you can expect when you enter the twilight years.' But it is hard not to think that my father's bewilderment is only temporary, and that behind it, his sharp critical mind is still alive and well. With this younger, firmer mind he will continue to read the letters I send him and write back—our correspondence is only temporarily interrupted.

The latest letter I have seen from him was not written to me but to one of his grandsons. My mother thought I should see it before she sent it. The envelope was taped shut with strong packing tape. The entire letter concerns a mathematical rhyme he copied from the newspaper. It begins:

> A dozen, a gross and a score
> plus three times the square root of four
> divide it by seven plus five times eleven
> equals nine to the square and not more.

Then he explains some mathematical terms and the solution of this problem. Because he changed the margins of his page to type the poem, and did not reset them, the whole letter is written in short lines like a poem:

> The total to be divided by 7 consists
> of the following:
> 12 plus 144 plus 20 plus 3 times
> the square root of 4.
> These are the numerals above the line
> over the divisor 7. They add up to 182,
> which divided by seven equals 26.
> 26 plus 11 times 5 (55) is 81.
> 81 is 9 squared.
> A number squared
> is a number multiplied by itself.
> The square of 9 is nine times nine or 81.

He goes on to explain the concept of squaring numbers, and of the cube, along the way giving the etymologies of certain words, including 'dozen', 'score' and 'scoreboard'. He talks about the sign for square root being related to the form of a tree.

I tell my mother the letter seems a little strange to me. She protests, saying that it is quite correct. I don't argue, but say he can certainly send it. The end of the letter is less strange, except for the line breaks:

> For me memory and balance fail rapidly.
> You are young and have a university library
> system for your use. I, who have
> a good home reference collection,

sometimes can get other people to
look up things for me, but it is not the same.
I have to explain that I have increasingly
lost my memory and sense of balance,
I can't go any where, not the libraries
or the book stores to browse. We have to pay
a young woman to walk out with me
and prevent me from falling
though I take a mechanical walker with me.
I don't mean it has an engine that propels it.
I do the propelling, but that it is
shiny and metal and has wheels. □

STATEMENT OF OWNERSHIP, MANAGEMENT, AND CIRCULATION

1. Publication Title: Granta
2. Publication No. 000-508
3. Filing Date: September 30, 1999
4. Issue Frequency: Quarterly (4 times per year)
5. Number of Issues Published Annually: 4
6. Annual Subscription Price: $34.00
7. Complete Mailing Address of Known Office of Publication: 1755 Broadway, New York, NY 10019-3780
8. Complete Mailing Address of Headquarters of General Business Office of Publisher: 1755 Broadway, New York, NY 10019-3780
9. Full Names and Complete Addresses of Publisher, Editor and Managing Editor: Publisher: Rea S. Hederman, 1755 Broadway, New York, NY 10019; Editor: Ian Jack, 2/3 Hanover Yard, Noel Road, Islington, London N1 8BE; Managing Editor: Karen Whitfield, 2/3 Hanover Yard, Noel Road, Islington, London N1 8BE
10. Owners: Granta USA LLC, 1755 Broadway, New York, NY 10019; NYREV, Inc., 1755 Broadway, New York, NY 10019; The Morningside Partnership, 625 N. State St., Jackson, MS 39202
11. Known Bondholders, Mortgagees, and Other Security Holders: None
12. Tax Status: Has Not Changed
13. Publication Title: Granta
14. Issue Date for Circulation Data: Fall 1999
15. Extent and Nature of Circulation: Average No.Copies Each Issue During Preceding 12 Months
a. Total No. of Copies: 79,519
b. Paid and/or Requested Circulation
1. Paid/Requested Outside-County Mail Subscriptions as Stated on Form 3541: 31,468
2. Paid In-County Subscriptions: 0
3. Sales Through Dealers and Carriers, Street Vendors, Counter Sales and Other Non-USPS Paid Distribution: 36,156
4. Other Classes Mailed Through the USPS: 168
c. Total Paid and/or Requested Circulation: 67,792
d. Free Distribution by Mail
1. Outside-County as Stated on Form 3541: 1
2. In-County as Stated on Form 3541: 0
3. Other Classes Mailed Through the USPS: 0
e Free Distribution Outside the Mail: 502
f. Total Free Distribution: 503
g. Total Distribution: 68,295
h. Copies not Distributed: 11,224
i. Total: 79,519
j. Percent Paid and/or Requested Circulation: 99%
15. Extent and Nature of Circulation:No.Copies of Single Issue Published Nearest to Filing Date
a. Total No. of Copies: 75,075
b. Paid and/or Requested Circulation
1. Paid/Requested Outside-County Mail Subscriptions as Stated on Form 3541: 31,465
2. Paid In-County Subscriptions: 0
3. Sales Through Dealers and Carriers, Street Vendors, Counter Sales and Other Non-USPS Paid Distribution: 29,662
4. Other Classes Mailed Through the USPS: 180
c. Total Paid and/or Requested Circulation: 61,307
d. Free Distribution by Mail
1. Outside-County as Stated on Form 3541: 1
2. In-County as Stated on Form 3541: 0
3. Other Classes Mailed Through the USPS: 0
e. Free Distribution Outside the Mail: 541
f. Total Free Distribution: 542
g. Total Distribution: 61,849
h. Copies not Distributed: 13,226
i. Total: 75,075
j. Percent Paid and/or Requested Circulation: 99%
16. Publication of Statement of Ownership will be printed in the Winter 1999 issue of this publication.
17. Signature and Title of Editor, Publisher, Business Manager, or Owner: I certify that all information furnished on this form is true and complete. Rea S. Hederman, Publisher

GRANTA

CLOSER

David Malouf

There was a time, not so long ago, when we saw my Uncle Charles twice each year, at Easter and Christmas. He lives in Sydney but would come like the rest of us to eat at the big table at my grandmother's, after church. We're Pentecostals. We believe that all that is written in the Book is clear truth without error. Just as it is written, so it is. Some of us speak in tongues and others have the gift of laying on hands. This is a grace we are granted because we live as the Lord wishes, in truth and charity.

My name is Amy, but in the family I am called Ay, and my brothers, Mark and Ben, call me Rabbit. Next year, when I am ten, and can think for myself and resist the influences, I will go to school like the boys. In the meantime my grandmother teaches me. I am past long division.

Uncle Charles is the eldest son, the firstborn. When you see him in family photographs with my mother and Uncle James and Uncle Matt, he is the blondest; his eyes have the most sparkle to them. My mother says he was always the rebel. She says, his trouble is he never grew up. He lives in Sydney, which Grandpa Morpeth says is Sodom. This is the literal truth, as Aaron's rod, which he threw at Pharaoh's feet, did literally become a serpent and Jesus turned water into wine. The Lord destroyed Sodom and he is destroying Sydney, but with fire this time that is slow and invisible. It is burning people up but you don't see it because they burn from within. That's at the beginning. Later, they burn visibly, and the sight of the flames blistering and scorching and blackening and wasting to the bone is horrible.

Because Uncle Charles lives in Sodom we do not let him visit any more. If we did, we might be touched. He is one of the fools in Israel—that is what Grandpa Morpeth calls him. He has practised abominations. Three years ago he confessed this to my Grandpa and Grandma and my Uncles James and Matt, expecting them to welcome his frankness. Since then he is banished, he is as water spilled on the ground that cannot be gathered up again. So that we will not be infected by the plague he carries, Grandpa has forbidden him to come on to the land. In fact, he is forbidden to come at all, though he does come, at Easter and Christmas, when we see him across the home paddock fence. He stands far back on the other side and my grandfather and grandmother and the rest of us stand on ours, on the grass slope below the house.

We live in separate houses but on the same farm, which is where my mother and Uncle James and Uncle Matt, and Uncle Charles when he was young, grew up, and where my Uncles James and Matt still work.

They are big men with hands swollen and scabbed from the farm work they do, and burned necks and faces, and feet with discoloured toenails from sloshing about in rubber boots in the bails. They barge about the kitchen at five o'clock in their undershorts, still half asleep, then sit waiting for Grandma to butter their toast and pour their tea. Then they go out to milk the herd, hose out the bails, drive the cows to pasture and cut and stack lucerne for winter feed. Sometimes my brothers and I go with them.

Working a dairy farm is a healthy life. The work is hard but good. But when I grow up I mean to be an astronaut.

Ours is a very pleasant part of the country. We are blessed. The cattle are fat, the pasture's good. The older farmhouses, like my grandfather's, are large, with many rooms and wide verandas, surrounded by camphor-laurels, and bunyas and hoop-pines and Scotch firs. Sodom is far off, but one of the stations on the line is at the bottom of our hill and many trains go back and forth. My Uncle Charles, however, comes by car.

His car is silver. It is a BMW and costs an arm and a leg. It has sheepskin seat covers and a hands-free phone. When Uncle Charles is on the way he likes to call and announce his progress.

The telephone rings in the hallway. You answer. There are pips, then Uncle Charles says in a jokey kind of voice: 'This is GAY 437 calling. I am approaching Bulladeela.' The air roaring through the car makes his voice sound weird, like a spaceman's. Far off. It is like a spaceship homing in.

Later he calls again. 'This is GAY 437,' the voice announces. 'I am approaching Wauchope.'

'Don't any one of you pick up that phone,' my grandfather orders.

'But Grandpa,' my brother Ben says, 'it might be Mrs McTaggart.' Mrs McTaggart is a widow and our neighbour.

'It won't be,' Grandpa says. 'It will be him.'

He is a stranger to us, as if he had never been born. This is what

Grandpa says. My grandmother says nothing. She was in labour for thirty-two hours with Uncle Charles, he was her first. For her, it can never be as if he had never been born, even if she too has cast him out. I heard my mother says this. My father told her to shush.

You can see his car coming from far off. You can see it *approaching*. It is very like a spaceship, silver and fast; it flashes. You can see its windscreen catching the sun as it rounds the curves between the big Norfolk Island pines of the golf course and the hospital, then its flash between the trees along the river. When it pulls up on the road outside our gate there is a humming like something from another world, then all four windows go up of their own accord, all together, with no one winding, and Uncle Charles swings the driver's door open and steps out.

He is taller than Uncle James or Uncle Matt, taller even than Grandpa, and has what the Book calls beautiful locks. They are blond. 'Bleached,' my grandfather tells us. 'Peroxide!' He is tanned and has the whitest teeth I have ever seen.

The corruption is invisible. The fire is under his clothes and inside him, hidden beneath the tan.

The dogs arrive, yelping. All bunched together, they go bounding over the grass to the fence, leaping up on one another's backs with their tails wagging to lick his hands as he reaches in to fondle them.

'Don't come any closer,' my grandfather shouts. 'We can see you from there.'

His voice is gruff, as if he had suddenly caught cold, which in fact he never does, or as if a stranger was speaking for him. Uncle Charles has broken his heart. Grandpa has cast him out, as you cut off a limb so that the body can go on living. But he likes to see that he is still OK. That it has not yet begun.

And in fact he looks wonderful—as far as you can see. No marks.

Once when he got out of the car he had his shirt off. His chest had scoops of shadow and his shoulders were golden and so smooth they gave off a glow. His whole body had a sheen to it.

Uncle James and Uncle Matt are hairy men like Esau, they are shaggy. The hair on their chest above the dip of their singlet is dark. But his chest and throat and arms were like those of an angel, smooth and polished as wood.

You see the whiteness of his teeth and, when he takes off his sunglasses, the sparkle of his eyes, and his smoothness and the blondness of his hair, but you do not see the marks. This is because he does not come close.

My grandmother stands with her hands clasped, and breathes but does not speak. Neither does my mother, though I have heard her say to my father, in an argument: 'Charlie's just a big kid. He never grew up. He was always such fun to be with.'

'Helen!' my father said.

I know my grandmother would like Uncle Charles to come closer so that she could really see how he looks. She would like him to come in and eat. There is always enough, we are blessed. There is an ivory ring with his initial on it, C, in the dresser drawer with the napkins, and when we count the places at table she pretends to make a mistake, out of habit, and sets one extra. But not the ring. The place stays empty all through our meal. No one mentions it.

I know it is Grandpa Morpeth's heart that is broken, because he has said so, but it is Grandma Morpeth who feels it most. She likes to touch. She is always lifting you up and hugging. She does not talk much.

When we go in to eat and take up our napkins and say grace and begin passing things, he does not leave; he stays there beside his car in the burning sunlight. Sometimes he walks up and down outside the fence and shouts. It is hot. You can feel the burning sweat on him. Then, after a time, he stops shouting and there is silence. Then the door of his car slams and he roars off.

I would get up if I was allowed and watch the flash flash of metal as he takes the curves round the river, past the hospital, then the golf course. But by the time everyone is finished and we are allowed to get down, he is gone. There is just the wide green pasture, open and empty, with fat, almost stationary clouds casting giant shadows, and the trees by the river in a silvery shimmer, all their leaves humming a little and twinkling as they turn over in a breeze that otherwise you might not have felt.

Evil is in the world because of men and their capacity for sin. Men fell into error so there is sin, and because of sin there is death. Once the error has got in there is no fixing it. Not in this world. But it is sad, that, it is hard. Grandpa says it has to be; that we must do what is hard to show that we love what is good and hate what is sinful, and the harder the thing, the more love we show Him.

But I don't understand about love any more than I do about death. It seems harder than anyone can bear to stand on one side of the fence and have Uncle Charles stand there on the other. As if he were already dead, and death was stronger than love, which surely cannot be.

When we sit down to our meal, with his chair an empty space, the food we eat has no savour. I watch Grandpa Morpeth cut pieces of meat with his big hands and push them between his teeth, and chew and swallow, and what he is eating, I know, is ashes. His heart is closed on its grief. And that is what love is. That is what death is. Us inside at the table, passing things and eating, and him outside, as if he had never been born; dead to us, but shouting. The silver car with its dusky windows that roll up of their own accord and its phone in there in its cradle is the chariot of death, and the voice announcing, 'I am on the way, I am approaching Nambucca Heads, I am approaching Lismore'—what can that be but the angel of death?

The phone rings in the house. It rings and rings. We pause at the sink, in the middle of washing up, my grandmother and my mother and me, but do not look at one another. My grandfather says: 'Don't touch it. Let it ring.' So it keeps ringing for a while, then stops. Like the shouting.

This Easter for the first time he did not come. We waited for the telephone to ring and I went out, just before we sat down to our meal, to look for the flash of his car along the river. Nothing. Just the wide green landscape lying still under the heat, with not a sign of movement in it.

That night I had a dream, and in the dream he did come. We stood below the veranda and watched his car pull up outside the fence. The smoky windows went up, as usual. But when the door swung open and he got out, it was not just his shirt he had taken off, but all his clothes, even his shoes and socks. Everything except his sunglasses. You could see his bare feet in the grass, large and bony, and he glowed, he was smooth all over, like an angel.

He began to walk up to the fence. When he came to it he stood still a moment, frowning. Then he put his hand out and walked on, walked right through it to our side, where we were waiting. What I thought, in the dream, was that the lumpy coarse-stemmed grass was the same on both sides, so why not? If one thick blade didn't know any more than another that the fence was there, why should his feet?

When he saw what he had done he stopped, looked back at the fence and laughed. All around his feet, little daisies and gaudy, bright pink clover flowers began to appear, and the petals glowed like metal, molten in the sun but cool, and spread uphill to where we were standing, and were soon all around us and under our shoes. Insects, tiny grasshoppers, sprang up and went leaping, and glassy snails no bigger than your little fingernail hung on the grass stems, quietly feeding. He took off his sunglasses, looked down at them and laughed. Then looked across to where we were, waiting. I had such a feeling of lightness and happiness it was as if my bones had been changed into clouds, just as the tough grass had been changed into flowers.

I knew it was a dream. But dreams can be messages. The feeling that comes with them is real, and if you grasp and hold on to it, you can make the rest real. So I thought: if he can't come to us, I must go to him.

So this is what I do. I picture him. There on the other side of the fence, naked, his feet pressing the springy grass. *Stretch out your hand*, I tell him. *Like this.* I stretch my hand out. *If you have faith, the fence will open before you, as the sea did before Moses when he reached out his hand.* He looks puzzled. *No,* I tell him, *don't think about it. Just let it happen.*

It has not happened yet. But it will. Then, when he is close at last, when he has passed through the fence and is on our side, I will stretch out my hand and touch him, just under the left breast, and he will be whole. He will feel it happening to him and laugh. His laughter will be the proof. I want this more than anything. It is my heart's desire.

Each night now I lie quiet in the dark and go over it. The winding up of the smoky windows of the chariot of death. The swinging open of the door. Him stepping out and looking towards me behind his sunglasses. Me telling him what I tell myself:

Open your heart now. Let it happen. Come closer, closer. See? Now reach out your hand. □

The Blood of Strangers

Stories from Emergency Medicine

FRANK HUYLER

"Utterly engrossing, moving, poetic accounts."

—*Kirkus Reviews*

This book is a visceral portrayal of a physician's encounters with the highly charged world of an emergency room.

$19.95 cloth

Luminous Debris

Reflecting on Vestige in Provence and Languedoc

GUSTAF SOBIN

Interpreting vestige with the eloquence of a poet and the knowledge of a field archaeologist, Sobin explores his elected terrain: the landscapes of Provence and Languedoc.

$45.00 cloth, $18.95 paper, illustrated

Room to Fly

A Transcultural Memoir

PADMA HEJMADI

"This book is at once a series of prose poems, a philosophy of aesthetics, and an exploration of cultures, written with such vivid immediacy and a language so beautifully crafted."

—Marguerite Guzman Bouvard, author of *Revolutionizing Motherhood*

$24.95 cloth

Children of a Vanished World

ROMAN VISHNIAC

Edited by Mara Vishniac Kohn and Miriam Hartman Flacks

Between 1935 and 1938 the celebrated photographer Roman Vishniac explored the Jewish *shtetlekh* of Eastern Europe. Seventy of those photographs are now available, accompanied by a selection of nursery rhymes, songs, poems, and chants for children's games in both Yiddish and English translation.

An S. Mark Taper Foundation Book in Jewish Studies, $25.00 cloth, illustrated

Dust

A History of the Small and the Invisible

JOSEPH A. AMATO

Foreword by Jeffrey Burton Russell
Illustrated by Abigail Rorer

Examining a thousand years of Western civilization—from the naturalism of medieval philosophy, to the artistry of the Renaissance, to the modern worlds of nanotechnology and viral diseases—*Dust* offers a savvy story of the genesis of the microcosm.

$22.50 cloth, illustrated

At bookstores or order 1-800-822-6657 **www.ucpress.edu**

UNIVERSITY OF CALIFORNIA PRESS

GRANTA

ASKING FOR IT

James Hamilton-Paterson

Having my hair cut one morning in February 1999, I fell foul of one of those barber-shop discussions which are a feature of life here in Italy. This morning's big issue happened to be the Italian Supreme Court's notorious decision, handed down the previous day, to quash the conviction of a forty-five-year-old driving instructor for raping his eighteen-year-old pupil. The reason given was that the girl had been wearing jeans, and the judges maintained that jeans are impossible to remove without the wearer's consent. The all-male discussion in the barber's followed fairly predictable lines, but the Supreme Court definitely lost the argument. There was clear majority agreement that nowadays, with so many violent lunatics around, women in such a situation were best not putting up too serious a resistance for fear of being killed. The problem, one customer sensibly observed, was how to convince a court of law that in asking not to be murdered you were not asking to be raped.

As the clippers buzzed about my ears I remembered a British high court judge in the 1980s who maintained that most women had a secret desire to be assaulted. I also remembered an earnest dinner party conversation rightly deploring this man's judgement that a particular rape victim had been 'asking for it'. Even so, I said, every citizen's having the right *not* to be assaulted was unfortunately not enough in the real world; adults had occasionally to take some responsibility for what happened to them. This was righteously howled down, one feisty lady going so far as to make vehement and incautious remarks about what she saw as my typical male insensitivity to rape. Ever since, it has rankled that for reasons of diffidence as much as of decorum I withheld the perfect riposte. Luckily for her, and unluckily for me, I was better qualified than she to speak on the subject.

In the spring of 1966 I was in Libya on my first job after leaving university, teaching for a year at a school in Tripoli. I was the only one of the British Council recruits who had chosen to live in an entirely Arab neighbourhood: a sandy, scrubby lot full of goats and the odd camel, a patch of land that has long since vanished under urban development. I was surrounded by a kind of village life that coexisted with what in those days was still a very small capital city.

At night the local people's huts and shacks were lit with pressure lamps rather than electricity, and by day the nearby dusty road was lined with stalls selling vegetables and cheap household goods. I got on fine with my Arab neighbours, buying eggs from some and little flat loaves from others, relationships that naturally improved the more I acquired a bit of the language. However, on my days off I took to escaping the noise by driving out into the coastal areas surrounding Tripoli. These were semi-desert, part citrus orchards and olive groves, mostly planted by Sicilian immigrants in the 1920s under Mussolini's 'Garden of Italy' scheme. Here were miles and miles of nothing, with ravishing views of empty coastline. I had bought a Ford Fairlane for fifty dollars from an American GI at nearby Wheelus Field, a huge air force base the USAF maintained until Colonel Gaddafi took over in the 1969 coup and kicked them out. I used to drive down empty tracks past the last signs of habitation, then park and go swimming or write letters home.

On the February afternoon that so nearly turned out to be my last I was lying on my stomach, half asleep and enjoying sunshine that was not yet strong enough to burn. Suddenly I was aware of a ring of figures looking down at me: five Bedouin pastoralists, to judge from their robes and sticks. The customary greeting I gave them was doubtless too casual, especially for a shirtless white foreigner wearing only a pair of jeans. The next thing I knew was that they had thrown themselves on top of me. I remember the smell of sheep's grease on their robes and the sand in my mouth. One knelt holding a large reddish rock with which he kept feinting at my head whenever I looked up or tried to protest. Beyond that I was quite unable to move. I can assure the Italian Supreme Court that jeans can indeed be torn off without the wearer's consent. Only at that point did I understand what was about to happen, and the realization seemed like a reprieve since I had assumed murder was uppermost in their minds. The relief was short-lived.

It was excessively painful and disagreeable, and it seemed to last rather longer than forever. Not once but five times, the men democratically moving around and taking over the rock in turn, each making it quite clear what would happen if I tried serious resistance. Insofar as I was capable of maintaining a clear thought, it was one of despair: that eventually, whether or not I resisted, they would kill me. Having gone so far, they would surely decide they had nothing more to lose and guarantee my silence by smashing my head with the rock and leaving me there. Thankfully, I had miscalculated. After *un mauvais quart d'heure* they dropped the rock by my head and got to their feet, laughing. Then all five of them spat at me and walked off, still laughing.

There is no point in dwelling on the agonizing drive back into town, the gore on the upholstery, the final humiliation of being examined by a roguish Yugoslav doctor in the old Italian hospital on the seafront ('Ah, my friend, it is spring!'). I soon realized why I had miscalculated my attackers' need to ensure my silence. They understood that nothing guarantees silence better than shame, and nothing exceeds the complete abjection of a male in a macho society who is raped. It was quite unthinkable to tell anyone at the British Council: their discomfiture would have been almost on a par with my own. The same went for the British Embassy. As for reporting the episode to the Libyan police, I would as soon have died. In fact, the sheer relief at being alive transcended everything and sustained me. It was some time before I could confide in the closest of my British colleagues, after first extracting oaths of everlasting secrecy from which this article now releases him. The weeks went by, and gradually it became clear that I hadn't sustained irreparable physical or psychic damage. Just one of those things, I came to think; just part of Life's Great Web, as Marcus Aurelius was irritatingly fond of saying. Let that be a lesson to you.

But what lesson, exactly? For a long time afterwards I interrogated my unconscious to discover if I might not have secretly desired and engineered the whole episode. Yet I knew I hadn't. Inevitably, my British friend told me how daft it had been to go sunbathing alone in North Africa. 'Just asking for it, you know,' he said. I had undoubtedly been excessively confident of who I was and what I was doing and of the Libyans in general whom I liked so much. On several occasions my students, who ranged in age from fourteen to forty-two, had invited me to their houses to meet their families. I once drove 160 miles into the desert with one to visit his home, which turned out to be several brown Bedouin tents. I was given the kindest and most dignified welcome imaginable. After eating we chatted around the fire beneath a desert sky crammed with immense and brilliant stars, criss-crossed by sudden meteorite trails which lit up the wilderness. Each time this happened someone passed a remark to the effect that God was very good; and the prevailing spirit of magnificence and well-being was so strong I could scarcely doubt it. This and similar experiences had left me with a considerable respect and affection for Libyans (which I retain to this day), plus—I suppose—a commensurate trustingness.

In a metaphorical sense, though, I surely had been asking for it by so cockily failing to take politics into account. This was the year before the Six Day War. President Nasser of Egypt was broadcasting almost nightly to the Arab world: long harangues whipping up nationalistic spirit, reminding Arabs of the triumph of Suez in 1956, lambasting Israel, the oil companies, the United States. There were already students in the school who showed increasing truculence. I knew the GIs at Wheelus seldom ventured off-base, and never alone. My Fairlane had steel clips under the dash where its previous owner had kept a baseball bat for self-defence. For all its Libyan number plate the car still had the old Wheelus sticker on it which I had not removed. My rapists, it seemed, had been committing a political more than an erotic act. I was violated because I was a white foreign male. I was not even a person but an object to be despised and humiliated. In my youthful British arrogance I had believed I was exempt from being thought anything other than benignly apolitical, and could in any case never be taken for an American. I had failed to read the signs and paid for my stupidity.

On balance I'm glad it happened in the days before obligatory courses of post-traumatic stress counselling became de rigueur. It never even crossed my mind that I wouldn't get over it. This is by no means to make a bluff, harrumphing point about rape victims needing to stop making a fuss and to pull themselves together. Such horrid incidents take different people in very different ways. Even at that time, though, I had a deep private belief that I would do better to chalk things up to experience than to think of myself in terms of victimhood. Besides, talking about it to a complete stranger would have made it far worse. I felt much too much of a fool, and needed to come to terms with it by myself and at my own pace.

By an odd coincidence the barber-shop conversation about the Italian lady with the jeans marked almost to the day the thirty-third anniversary of an episode which taught me that the egoistic assertion of innocence is never enough. You need to have all your wits about you all the time. You need to wonder whether, even with your mouth tightly closed and jeans tightly buttoned, you are not actually asking for something. Simply by being too innocent, too ignorant, too *arrogant* even, you may be asking for a demonstration that being violated can have its uses; that ends you had not given thought to might be served. A hard lesson, but a quite useful one. □

GRANTA

FIRST CUT

Jonathan Kaplan

LEARNING TO BE A SURGEON
UNDER APARTHEID

Jonathan Kaplan

I grew up with the expectation that I would serve. One of my mother's brothers had been through the Somalia campaign as a regimental surgeon in the King's African Rifles. The other had been a sapper, clearing German minefields under fire in the Western Desert. My father spent five years in uniform, in Africa and Europe, treating the wounded in tented field hospitals. His medical colleagues—our family friends—had been there too. We were a medical family: my father the orthopaedic surgeon, his brother the virologist; my mother the pathologist, her brother the urologist. In Durban, wherever we went, we got respect. People would approach my father, expecting that he should instantly remember the history of their pain and survival. He used the trick (I have since used it myself) of asking to see their scars, and from the track of the knife he would recall first the operation, then the problem, and often, finally, their names. Among these erstwhile patients, as well as among the nurses and doctors I met as I trailed my father on his rounds through the hospital wards, the assumption was clear: I too would become a doctor, and serve. Exactly what form that service would take was uncertain; to my relief there seemed to be no great, impending conflict in which I would be tested.

I was accepted into the School of Medicine at Cape Town University, and, beneath the loom of Table Mountain, found a new burden of tradition. The university library contained the same leather-bound volumes by Wells and Kipling that my father had read. In the chemical reek of the dissecting rooms I studied the same intricate anatomy texts, and laughed at the same practical jokes involving cadaver fingers slipped into the lunch boxes of the unsuspecting. The senior anatomist—an elderly rake who wore a linen suit and sported the panama hat, white goatee and moustache that Colonel Sanders was to make famous—had been there for four decades, and talked wistfully of the 'gentlemen' he had taught before the war. He would hold tea parties in his office for groups of old ladies, trying to coax them into leaving their bodies to science. Afterwards he would take them on a tour of the dissecting rooms, warning us in advance to be on our best behaviour. 'Think of yourselves resting here, girls,' he would say, patting the enamel tables, 'at peace in the hands of these young men,' and the ladies would giggle and gasp, and, presumably, be seduced.

These first years of study were basic blood and bones: anatomy, physiology, pathology and bacteriology, pharmacology. Some took their studies seriously, attending every lecture and reading textbooks into the night, but myself and my friends found enough diversions to prevent us from learning any more than we needed. There was surfing and diving and cinemas and parties and pinball dives, and all-night clubs near the harbour full of prostitutes and drunken sailors. There was a feeling among us that our studies wouldn't really start until we saw our first live patients in a couple of years' time.

So the first time I got blood on my hands had little to do with my studies. It began, improbably, in the middle of a dull basic-sciences lecture. A small group of students had marched through the centre of Cape Town that morning, carrying banners that called for an end to apartheid. By lunch time they were ranged on the steps of the Anglican cathedral behind the Parliament buildings, their banners held aloft, when the police arrived. A stand-off ensued in the warm sunshine, with motorists steering carefully along the road between the opposing groups. Though the police seemed reluctant to move on the students in such a public place, riot-squad reinforcements were gathering in the side streets, and student runners were sent to the campus to ask for help.

I was drowsing over my notes when there was the sound of running feet in the corridor outside. The door to the lecture theatre opened with a crash. A face peered in and addressed us, ignoring the man at the podium. 'There's going to be trouble at St George's Cathedral; hundreds of cops, and riot trucks. We need lots of people there; they can't arrest everyone.' A couple of my friends stood up. After a moment's hesitation, I joined them. Perhaps ten of us, in that class of a hundred, made for the door. Outside it was clear that there had been a much better response from the liberal arts faculties, for all over campus students streamed out of the buildings and jostled for lifts, piling into cars and pick ups and VW buses that roared off down to the highway that led to town.

We approached the cathedral from the back, through public gardens unusually empty of sweepers and gardeners and nannies with their infant charges. From ahead came a thready chanting, and a thumping sound that I couldn't identify. Rounding the building, we came to where the battle lines were drawn. A host of students, men and women, occupied the stone steps of the cathedral and the wide pavement in front of it. Across the street stood a phalanx of riot police in solid rows. Steady as a heartbeat, they struck their batons against the square perspex shields that they carried. The crowd flinched at each blow, shrinking back towards the cathedral steps. Then a colonel stepped forward, sunlight blinking off the braid on his cap. In one hand he held a yellow megaphone.

'This is a prohibited gathering.' The metallic warp cut through the sudden silence. 'You have thirty seconds to disperse.'

He stood there in his dark tunic, the bright yellow cone raised to his mouth.

'It's Daffy Duck!' yelled a wag in the crowd, and a roar of laughter drowned out his next words. Abruptly, the colonel turned to the police lines and raised an arm. There was a crack and two tear-gas canisters curved skyward, trailing arcs of haze. They landed in the street and rolled towards us, squirting smoke. A student scooped one up and threw it back into the police ranks, where it fumed and spluttered under their feet. Gagging and swearing, the riot cops reeled, then charged in a body, their long batons raised. The banner-holders in the front went down under a storm of blows, and were dragged across the road to the waiting trucks. The rest of us fled up the cathedral steps, new canisters churning white clouds under our feet. We kicked them off the wide top step and stared in horror at the melee below, where people screamed and choked in the rising gas and cowered under flailing batons.

Men and women leaped up the steps, their arms outstretched towards us, while red-faced riot police grabbed at their clothes and hurled them back down, kicking them as they fell. A grisly tug-of-war developed in front of me: we caught hold of a girl's hands and tried to pull her up to safety, while the police continued to rain blows on her back and legs. There was a shouted command and she fell, sobbing, into our arms. The police line retreated, step by step, exposing a wasteland of blood-splashed stone and lost shoes. I stood at the top of the steps between the open cathedral doors. My eyes were streaming; the gas stung my lips and smarted where it found moisture on my sweating face. People retched and coughed. Some helped to pass the injured to the rear, and carry them into the nave. Others screamed insults at the police, calling them slime and filth, and Boer baboons.

A breeze turned the scraps of paper in the street, thinning the tear-gas haze. The noise of the city returned and I could hear the voices of office workers watching us from the windows of the building opposite. Then the colonel's megaphone screeched again.

'You are all under arrest!'

From the steps came ragged laughter and shouts of defiance.

Then the police charged and the students recoiled. Those who could fled back into the church, the press of bodies carrying me with it. Over their heads I could see the flash of falling batons and hear the crack as they made contact. A tear-gas canister was bowled through the opening and then the police pushed the doors shut with a crash on the daylight outside. Some students sprinted down the aisles to escape through the transepts, but those doors too were slammed shut before they reached them. We were sealed inside. From the street came cries, and the sound of beatings.

The gloomy nave was filled with people. Some cried, or ran about frantically, their chests heaving. Others staggered, their hair matted with blood from head wounds. The shock of confrontation had revealed us for what we were: a bunch of self-styled rebels without cohesion, amateurs at confronting the State. Someone had clapped a cleaner's bucket over the tear-gas canister, but trails of smoke leaked out along the floor. It was not only the gas that made our eyes burn. I collapsed on a pew and lit a cigarette, my hands trembling. 'Not a fastidious churchgoer, I see,' said a voice beside me. I looked up and recognized the speaker, a medical student from the year above me. Stefan gazed around at the defeated mob and shook his head. 'Looks like Casualty on a Saturday night,' he said. 'Smoke up, and we'll do something constructive.'

This was my first taste of trauma, but Stefan seemed to know what to do. He stood on a pew and addressed the refugees, his voice cutting through the moans and whimpers.

'Let's get the injured seen to,' he said, 'anyone got some clean cloth?'

A girl pulled a blouse from her backpack and held it up. Someone else produced a white lab-coat, and a couple of handkerchiefs were handed forward.

'Bring all those that have been hurt here, to the front,' said Stefan. He began to tear the fabric into strips using a pen knife. Wounded people started to emerge from the shadows. I looked at their ragged cuts and thought I might faint. I set to work nervously, rolling the cloth into pads and holding them against gashed scalps to staunch the bleeding. Recovering from their shock, others came to help. Stefan appeared at my side.

'Reassure them,' he said softly, 'tell them head wounds always bleed a lot, but they soon stop. Tell them it's going to be OK.'

I was struck by the immediate calming effect of his voice. I relayed the message to my helpers, and noticed how they too seemed heartened.

Stefan had gathered the worst tear-gas victims at the font. Some could hardly see between their swollen eyelids. He spoke to them gently as he bathed the blistered skin. 'Don't worry. It will burn at first when the water reacts with the chemicals. It'll stop after a few seconds.' Here, too, his voice worked like a tranquillizer, and I began to understand a little of what healing involved.

I had treated my first casualties, however minor, and embraced my first cause. 'The Siege of St George's' they called it in the papers the next morning, and those of us who had been there gained a brief notoriety. A few people, after showing off their bruises, went on to make names for themselves as political activists. One was my friend Stefan. For a while I shared a student squat with him and Neil and Nigel, the Marxist-Lentilists, who shared an admiration for Albanian communism and a conviction that meat, or fruit, or anything but the most rigorous of subsistence diets signified bourgeois softness and betrayal of the oppressed masses. They shared their spartan meals with some coloured children who slept rough in the cemetery behind the house, and laughed when our possessions were regularly stolen—'redistributed'—by the most enterprising among them.

I didn't really mind the absence of luxuries. I was short of money and augmenting my living allowance by working as a mechanic, rebuilding the engines of the VW buses and Beetles that were the most popular student transport. Our kitchen was always full of people, talking socialism through the night. I didn't pretend to be an activist, but I was now aware of the political aspects of studying medicine in South Africa, as one of the select minority who qualified. The irony of this privilege became apparent when we started our clinical training. Our professors adhered to the standards of the English medical schools from which most of them had graduated. Groote Schuur hospital was an international centre of excellence; it was here that the world's first heart transplant had been performed in 1967, and overseas doctors felt honoured to work in the department of cardiac surgery and other specialities. One day we too would enter that elect society of healers and begin to make a difference to humanity. Our medical training was rigorous and complete, for we had an abundant supply of 'clinical material'; the poor from the townships and bleak rural homelands.

We would see pathology that had all but disappeared in the developed West. TB patients coughed up bloody sputum, their heaving chests resonant from cavities where the disease had corroded their lungs. On the neurology wards a patient, asked to stand, would reel when he closed his eyes, and walk with stamping, uncertain feet. 'Come now,' our tutor would challenge, 'are we looking at beriberi or General Paresis of the Insane?', and we would strain our diagnostic faculties to try to distinguish vitamin-deficient dementia from delusions of grandeur, and to identify the vacant face and irregular pupils of advanced syphilis. Schizophrenics would be admitted to the psychiatric hospital with florid catatonia, holding for hours the positions in which their ductile limbs were placed. By the time some cancer patients reached us from the rural areas their tumours would be huge and ulcerating, no-hope opportunities for the surgeons to demonstrate their cutting skills to us.

There were also opportunities to study more acute surgical crises. Violence seemed to be the main export of the Cape Flats townships. Those of us who wished could spend nights working in Accident and Emergency, clamping arteries and stitching wounds. Excitable camaraderie embraced all of us facing that steady tide of perforated bodies, as we worked together to stop bleeding and stabilize vital signs. I began to gain a little more confidence in my skills and judgement, but remained in awe of the registrars and consultants who stood solid in that workshop of pain, making decisions about saving people's lives. It was terrifying to imagine that I might ever have to shoulder such responsibilities myself.

Other experiences provided a vertiginous awareness of our own mortality. We saw patients pass through the terminal stages of illness, and hovered at the fringes of unsuccessful resuscitations. Learning clinical pathology, we crowded around the autopsy tables to see the face of victorious disease. Probably for the first time, I truly realized that one day I would die. It was easy, and deeply disturbing, for me to imagine myself on the slab, sliced and gutted, with the pathologist opening my chest with a buzz saw and his assistant sluicing away the blood clots. Most graphic were the sights in the police mortuary, where, during our study of forensic medicine, we would see every permutation of unnatural death.

The white bodies tended to be tidier. There was a regular attrition among young men in that society, who went scuba-diving and hang-gliding and rock-climbing, or drove too fast on winding mountain roads. A few students, beaten down by loneliness or the fear of failure, would hang themselves or take overdoses. In the 'non-white' mortuary (here, too, the principle of racial segregation was observed) the corpses were less reposeful, dead from spear-thrust, gunshot and axe. Bodies were disembowelled, or bled dry from multiple chop-wounds, or contracted and charred by fire. They came from a place beyond the frontier of our known lives, where other rules appeared to prevail.

We felt a sort of horror about that place. People slaughtered each other there in a malevolent frenzy. One day, I saw the body of a young woman on the autopsy table. She was beautiful. Even the coarse line of undertaker's stitches that ran from her neck down between her breasts to her pubic hair could not diminish her perfection. She had bled to death; gang-raped and then despatched with a bottle kicked up her vagina, which had shattered, slashing the arteries in her pelvis. The social theorists would explain such incidents as the product of economic despair, or rage, at the impotence that apartheid had produced among the dispossessed. I felt dizzy, terrified, at the thought of such contemptuous destruction. The only way to deal with the fear was to keep it at bay through clinical detachment, clinical study.

So we lay on the beach and studied, slept and studied, fell in love and studied. A number of my classmates were pairing off, getting married, setting up medical partnerships for the future. Others were planning to specialize, dreaming of a secure future of private practice and social standing. When I visited Durban my parents' friends smiled at me, and nodded their approval. 'You'll do orthopaedics, like your father,' they suggested. 'He'll want you in the practice. One day he'll need someone to step into his shoes.' The idea seemed too improbable. The charm of the city's avenues of jacaranda trees, the genteel respect of my father's patients, even his worthy work at the black leper hospital up the coast, appeared irrelevant and transitory. Something apocalyptic was about to happen. I didn't know what, but it was sure to change everything.

In 1975 the South African army invaded Angola. The previous year there had been a coup in Portugal, led by young officers against a senile military government. The officers objected to the slaughter of so many young conscripts in the Portuguese colonies of Angola and Mozambique, where they were fighting an unwinnable conflict against black independence forces. Their first move was to divest Portugal of its overseas possessions. Suddenly the colonial authorities were gone, along with many of the white settlers. Forces of the main independence movement, the MPLA (Popular Movement for the Liberation of Angola) entered the capital. Shortly afterwards there was heavy fighting to the south of the city, and a column of tanks and troops rolled in, white men speaking Afrikaans. The South African army was operating outside its country's borders for the first time since the Second World War.

I expected, like all white males in South Africa, to do National Service. Most were called up directly on leaving school at sixteen or seventeen to spend a year in desolate base towns in the Karoo or the Highveld being bullied through drill and inspections by Permanent Force sergeants. Or you could apply for deferment to go to university, after which you were called up anyway. For most, service in the South

African Defence Force offered the prospect of a long period of dullness, enlivened only by the opportunity for some gratuitous damage to government property such as rolling a Bedford truck. The army had a high rate of serious motor accidents. Only graduating doctors could find any merit in this; drafted into the medical corps after a year of hospital internship, one might see some traffic trauma between treating conscripts' athlete's foot.

Now all that changed. The Angolan invasion had been repelled by Cuban troops airlifted in to help the MPLA. Driven back to South West Africa, the army dug in along the border with Angola. The 'operational zone' extended from the Atlantic coast in the west to Rhodesia, where Ian Smith's government was losing its own war against black guerrilla forces. It was in the operational zone that you now did your service, which was extended to two years. From the border district of Ovamboland constant attacks were launched into Angola. Even Ovamboland was enemy territory; the people there supported the South West Africa People's Organization, whose military wing was waging its own struggle against the South African occupiers.

The next year things got worse. In 1976 the Pretoria government decided that black schoolchildren across the country should be taught in Afrikaans. There was enormous resentment against the decree. It was pointed out that few children, or their teachers, knew the language. Petitions were submitted, school deputations sent to the government. All were ignored. Schoolchildren poured out of their schools on to the streets of Soweto, waving crude placards. The police opened fire, killing some children and wounding many others. The accumulated pressures of almost thirty years of apartheid could no longer be contained. Pupils, parents, workers marched on every symbol of the hated system: schools, administration offices, government beer-halls. Many were burned down. Roads were blocked with flaming tyres. For two days the police couldn't enter Soweto, until they came in armoured cars. It took months to crush the uprising in the townships around Johannesburg, by which time it had spread across the country.

Many hundreds of blacks died, and a few whites, killed by mobs after driving too close to the townships and getting caught in the conflagration. Suddenly, all those fears of ravening black hordes seemed about to become reality. As unrest became endemic, the tacticians of apartheid declared that the 'Total Onslaught' was upon us, and a 'Total Strategy' was needed to counter it. The army, already committed to an aggressive defence of the nation's borders, would now be sent into the townships as well. The war was everywhere, but it hadn't yet touched me directly. In the temporary stillness of the storm's centre I concentrated on learning my art.

There is a unique thrill to operating. Opening a belly, for example, and knowing how the layers of the abdominal wall will cleave under the line of the knife. The skin, bronzed by the coating of sterilizing iodine, must be opened in a single sweep, for its tension pulls the wound-ends apart, and later extensions to the cut will look dog-eared and ragged. Under the skin lies fat, creamy or a rich yellow, dense or semi-liquid, according to body type and diet. As it parts, the first drops of red are starting from the cut surfaces—they are promptly sealed by cautery forceps, and a wisp of blue smoke and brief smell of barbecue rises under the theatre lights.

Then comes the muscle layer, easiest to split along its fibrous junction in the midline. This must be divided with care, for immediately beneath it lie delicate structures—the sliding contents of the abdominal cavity and the delicate film of the peritoneum that sheathes them. A small hole is made with scissors. The cut gapes like a buttonhole. A pair of fingers slide behind the muscle sheath, the first intimate contact with the patient, and the scissors advance, clipping through fibres that grit faintly between the steel jaws.

The peritoneum itself is cut next, its milky blue membrane retracting like an anemone. Retractors are hooked into the wound edges and the frame cranked apart, and a new territory is revealed. Loops of neatly layered bowel pulsate in slow waves like wind over a cornfield. The sharp edge of the liver, a rich brown, forms a notched line below the ribcage, and nuggets of fat gleam between the fine vessels that fan out between the translucent layers of the mesentery. A faint odour, fresh yet slightly sour, rises from the exposed tissue.

Not every abdomen looks like this inside. Sometimes the fine architecture has been blasted and torn. Such bellies might carry a warning: the blue hole of a bullet wound or the pout of a stab.

Sometimes there is only the sullen crescent of a bruise beneath the ribs that tells of a blow sufficient to rupture the delicate organs within. A common factor is rigidity of the abdominal muscles, 'board-like', as the textbooks call it, fixed in an involuntary spasm that attempts to guard against the pain of movement. The patient may be in shock, with a high pulse and falling blood pressure, and getting him to surgery will be a priority. As soon as he is stable enough to endure the hazards of an anaesthetic, and sometimes before, while resuscitation is still underway, the abdomen is opened.

In such cases, the first thing that strikes one is the smell, the reek of an abattoir. A swill of blood, bile and faeces obscures the clean structures, signifying ruptured viscera and vessels. Bowel can wait a while for patching; bleeding can't, and while the anaesthetist pumps blood into neck or arm veins, the surgeon looks for where it leaks, and he sweats. Even old hands, veteran operators, feel fear as the dark blood wells from down where the great vessels lie. Sometimes I still dream about that feeling of helplessness, when my knowledge seems useless against the implacable approach of death. It began when I opened my first patient, in a hospital near the edge of Cape Town.

Conradie was an old army hospital, now converted to civilian use. It included a spinal unit, general medical and surgical wards, a paediatric department and a small neurosurgery unit. Long barrack wards with wide verandas lay among a grid of paths, along which paraplegics raced in their wheelchairs. Khaki-clad convicts from a local jail mowed the grass and dressed the regimented flower beds, while prison officers sat in the shade and supervised the work, pointing with their thermos flasks. As a district hospital with a reputation for roughness, it didn't attract the high-flyers, who preferred the academic ambience of the university teaching hospital. It was here that I came to take up the post of surgical house officer shortly after graduating from medical school.

Conradie Hospital lay in an unusual position. On one side stretched the expansive avenues and bungalows of Pinelands, a white suburb of watered lawns, where civil servants retired to bully their servants. The Cape Flats began on the other, a mosaic of concrete cube-houses and ribbon roads that zoned the grey beach-sand into 'townships'—Mitchell's Plain for 'coloureds', Nyanga, Langa and Gugulethu for blacks—and between them stunted jungles of scrub willow that hid the unmapped tracks and shanties of the 'informal settlements' thrown up by squatters from the hinterland. The hospital served all races, after a fashion—its patients were delivered in racially specific ambulances to segregated casualty departments.

It was often busy. The odd solid citizen from Pinelands, with diabetes or an asthma attack, would arrive in 'white' Casualty, expecting instant service from the single medical officer on night duty. Across the hall, on the 'black' side, victims of assaults, traffic accidents and incomplete abortions would arrive thoughout the evening, filling the benches in the waiting room. Now and then a turf-fight would break out between coloured gangs, and the corridor would be flanked with trolleys from which slashed Gypsy Jokers and Manhattans, their tattoos smeared with blood, would scream threats at one another while the walking wounded grappled in the reception area, feet slipping on the bloody floor. Those too embattled to have their injuries treated would be separated by the cops, cruel but impartial, who would club the casualties back into line. 'Listen to the doctor,' they'd order. 'You cunts can carrying on killing each other outside when he's finished.' On my second night on duty a big-bellied sergeant, mug of tea at his elbow, showed me how to put a drain into the chest of a stab victim with a collapsed lung. Sometimes he pitched in as an extra medic, cobbling together ragged machete wounds with big, efficient sutures.

In South Africa, that passed for normal hospital life. Its even tenor was about to be disrupted. Unrest had been simmering in the black townships around Cape Town, and the authorities now decided to suppress it. One morning I drove to work past convoys of police trucks on their way to Langa and Nyanga and Gugulethu, their windscreens blanked with steel mesh. Over the course of that baking, windless day the confrontation seemed to have been suspended. A sweaty contingent of riot police lounging at the hospital gates announced that the demonstrators had been dispersed or arrested. Nevertheless the hospital staff were generally on edge, and by four p.m. those who were able to had left, to make sure that 'everything was all right at home'. I stayed, because I was the medical officer on duty that night.

By sunset the casualty department would usually start to fill with the evening's crop. It remained empty. I stood outside in the dusk, feeling the overheated stillness of the day give way to a steady east wind. With it came a smell of woodsmoke and the crackle of shots, rising and falling like the approach of a brush fire. A helicopter clattered overhead, and then another, heading for the townships. A column of smoke rose against the darkening sky. From the distance came the sound of sirens. I thought I knew what was coming. I recalled the stories of war service I had been hearing ever since I was a child.

The first ambulance swung on to the tarmac apron outside Casualty. Another was just behind it, and another, and a snake of flashing lights that stretched back down the road. It was suddenly clear that my training hadn't prepared me for anything on this scale. I fled into the building, from which startled nurses were beginning to emerge, pushing trolleys. Panicking, I asked the receptionist to call the switchboard and get them to page every doctor they could reach. The casualty staff were already mobilizing. Orderlies were opening crates of intravenous fluid, and hanging bottles in jingling bunches from the drip stands. Hastily arranged stacks of dressing packs and chest-drain kits spilled across the floor. Outside, under the arc lights, each ambulance disgorged its load of six or eight bodies directly on to the ground, limbs tangled. We pulled them apart, sorting the dead from the living, and lifted those who were still breathing on to the trolleys. Then we ran with our limp cargoes into the treatment area.

The bodies were full of holes. Dark blood welled from punctured skin, or jetted red from open arteries. I ran from wound to wound with a tray of instruments, clamping bleeding points, while the senior sister slid a drip line into each patient who required one. A group of boys in football kit had been shot at from above (I heard later that a police helicopter had circled above their playing field, spraying it with automatic rifle fire). We had left all but one outside among the dead; from my forensic studies I recognized the effects of high-velocity bullets; muscle and bone had exploded, leaving stark cavities of shattered flesh. We took the sole survivor into the Casualty theatre. He was unconscious, and an entrance wound at the base of his neck bubbled and sucked. I closed it hastily, then stuck a drain into his chest. Blood flooded through the tube, filling the drain bottle, as his last breath gurgled in his throat.

Many of the casualties had been hit by shotgun fire on their legs and backs, and were peppered with pellets that made hard mounds under the skin. These could wait till later. Some had lost great ragged bites of tissue from the blasts. We packed their wounds with dressings and moved on. Others had been struck by pistol bullets—I could tell by the neat blue holes—but some of these wounds showed the scorched edges of close-range shots. An ambulance driver told me why.

'The cops and soldiers make the sweep, shooting from the armoured cars. If they see someone at the end of the street they blaze away, because they're frightened that the kids will get them with petrol bombs if they let them get too close. Then they call us in to pick up the bodies, and move on. When we reach the wounded their friends sometimes try to pull them away, or attack us, and we've got to defend ourselves.' He patted his side, where a revolver hung. 'Most of the crews carry guns. When we've shot them we throw them in the back and bring them here, with all the rest.'

By now a few doctors had arrived and were taking over treatment and resuscitation. An anaesthetist had also appeared, and he and I checked on the patients who needed urgent surgery. My job as duty doctor, as soon as I was relieved in Casualty, was to get the most acute case into theatre and prepared for operating while the surgical registrar was on his way.

I had dealt almost mechanically with the carnage in Casualty, but now, as I tried to make a clinical decision, I was abruptly aware of my lack of experience. Apprehensively, I pointed out a youth on a nearby trolley. Although we had been pouring fluid into his veins his blood pressure was almost unrecordable. Two small holes in his abdomen indicated the path of the bullets that had struck him down.

'We've got six units of blood on the way for him,' I told the anaesthetist. 'It looks like the upper round might have hit his liver. There's also an exit wound in his back, near his left kidney. I'd say his condition is the most critical.'

'I think you're right,' said the gas man, 'he's first for the chop.'

We shunted the trolley through the theatre doors. By the time I'd changed into a cap and mask, the orderlies had the patient on the table with his clothes cut away, and the anaesthetist had begun his work. I scrubbed my hands and forearms, watching as he slid a tube into the unconscious youth's throat. The ventilator started its steady sighing. Gowned and gloved, I wiped the rigid belly down with iodine and framed it in green drapes. The anaesthetist flung an empty blood-bag on the floor and connected up a new one, pumping at the pressure cuff to squirt it through the drip as fast as possible. He turned to me and shook his head. 'He's sliding. You may save him if you get him open quick.'

'But the registrar isn't here yet.'

The theatre sister looked at me across the sterile drapes. 'If you wait any longer it'll be too late,' she said. 'You may as well do the best you can.'

I took the knife from her, and held it uncertainly. I had made a few small incisions before, removing minor lumps and bumps. I had assisted other surgeons, but I had never cut into a belly myself. Taking a deep breath, I placed two fingers at the lower end of the patient's sternum, and poised the blade below them. Then, tentatively, I drew the scalpel down to the umbilicus. A faint line, fine as a cat scratch, showed my failure. 'Harder,' said the sister, 'as though you're slicing steak.'

I cut again, more strongly, and the skin opened reluctantly, fighting the blade. The youth's spare body carried almost no fat, and I picked my way through lean muscle. Revealed, the pale translucency of the peritoneum was dulled by an underlying blue-black shadow.

'Blood,' said the sister, 'his belly's full of blood. I've got the suction ready.'

I lifted a fold of the membrane between two artery clips, and snipped the raised edge. Immediately, the sister plunged the nozzle of the suction line into the gap, where it slurped and hiccuped, swallowing fluid and dark clots that rushed away down the plastic hose.

'Quickly,' called the anaesthetist, fussing over his readings, 'get in there and find the bleeding.'

I glanced at the window into the scrub room, hoping desperately to see the registrar. I thought I might faint. Trembling, I opened the peritoneum and laid it back. Blood lapped at the wound edges and overflowed on to the floor while the suction line choked, and cleared. For an instant I saw a pit of lacerated liver and leaking bile. Then blood welled up again, from some deep recess of the wound.

Shreds of yellow shit floated in the mess. I felt utterly alone. Time seemed to be rushing by, measured by the rapid tick of blood hitting the floor.

'Give me the biggest swab, no, three of them.'

I balled the big gauze compresses and thrust them into the depths beneath the liver's edge. I wrapped another round a piece of punctured bowel and sluiced out the abdomen with fresh saline. Slowly and then faster the debris cleared, hoovered up by the voracious sucker. I began to recognize some anatomy.

One of the bullets had struck beside the umbilicus, punching through some loops of small bowel before exiting through the back, close to the edge of the left kidney. I looked below the drapes to the catheter bag hooked to the operating table's edge. The urine in it was pale and clear; the kidney hadn't been hit. It was the other shot that had done most damage. It had struck the liver, shattering part of it, and evidently damaging the biliary system. Then it had travelled on to unknown, mortal regions, where the portal and hepatic veins run into the liver, and the great, thin-walled vena cava drains the lower body, carrying blood back to the labouring heart. The wad of gauze I had packed in there was sodden with blood. I didn't want to move it, but I had to.

I found the gall bladder where it lay beneath the liver. It had been perforated, and I clamped the hole with forceps to stop more bile leaking out. Then, lifting the clamp gently forward, I traced the bile duct back into the mess below. It seemed undamaged, and for the first time I began to hope; perhaps the bile leak was from the hole in the gall bladder, and the delicate biliary system itself was still intact. I peeled back the sodden compress, bit by bit. Blood oozed from a star-shaped fissure in the under-surface of the liver. It coursed thickly from one edge of the crater, where it appeared that a branch of a vein had been torn. I tried to clamp it, but the jelly-like liver crumbled under the steel jaws. Hoping that I was doing the right thing, I placed a couple of wide catgut stitches through the area, tightening the knot with caution so that it wouldn't cut out of the tissue. The bleeding dwindled as the surface of the laceration began to clot. I straightened up and looked over at the anaesthetist, who lifted his thumb and nodded. I nodded too, wildly, because I could see the registrar coming through the theatre doors behind him, snapping on his gloves.

It took another hour to trace each source of bleeding and explore the bullet tracks. We lifted every inch of intestine, inspecting it for holes. Some small punctures could simply be closed with sutures, but other sections looked bruised and torn. Damaged gut heals poorly, so we cut out these sections between clamps and rejoined the ends with close, neat stitches. Fortunately the large bowel appeared intact, for any injury to it would have needed a colostomy to rest the repaired area while it healed. Finally we flushed out the abdominal cavity again, washing clots and flecks of bowel content from between its folds. A couple of drainage tubes were laid—behind the liver and the repaired bowel, where leakage or infection might occur—and I carefully joined the layers of the abdomen. The last line of sutures closed the skin. I lifted off the drapes and looked at this small battlefield. The skin-stitches ran like a zipper down the midline. Red rubber tube drains jutted to the right and left, and neat oval wounds marked the trimmed bullet holes. Inside this arena I had been lost, and then restored. I had learned that I could cope.

The army was waiting to pounce on me as soon as I finished my year of internship, to draft me, short-back-and-sides, into the service. Despite the prospect of two years in uniform, plus a further three months a year thereafter at the army's whim, it was hard to contemplate voluntary exile. I could go to England, where my medical degree would be recognized, or join my family in the United States, where my father had taken up a professorship at a medical school in New York. But the truth was, I wanted to stay.

Surgery, it seemed, was what I wanted to do, to feel that rush of confidence as my hands negotiated the intricate demands of operating. If I stayed in South Africa, I knew that I would do a lot more trauma work. Every evening I would drive home from the hospital, through the steep Constantia valley, and park on a farm track under the trees. A scramble up a rutted path brought me to my house, a bungalow dressed in flowering creeper that gazed out across the Cape Flats to the sawtooth range of the Hottentots Holland mountains lit by the sunset. Each morning I would leave the calm of that charmed place, and plunge back into hospital life; challenging and exhilarating. It seemed unlikely that I would find another country that could provide such a way of life.

We young doctors discussed the issue exhaustively. My radical friends said change was inevitable, even if it was to be through bloody revolution, and they wanted to see it happen. To do so they would have to remain in South Africa, which meant going into the army. Others took an ethical standpoint: a doctor was a doctor, in uniform or out, and on National Service one was still trying to heal people. My friend Stefan had been a strong supporter of this view. Called up several months before, he was now stationed somewhere on the Angolan border. As yet I hadn't heard from him, but I knew he was due for leave before the end of the year. I was looking forward to seeing him and laughing at his haircut, and finding out whether he was managing to survive the army with his principles intact.

When Stefan returned to Cape Town, however, he made no effort to get in touch with me; I wasn't aware that he was back. Then one day I received a message that he wanted to see me. Wondering why he hadn't called himself, I went to see him one evening at a flat where he was staying with some people I'd never met before. The man who answered the door seemed suspicious of me, but a high and unfamiliar voice behind him instructed him to let me in. Stefan sat in the lounge. His face looked hollow, as though something vital had been squeezed from it. His embrace was perfunctory.

'How was basic training?' I wanted to know. 'How was the border? How did you manage to get leave so soon? I wasn't expecting you for another two months.'

'Have a drink,' he replied, pouring me a brimming glass of neat vodka. He took a swallow from his own glass then topped it up, and placed the bottle beside the leg of his chair.

'Let me tell you what it's like,' he said, lighting a cigarette. I'd never seen him smoke before.

Stefan had been sent first to Oshakati, a small town forty miles south of the Angolan border, where he'd been put to work in the main hospital. It was busy. The army was in Angola, long-range infiltrations, and every now and then a patrol would get ambushed and be brought in by helicopter. 'We'd also get black civilians, sometimes a busload who'd hit a mine, and patch them up; trying to win their hearts and minds, even if they lost their arms and legs.' Most of the mines were laid by their own people, SWAPO guerrillas, who were trying to kill the occupiers, the South Africans. 'If the South Africans hadn't been there, neither would the mines,' Stefan said. 'All these people wanted was for us to leave, yet there I was, an army doctor, trying to help them. The result was incomprehensible confusion, for them and me.'

Then he'd been sent to the forward base at Oshikango, on the border, to relieve an army doctor who was down with malaria. One night, after he had been there for about a month, he was woken and told to report to the hospital. A group of men in camouflage kit were standing around a stretcher. On it lay a black man, shot through the thigh, gasping in pain. 'I checked him over. I got a drip running, and drew up some antibiotics. The officer in charge checked the ampoules. He had a full beard, he looked like a pirate.'

The officer told Stefan: 'I don't want you giving him any painkillers, doc. He's a fokkin terrorist. We need him to talk.'

Stefan objected that the man's thigh bone was fractured; it would need to be stabilized, otherwise he would bleed to death.

'Do what you like, doc, put it in a splint,' the officer said. 'You can have him back when we've finished with him.'

Stefan strapped the man's leg into a frame. Then the officer gave an order, and four black troopers picked up the stretcher and took him away.

Stefan said: 'Over the sound of the generator I thought I could hear screaming. I went to find the senior duty officer and told him they were questioning a prisoner and denying him proper medical treatment. He said there was nothing he could do; the others were a police counter-insurgency unit, not under army control, and I should go back to sleep. I couldn't. I sat in the dispensary, trying to read. The screaming went on, sometimes drowned out by the roar of a truck engine.'

A police trooper came running in and told Stefan to bring his bag. He sprinted across to their camp. An arc light was strung between a pair of Casspir armoured personnel carriers and beneath it a group of men stood around a figure on the ground.

'He's passed out, doc, just when we were getting somewhere,' the officer said. 'You have to bring him round.'

Stefan said: 'There was a terrible smell, like burning meat. The skin on the man's legs and back was scorched off, hanging in long strips. He was unconscious.' The splint had been discarded, and the end of his fractured femur stuck through the flesh. Stefan asked what had happened to him, how he'd got burned.

The bearded policeman had laughed.

'We had a barbecue. We put him on the exhaust pipe of the Casspir and let him cook. It always works. Plus we gave his leg a twist, to help him concentrate.'

Stefan said the man needed to go to hospital; he could die.

'He'll die anyway,' said the officer, 'we don't take prisoners. Just give him an injection or something to wake him up for a while before he goes.'

Stefan pulled out an ampoule of calcium solution and cracked it open.

'No painkillers, doc,' warned the officer.

'No painkillers,' Stefan had said, injecting the calcium into the drip line, 'he's in shock. I'll try to jolt his heart a bit, to bring him round.'

The man opened his eyes, and took a deep, racking breath. The policemen began to pull him upright.

His mouth opened, then he arched his back convulsively and died.

'Shit,' said the captain, 'he was starting to talk. I suppose he was just too far gone, hey, doc?'

'Too far gone,' Stefan had agreed.

He went on: 'I went back to my cot. I lay down, but at once the horror of what I had done overwhelmed me. I had just murdered someone. I hung on to the edge of the bed, shuddering with fear.'

Then he'd opened his medical bag and taken out the pethidine that he'd been forbidden to give the wounded man. He'd drawn it into a syringe, and injected it into his arm.

Stefan subsided into his chair. His thin hands vibrated where they clasped the armrests.

'I managed to last another three weeks, stealing pethidine from the dispensary and shooting up every night. When I tried to sleep I couldn't bear the solitude. I came down with malaria, and was sent back to Oshakati. I knew one of the doctors there, and he had me transferred to the military hospital here in Cape Town. Ten days ago I bribed an orderly to get me twenty ampoules. Then I walked out and came here.'

He rolled up his sleeve, and I saw that his arm was a mesh of bruises.

Stefan said that Mark, the owner of the flat where we were talking, was a psychiatrist and trying to help him. 'In the meantime I'm trying to avoid the drugs, by using this.'

Stefan sucked deeply from his glass of vodka. He gagged, and drank again.

'You won't see me for a while. Tomorrow I'm being moved to somewhere safer. Mark's making plans to get me out of the country.'

'What about your family? Your friends?'

Stefan shook his head.

'They'll hear from me, once I've made it overseas. Don't tell anyone you've seen me. And don't believe that bullshit I used to give you about being able to keep your humanity by being a doctor. It isn't true. There are situations where that option simply doesn't exist.'

□

NOTES ON CONTRIBUTORS

Raymond Carver's recently discovered stories will be published in an expanded edition of his uncollected fiction and prose, retitled *Call If You Need Me*, to be published by Knopf in the US and Harvill in the UK.
Lydia Davis is the author of two collections of stories, *Break it Down* and *Almost No Memory*, both published by Farrar, Straus & Giroux. She is translating a new version of *Swann's Way* for Penguin Classics.
Keith Fleming's memoir about his adolescence, *The Boy with the Thorn in His Side*, will be published in April by William Morrow.
Ruth Gershon's autobiographical piece about growing up in the rag trade in London, 'A Life in Clothes', appeared in *Granta* 65.
James Hamilton-Paterson's most recent book, *America's Boy,* was published in 1998 by Granta Books in the UK and Henry Holt in the US. His piece 'Sea Burial' appeared in *Granta* 61.
Aleksandar Hemon lives in New York. His first book, *The Question of Bruno*, will be published in spring 2000 by Picador in the UK and Doubleday/Nan Talese in the US.
Peter Ho Davies's story collection *The House at the End of the World* won the Macmillan Silver Pen Award in 1999. His second collection, *Equal Love*, will be published by Granta Books in the UK and Houghton Mifflin in the US.
Jonathan Kaplan has worked as a physician and surgeon in Britain, the US, Africa, the Far East and South America. His book, *The Dressing Station*, will be published by Picador in the UK and Grove Atlantic in the US in 2001.
David Malouf's books include *An Imaginary Life*, *The Great World* and *Remembering Babylon*, which was shortlisted for the Booker Prize and won the IMPAC Prize, and most recently *The Conversations at Curlow Creek*. His new story collection, *Dream Stuff* (Chatto & Windus/Pantheon), is published next spring.
Daniel Meadows is photography tutor at the Centre for Journalism Studies at Cardiff University. He is currently working on a book about the Free Photographic Omnibus, 1973–1999.
Orhan Pamuk's most recent novel, *The New Life*, was published by Faber in the UK and Farrar, Straus & Giroux in the US. His new book, *Call Me Crimson* (Faber/Knopf), will be published in the autumn of 2000. He lives in Istanbul.
W. G. Sebald lives in East Anglia. He is the author of *The Emigrants* and *The Rings of Saturn*, both published by Harvill in the UK and New Directions in the US. 'Going Abroad' is taken from his forthcoming book *Vertigo* (Harvill/New Directions).